THE INTERNATIONAL ASSOCIATION FOR COPTIC STUDIES

ACTS OF THE
FIFTH INTERNATIONAL CONGRESS
OF COPTIC STUDIES

WASHINGTON, 12 – 15 AUGUST 1992

VOLUME 1

REPORTS ON RECENT RESEARCH

Edited by Tito Orlandi

ROMA – C.I.M. – 1993

Impaginazione effettuata presso il C.I.S.A.D.U. (Centro Interdipartimentale di Servizi per l'Automazione nelle Discipline Umanistiche), Università degli Studi di Roma – La Sapienza.

ISBN 88-85354-02-5

Centro Italiano Microfiches
Piazzale di Ponte Milvio 28
I - 00191 Roma (Italia)

TABLE OF CONTENTS

PREFACE

It is a great pleasure to present this volume, which contains the Reports given in the plenary sessions of the Fifth Congress of the International Association for Coptic Studies which for the first time I could not attend,[1] but which I know to have been quite successful as an occasion to share important progress in the field of Coptic studies. For all this the efforts of the convenor, David Johnson (and the Catholic University in Washington), deserve our hearty gratitude.

The publication of the Acts of the Congresses preceding this one were entrusted to the different Congress Secretaries, and therefore are not part of one special collection. It seems convenient to mention them once again:

Cairo Congress, 1976: R. McL. WILSON (ed.), *The Future of Coptic Studies*, Leiden, Brill, 1978 = Coptic Studies 1.
R. McL. Wilson (ed.), *Nag Hammadi and Gnosis, First International Congress of Coptology, Cairo, December 1976* = NHS 14, Leiden, Brill, 1978.
1. Internationaler Kongress für Koptologie, Kairo 08.-18. Dezember 1976 = Enchoria 8 (1978), Sonderband, Lieferung II.

Rome Congress, 1980: Tito ORLANDI - Frederik WISSE (eds.), *Act of the Second International Congress of Coptic Studies, Roma, 22-26 September 1980*, Roma, CIM, 1985.

---

1. I wish to take the occasion to thank again all those colleagues who have expressed sympathy and concern, and who made me feel once more how much our Association has been successful in developing an environment not only of scientific but also of deep human relations.

Warsaw Congress, 1984: Wlodzimierz GODLEWSKI (ed.), *Coptic Studies. Acts of the Third Int. Congr. of Coptic Studies, Warsaw, 20-25 Aug. 1984*, Warszawa, PWN - Państwowe Wydawnictwo Naukowe, 1990.

Louvain-la-Neuve Congress, 1988: *Actes du IVe Congrès Copte. Louvain-la-Neuve, 5-10 septembre 1988*, édités par M. RASSART-DEBERGH et J. RIES, I. *Art et Archéologie*; II. *De la linguistique au gnosticisme*, Louvain-la-Neuve, 1992.

The delay between the date of the Congresses and the publication of the Acts, varying from 4 to 6 years (except for the first Congress), has been judged by the Board and the Assembly[2] to be too long, though unavoidable when adopting the traditional editorial and printing procedures. It was thus decided that this time speed of publication was to be preferred to elegance.

The result of this decision is the present three-volume set, which therefore need not be described here. I emphasize, however, that also this first volume, whose appearence is nearest to the traditional one of the linotyped book, has not been copyedited, and each contribution shows the personal preferences of its author in every aspect, from the division of the sections to the use of italics, quotation marks, etc., to the presentation of the bibliography. It may be added that the use of italics depends sometimes on the «portability» of the diskettes; and that the peculiar position of certain footnotes depends on an unavoidable feature of the formatting programme which I used.

As usual, Stephen Emmel assisted the editors in the whole process of the preparation of the three volumes, with his well known competence and good disposition.

Tito Orlandi

---

2.   Cp. Newsletter/Bulletin d'Information of the IACS, n. 31, p.4 ff.

HEINZGERD BRAKMANN

NEUE FUNDE UND FORSCHUNGEN
ZUR LITURGIE DER KOPTEN (1988-1992)

Otto Nussbaum zum 1. 7. 1993

Forschungen zur Liturgie der Kopten standen unter dem Verdacht der Unerheblichkeit und Esoterik. Beides ist inzwischen widerlegt. Wer heute koptische Studien, gleich welcher Art, betreibt, behandelt bekanntlich in der Regel etwas, das für den Gottesdienst geschaffen, in ihm benutzt, durch ihn tradiert wurde oder aus ihm lebt wie die koptische Kommunität der Gegenwart. Wie 1988 in Louvain-la-Neuve wendet sich deswegen mein heutiger »report« nicht an Spezialisten, sondern skizziert zu allgemeinerem Nutzen das Panorama unseres Forschungsgebietes. Darin eingezeichnet sind jeweils Fundstellen und Arbeitsfelder der vergangenen Olympiade.[1]

Das Ziel unserer Wissenschaft ist unverändert die Erforschung der Liturgiegeschichte der Kirche Ägyptens,[2] besonders ihrer stilbildenden Zentren, sowie die genetische Erklärung der einzelnen gottesdienstlichen Feiern mit ihren sämtlichen, auch nonverbalen, Gestaltungselementen.

Drei Unterscheidungen sind hilfreich: 1) zeitlich - vor und nach der Spaltung des Patriarchats infolge Chalkedons, 2) personell - zwischen dem Gottesdienst der Mönche und dem der Gemeinden in der Welt

---

1. Für Einzelheiten s. die anschliessende Bibliographie. Auf dort verzeichnete Titel wird im Text aus Platzgründen nur in allgemeiner oder andeutender Form verwiesen.
2. Forschungsobjekt kann, aus hier erneut verdeutlichten historischen Gründen, nicht allein der Kult oder -anteil in koptischer Sprache sein, sondern nur der Gottesdienst der christlichen Ägypter insgesamt, zu berücksichtigen sind damit letztlich alle Liturgien im Patriarchat von Alexandreia.

(»Kathedraltradition«), 3) regional - zwischen Alexandreia und
Ägypten sowie dessen Norden und Süden. Zwischen Epochen, Gruppen und Gebieten herrscht, auch über die Grenzen des Nillandes hin-
weg, Abhängigkeit, Austausch, Verdrängung, keine Isolation.

I

Unsere Kenntnis der vorchalkedonischen Liturgiegeschichte
Alexandreias und Ägyptens beruht auf unmittelbar für den Gottesdienst bestimmten Texten und Nachrichten in der Literatur früh- und
hochpatristischer Zeit.

Unterschätzte Auskünfte über die Liturgie des 2. Jh. in der ägyptischen Provinz bietet nach R. Warns der sog. 2. Klemens-Brief. Weiterhin ungebrochen ist, wie die Bibliographie erweist, das Interesse an
Gottesdienst und Psalmenrezitation im frühen Mönchtum, neuerwacht
das für Sonderbräuche der Melitianer. Einen Forschungsschwerpunkt
der letzten Jahre bilden die Osterfestbriefe der alexandrinischen Patriarchen, wesentliche Quellen für die Geschichte der Fastenzeit und der
damit verbundenen Frage nach den Taufterminen in Alexandreia und,
möglicherweise unterschiedlich, in Ägypten.

Neufunde oder neue Identifikationen alter gottesdienstlicher Texte
betreffen griechische Lektionar- und Anaphorenfragmente, darunter,
durch den unvergessenen K. Treu,[3] einen weiteren frühen Zeugen der
Markos-Anaphora[4] (P. Vindob. G 26134; van Haelst[5] nr. 1024). R. P.
Roca-Puig versandte als Weihnachtsgeschenke ergänzende Exzerpte
zu Eucharistiefeier und Krankenliturgie aus dem Papyruskodex des 4.

---

3.   In seiner Berichterstattung über neupublizierte griechisch-christliche Papyri (K.
Treu, Christliche Papyri, in: ArchPapForsch 19 [1969] 169-205 [mit Rückblick bis
1940]; 20 [1970] 145-152; 21 [1971] 207-214; 22/23 [1974] 367-395; 24/25 [1976]
253-261; 26 [1978] 149-159; 27 [1980] 251-258; 28 [1981] 91-98; 29 [1983]
107-110; 30 [1984] 121-128; 31 [1985] 59-71; 32 [1986] 87-95; 34 [1988] 69-78; 35
[1989] 107-116), also ein halbes Jahrhundert Forschungsgeschichte beobachtend
und mitgestaltend, hat K. Treu die Liturgica stets mit besonderer Aufmerksamkeit
bedacht. Der Tod des Berliner Gelehrten († 7. Juni 1991) bedeutet daher auch für die
Liturgiewissenschaft einen schmerzlichen Verlust.
4.   Neuausgabe durch J. Hammerstaedt, Köln, in Vorbereitung.

Jh. in Barcelona (van Haelst nr. 862/4 + 1210) und verspricht eine vollständige Edition der Anaphora für die Bonner Neubearbeitung der Anthologie »Prex Eucharistica«. Sein Kodex gehört offenbar zu den Stücken, die Anfang der 50er Jahre, wie es heisst, in der Umgebung von Pabau gefunden wurden.[6] Auf bemerkenswerte koptische Anaphorenzitate in T. Orlandis Schenute-Exhorte macht A. Grillmeier aufmerksam.

Studien zur Prex Eucharistica nehmen in der Bibliographie wachsenden Raum ein, entwickeln sich zu einer Spezialdisziplin der Liturgik. Für uns wichtig sind zwei relativ gesicherte Ergebnisse: 1) zwischen der alexandrinischen Markos-Anaphora und dem römischen Canon Missae bestehen Verwandtschaftsbeziehungen, die auf einen frühen Austausch hinweisen (E. Mazza). 2) die sog. alexandrinische Basileios-Anaphora ist eine später leicht ägyptisierte Arbeit ihres Namenspatrons, wahrscheinlich noch im 4. Jh. durch monastische Besucher des Kirchenvaters aus Kappadokien nach Ägypten gebracht (J. Fenwick). Erhärtet wurde, trotz gelegentlichen Widerspruchs, die Erkenntnis, dass das Serapion-Euchologion den Namen des Athanasiosfreundes zu Unrecht trägt. Es verfälscht theologisch wie liturgisch eine Vorlage, für die aufgrund der eingeschlossenen Bischofsordination stadtalexandrinische Herkunft nicht auszuschliessen ist.

Erschienen ist eine verbesserte Auflage der rekonstruierten Traditio apostolica, früher gern Ägyptische Kirchenordnung genannt. Aus ihren ägyptischen Ausgestaltungen erwartet neue Behandlung das in Rezension E in Auszügen enthaltene, m. E. stadtalexandrinische, Euchologion des 5. Jh.[7] In etwa dieselbe Zeit datieren möchte ich die aus

5.   J. van Haelst, Catalogue des papyrus littéraires juifs et chrétiens (Paris 1976). Der Inhalt dieses auch für Koptologen nützlichen Kataloges griechischer Texte ist breiter, als es sein Titel vermuten lässt. So sind z.B. auch Fragmente später koptischer Pergamentkodizes aufgenommen, sofern sie auch griechisches Material tradieren.

6.   J. M. Robinson, The First Christian Monastic Library, in: W. Godlewski (ed.), Coptic Studies. Acts of the Third Intern. Congress of Coptic Studies, Warsaw 1984 (Varsovie 1990) 374. 377 nr. 38 (dort falsch: »The Greek liturgical text is unpublished«); vgl. aber R. Kasser, Status quaestionis sulla presunta origine dei cosiddetti Papiri Bodmer, in: Aegyptus 68 (1988) 191-194.

einer äthiopischen Synaxar-Handschrift bekanntgewordene singuläre
Katechese aus Patriarchat oder Stadt Alexandreia mit Anweisungen an
Neugetaufte zur participatio activa bei der Messfeier.[8]

II

Die auf Chalkedon und die postchalkedonischen Wirren folgende
Neuorganisation des alexandrinischen Patriarchats der Konzilsgegner
knüpft in der Liturgie an heimische Traditionen an, bringt zugleich
nicht unerhebliche Neuerungen mit sich.

Lange feststellbar ist die herkömmliche Gliederung in die drei Re-
gionen Alexandreia, Nord- und Südägypten. Auch in Gemeinden und
Klöstern der ägyptischen Provinz bleibt die griechische Sprache
zunächst präsent bei Bibellesung, Gebeten und Gesängen, teils mit,
teils ohne koptische Übersetzung, auf Dauer erhalten auffälligerweise
in Formeln, die das Volk angehen. Ergänzende Belege dafür bilden
neuendeckte griechische Hymnen in Papyrusabschriften der ersten
postchalkedonischen Jahrhunderte, darunter ein Osterlied (P. Berol.
21329) und ein Text zu Ehren des alexandrinischen Märtyrerbischofs
Petros (P. Vindob. G 19 934 Bl. 1a). Solch unbefangener Gebrauch
des Griechischen im Gottesdienst der Kopten wie in den Festbriefen
der koptischen Patriarchen bis wenigstens zum Schreiben Alexanders
II. (704-729) v.J. 713 oder 719 (van Haelst nr. 621) stützt nicht gerade
Versuche, die Loslösung der koptischen von der Reichskirche zu
deuten als »national movement in disguise«.

---

7. Massgebliche Ausgabe: H. Duensing, Der aethiopische Text der
Kirchenordnung des Hippolyt = AbhGöttingen 3, 32 (Göttingen 1946). Aus dem
Eigengut der Trad.-Apost.-Rez. E besitzen liturgiegeschichtliche Bedeutung vor
allem 1) die Ausweitung der Eucharistietexte nach Bischofswahl und -weihe im
Kap. 5 um die priesterlichen Formeln und zugehörigen Rubriken des
Kommunionteils und des Ritus conclusionis der Messe (äth. Kap. 21) und 2) ein
langer Einschub mit 15 Gebeten und 12 Rubriken zwischen Kap. 30 und 31 von B.
Bottes Trad.-Apost.-Rekonstruktion (äth. Kap. 39 [40]), in Überschrift und
Schlussformel als »Ordnung der Taufe« bezeichnet.
8. R. Beylot, Sermon éthiopien anonyme sur l'eucharistie, in: Abbay 12 (1983)
79-116; G. Colin, Le synaxaire éthiopien. Mois de Terr = Patrologia Orientalis 45, 1
(Turnhout 1990) 212-231.

Selbstverständlich fortgeführt wurden auch die traditionellen Gedächtnisfeiern Christi, der Heiligen und der verstorbenen Christgläubigen. Von bleibender Sorge für die Verstorbenen durch Totenklage, Fürbitte und Pflege ihrer Memorialtage zeugen die von M. Hasitzka edierten Wiener koptischen Papyri des 7./8. Jh. Veränderungen des Festkalenders hingegen dokumentiert der dem 6./7. Jh. zugewiesene P. Iand. inv. 318. Zum einen verzeichnet er, zT. unter abweichenden Daten, schon früher verehrte Mönchsheilige wie Phib u. Apollo, auch Apa Bane, dessen Mumie man jetzt gefunden glaubt, zum andern berücksichtigt er das bei den Kopten offenbar als Reaktion auf Chalkedon eingeführte Gedächtnis der Dormitio Mariae sowie ausdrücklich Patriarch Severos von Antiochien († 538), dessen Beitrag zur ägyptischen Kirchen- und vielleicht auch Liturgiegeschichte noch heute regelmässige Namensnennung im koptischen Gottesdienst würdigt. Die Eucharistie wird weiterhin sowohl am Abend des Samstags wie am Morgen des Sonntags gefeiert, wie man dies schon im 5. Jh. überall in den Städten und Dörfern Ägyptens tat, Alexandrien ausdrücklich ausgenommen. In Klöstern nutzte man die Zwischenzeit zur Rekreation und, wie die von D. Johnson edierte Zenobios-Vita lehrt, zu nicht immer brüderlichem Gespräch. Mit der Abendmesse des Samstags hängt zusammen die in Ägypten noch spät anzutreffende Nichtbeachtung der eucharistischen Nüchternheit. Schenute hatte das Essen vor der Kommunion noch mit der Belastung seiner Landsleute durch Feldarbeit entschuldigt. Abraham von Hermonthis († 620?) und Patriarch Michael I. († 768) kämpften dagegen mit der Waffe der Exkommunikation.[9] Von diesem Kampf zeugt nun auch das von M. Krause bearbeitete Ψήφισμα P. Pierpont Morgan inv. 660. B. 12. Der Priesteramtskandidat verpflichtet sich darin ausserdem, keinen Altar mehr als einmal am Tag für die Eucharistiefeier zu benutzen. Dieses sog. Binationsverbot urgiert ähnlich das koptische Briefcorpus Petros' I. von Alexandrien,[10] das in etwa dieser Zeit gefälscht worden sein dürfte.[11]

9.   Vgl. H. Brakmann, Zur Geschichte der eucharistischen Nüchternheit in Ägypten, in: Muséon 84 (1971) 197-211.
11.   Anders T. Vivian, St. Peter of Alexandria (Philadelphia 1988) 54-57.

Das zuvor sicher schon für Bibellesung, Psalmen- und Privatgebet gebrauchte Koptische dringt offenbar erst jetzt stärker ein in den Bereich priesterlicher Amtsgebete, der Anaphoren usw. Jedenfalls werden alle bekannten koptischen Euchologion-Handschriften um oder nach 600 eingeordnet. Doch bleibt daneben griechische Euchologie auch im Süden des Landes in Gebrauch, wie zB. der vielbesprochene eucharistische Papyrus (van Haelst nr. 737) aus dem Apollo-Kloster bei Balai'zah belegt. Am ausdauerndsten, wenngleich kaum mit bestem Verständnis, bekanntlich in Nubien. Von dort wird erstmals ein Textfund aus der Initiationsliturgie gemeldet (P. Macquarie inv. 374). Die Ausgabe weiterer griechischer Priestertexte aus Qasr Ibrim durch W. H. C. Frend (and friends) steht vor der Auslieferung.[12] Wie ihre Vorgänger ist sie nützlich, doch kaum definitiv. Die liturgiewissenschaftliche Untersuchung der in Nubien gefundenen Orationen und der Fragmente von Markos-[13] und Präsanktifikatenliturgie[14] bleibt Desiderat.

Die wesentliche liturgiegeschichtliche Neuerung dieser Epoche besteht darin, dass sich die koptische Kirche für Eucharistie und andere sakramentliche Feiern Ordnungen der Kirche Syriens zum Vorbild nimmt. So bildet in ihr nicht die Markos-Liturgie alexandrinischer Herkunft das eucharistische Normalformular, sondern die neugestaltete, sog. ägyptische Basileios-Liturgie. Sie verbindet die eingemeindete kappadokische Anaphora gleichen Namens und wenigstens zT.

---

10. PsPetr. I Alex. epp. frg. 1 (ed. W. E. Crum, Texts attributed to Peter of Alexandria, in: JournTheolStud 4 [1903] 389/912); vgl. H. Brakmann, Alexandreia und die Kanones des Hippolyt, in: JbAntChrist 22 (1979) 146 mit Anm. 43.

12. Falsch sind übrigens alle Zitate von »W. Frend, The Greek Liturgical Papyri from Qasr Ibrim (London 1981)«. Das angekündigte Buch ist weder erschienen noch weiterhin geplant.

13. Vorläufige Ausgabe: W. H. C. Frend / G. Dagras, A Eucharistic Sequence from Q'asr Ibrim, in: JbAntChrist 30 (1987) 90/8, 2 Taf.

14. Neben die beiden bisher bekannten Zeugen dieser Liturgie (s. H. Brakmann, Zu den Fragmenten einer griechischen Basileios-Liturgie aus dem koptischen Makarios-Kloster, in: OrChr 66 [1982] 120f Anm. 14f) tritt jetzt der noch unedierte Neufund von 1992 aus Old-Dongola (für Informationen darüber danke ich W. Godlewski und A. Łajtar).

einheimische Orationen mit einem syrisch geprägten Zeremoniell. Falls sich ihr neuer Rang bereits in dem unter Benjamin I. (624-665) gefertigten Diptychon der Diözese Hermonthis (van Haelst nr. 1052)[15] spiegelt, ist diese Liturgiereform spätestens unter seinem Patriarchat erfolgt. Wahrscheinlich liegen die Ansätze früher. Severos von Antiochien und Timotheos III. von Alexandrien (517-535) bleiben die bekanntesten Liturgiker im Ägypten des vielleicht entscheidenden 6. Jahrhunderts. Jedenfalls wird der antiochenische, nicht der alexandrinische Typ[16] der Prex Eucharistica massgeblich für Neuschöpfungen von Anaphoren, zB. die beiden Formulare in E. Lannes Euchologion des Weissen Klosters (»Z 100«),[17] die G. Maestri in das 7. Jh. datieren möchte.

Die Grundstruktur der koptischen Messfeier dieser Zeit wird erkennbar in einer jener partiell auch im Benjamin-Schrifttum greifbaren Mönchsgeschichten,[18] deren Ge'ez-Übersetzung V. Arras unlängst ediert hat.[19] Der Wortgottesdienst weist schon die vier rein neutestamentlichen Lesungen auf. Die Eucharistiefeier im engeren Sinn beginnt noch mit dem Anlegen der liturgischen Gewänder und der Übertragung von Brot und Mischwein zum Altar.[20]

---

15. Dort nachzutragen: heute im British Museum, London.

16. Zu den Notae characteristicae beider Typen s. A. Hänggi / I. Pahl, Prex Eucharistica (Fribourg 1968) 101. 204f.

17. Die liturgischen Kodizes des Weissen Klosters benenne ich, in Ermangelung eines allgemein anerkannten Verfahrens, im Anschluss an die Numerierung Zoëgas; stets mitgemeint sind also die Komplementblätter der Borgia-Kollektion und anderer Sammlungen.

18. Vgl. Quadraginta historiae monachorum 9 (CSCO 506/Aeth. 86, 57-63 Arras) mit C. D. G. Müller, Die Homilie über die Hochzeit zu Kana und weitere Schriften des Patriarchen Benjamin I. von Alexandrien (Heidelberg 1968) 132-269. Zur Frage der Echtheit der Benjamin-Schriften s. H. Brakmann, Zum Pariser Fragment angeblich des koptischen Patriarchen Agathon. Ein neues Blatt der Vita Benjamins I, in: Muséon 93 (1980) 299-309, bes. 308.

19. Siehe die vorige Anm.; zur arabischen Version der Sammlung s. vorerst W. E. Crum, A Nubian Prince in an Egyptian Monastery, in: Studies presented to F. Ll. Griffith (London 1932) 137-148.

20. Quadraginta historiae monachorum 35, 3 (CSCO 506/Aeth. 86, 154f Arras).

III

Alexandreia verdient weiterhin gesonderte Betrachtung. Hier muss bald nach Ansiedlung von Patriarchen der Kopten die Ordinationsliturgie ihre massgebliche Gestalt gefunden haben; denn die Ordnung der Patriarchenweihe nennt Örtlichkeiten der spätantiken Stadt ausdrücklich beim Namen.[21] Auffällig ist der bleibend hohe Anteil des Griechischen in diesem Ordo bohairischer Liturgie, eines von mehreren Indizien,[22] dass sich in und um Alexandreia griechische Gottesdienstsprache noch eine ganze Weile nicht allein auf Melchiten beschränkte.[23]

Kennzeichnend für die »neo-alexandrinische Liturgie«[24] postpatristischer Zeit ist die Aufnahme pseudapostolischer Texte syrischer Herkunft, so der Ordinationsgebete aus den Apostolischen Konstitutionen und dem Testamentum Domini. Die arabische Übersetzung der bis auf liturgische Exzerpte verlorenen koptischen Fassung des Testamentum tradiert Stücke eines alexandrinischen Euchologions,[25] nach A. Baumstark aus dem 6., nach Th. Scherman, wohl zutreffender, aus dem 9. Jh.[26] Sie zeugen von dem offenbar gescheiterten Versuch, die eigene Markos-Anaphora der auswärts vorherrschend gewordenen

---

21. Nachweise bei H. Brakmann, Σύναξις καθολική in Alexandreia, in: JbAntChrist 30 (1987) 87f.

22. Vgl. ebd. 88 Anm. 109.

23. Nach der arabischen »Beschreibung der Kirchen und Klöster Ägyptens« eines koptischen Autors des 13. Jh. wurden in Samannud und zwei weiteren Städten die liturgischen Gebete in griechischer Sprache rezitiert (Bishop Samuel [ed.], Abu al Makarem, History of the Churches and Monasteries in Lower Egypt in the 13th Cent. [Cairo 1992] 64) und »All that is read in the churches of Alexandria, is in the Roman language (Latin [sic!]), except that which is read in the church known as Al-Qamga, which is read in Coptic« (ebd. 202).

24. Die Bezeichnung ist gewählt, um die vom koptischen Patriarchat ausgebildete Form zu unterscheiden von der »alt-alexandrinischen« der Kirchenväterzeit.

25. Ausgaben: A. Baumstark, Eine aegyptische Mess- und Taufliturgie vermutlich des 6. Jh., in: Oriens Christianus 1 (1901) 1-45; I. E. Rahmani, Les liturgies orientales et occidentales (Beyrouth 1929) 446-470.

26. Baumstark a.O. 4; Th. Schermann, Ägyptische Abendmahlsliturgien des 1. Jahrtausends (Paderborn 1912) 190.

Basileios-Liturgie anzugleichen, überliefern ferner Texte einer Initiationsliturgie mit Weihe der Öle, des Taufwassers und Spendung von Taufe, Firmung und Erstkommunion in ein und derselben Feier, wie dies noch Makarios von Memphis (Ende 10. Jh.) als vergangene Übung, nicht mehr lebendigen Brauch Alexandriens kannte.[27] Als Katechese wurde dabei die dem Testamentum Domini entnommene »Mystagogia« verlesen, die verbunden mit der später vornehmlich im Wadi-Natrun oder in Kairo gefeierten Myronweihe Bestandteil koptischer Liturgie blieb. Die Verabreichung von Milch und Honig an die Neugetauften belegt, dass man nach Chalkedon in Alexandreia durchaus an alt-alexandrinische Traditionen anzuknüpfen verstand.

IV

Gefestigte Liturgie in sahidischem Milieu wird sichtbar mit der Würzburger Tafel K 1019 etwa des 8./9. Jh., einem jener Holzbretter, die wohl als Memorier- oder Vorlesehilfe dienten. Der in Griechisch und Koptisch aufgeschriebene Hymnus auf Christus und Maria findet sich auch im »Brevier« Pierpont Morgan 574 aus dem Michael-Kloster im Faijum. Eine Ausgabe seines Antiphonars M 575 wird in Münster vorbereitet.

Seine Arbeiten zum Psalmengebrauch südägyptischer Liturgie setzt H. Quecke fort. Die inzwischen auch von anderen beachteten »Hermeneia«, meist nach gleichem Stichwort centoartig zusammengestellte koptische Psalmverse, wurden inhaltlich abgestimmt im Gottesdienst eingesetzt. Dies zeigt erneut die von A. Alcock veröffentlichte »Hermeneia«-Ordnung einer Eheschliessung aus Oxyrhynchos (P. Oxy. 5B/125A [1-2], ca. 11. Jh.) und ebenso die gelegentliche Nutzung eines sahidischen »Hermeneia«-Textes bei der Myronweihe in Unterägypten.[28] Quecke weist neu hin auf ein durch

---

27. L. Villecourt, La lettre de Macaire, évêque de Memphis, sur la liturgie antique du chrême et du baptême à Alexandrie, in: Muséon 36 (1923) 33-42.
28. L. Villecourt, Un manuscrit arabe sur le saint Chrême dans l'église copte: RevHistEccl 18 (1922) 6. Weitere sahidische Texte (welche?), die bei solchem Anlass Verwendung fanden, sollen in einer Handschrift des Athanasios von Qus in Kairo (Cairo 723, 1/Lit. 106, 1 [a. 1377]) enthalten sein.

mehrere Handschriften vertretenes zweites Corpus andersartig aus-
gewählter Psalmverse, diesmal in griechischer Sprache, die ebenso
zum verbreiteten gottesdienstlichen Repertoire des Südens gehörten.

Isoliert neuerlich vorgelegt wurde ein Blatt (van Haelst nr. 1047)
aus einer partiell rekonstruierbaren Handschrift des Weissen Klosters
(»Z 108, 3«).[29] Die Gesänge mit Trishagion gelten seit C. Wessely als
»Gebet bei der Nilschwelle«.[30] Die geschilderte Situation der Beter
lässt an Verwendung im Morgenoffizium denken.

Aus den Resten sahidischer Euchologien bespricht H. Quecke ein
bisher unediertes, doch textgeschichtlich wichtiges Fragment der
Basileios-Anaphora (Cod. Vat. copt. 103, 2). Ein zweites Euchologion
des Weissen Klosters, »Z 110«, nimmt durch Zuweisung mehrerer
Blätter deutlichere Gestalt an.[31] Nachprüfung ergab, dass die in der
Literatur mehrfach angeführten sahidischen Marien-Anaphoren (van
Haelst nr. 1045f) ihre Existenz allein missverstandenen Beschreibungen Zoëgas verdanken.[32] Die äthiopischen Marien-Anaphoren
wiederum sind inzwischen als späte einheimische Schöpfungen erkannt wie ebenso die meisten dortigen Sonderanaphoren,[33] auch wenn
sie alexandrinisch-ägyptische Namen tragen wie Athanasios, Kyrillos
und Kyriakos von Behnesa.

Eine grössere Anzahl von zum Teil zweisprachigen Lektionaren,
weithin aus dem Weissen Kloster, bietet liturgiewissenschaftlicher
Auswertung an die fortgeführte Münsteraner Liste der sahidischen
Handschriften der Evangelien. Neben eigentlichen Evangeliaren um-
fasst sie gemischte Lektionare verschiedener Typen,[34] die auch bei
den an Aktualität gewinnenden Forschungen zur alttestamentlichen

---

29. Verzeichnis der Fragmente: Quecke, Rec. Layton 239; vgl. Schmitz / Mink Sa
342L.
30. Parallelen nennt W. E. Crum, Bibliography: Christian Egypt, 1915-1916, in:
JournEgyptArch 4 (1917) 48f.
31. Layton nr. 66.
32. Für die Überprüfung danke ich E. Lanne, Chevetogne.
33. Dazu vgl. man neben E. Hammerschmidt, Studies in the Ethiopic Anaphoras.
Second revised Edition (Stuttgart 1987) besonders Getatchew Haile, Religious
Controversies and the Growth of Ethiopic Literatur in the Fourteenth and Fifteenth
Centuries, in: Oriens Christianus 65 (1981) 102-136.

Schriftlesung im christlichen Gottesdienst Beachtung verdienen wie erst recht das reine AT-Lektionar »Z 32«, über das P. Nagel vorerst an abgelegenem, doch liebenswertem Ort berichtet.[35]

In den späten sahidisch-arabischen Pascha-Lektionaren »Z 99« und Cod. Huntington 5 erkennt U. Zanetti Zeugen südägyptischer Traditionen, in denen bereits bestimmender Einfluss des Nordens zu spüren ist. Skeptisch zum Wert von R.-G. Coquins »nouveau témoin« der oberägyptischen Rezension des arabischen Synaxars äussert sich J. Doresse, nach dem diese Rezension möglicherweise stets Stückwerk blieb.

Deutlich dürfte hier erneut geworden sein, dass der Schlüssel für das Verständnis diverser Einzelstücke, aber auch der wenigen vollständigen liturgischen Bücher des sahidischen Dialekts zu suchen ist in den verstreuten Liturgica des Weissen Klosters. Allein sie repräsentieren alle Arten von Büchern, die von den verschiedenen Akteuren des Gottesdienstes benutzt wurden, Euchologien, Diakonalien, Homiliare, Typika usw. Sie müssen gemeinsam studiert werden, weil sie erst in der Zusammenschau ein vollständiges Bild der Feiern abgeben. Die Erfassung der erhaltenen Fragmente hat in den letzten Jahren bedeutende Fortschritte gemacht. Weitere, so die angekündigte Bearbeitung der Bestände der Pariser Bibliothèque Nationale durch A. Bouvarel-Boud'hors, werden erwartet. Die schon jetzt wiederholt beobachtete Mischung von biblischen, literarischen und liturgischen Texten in einem Band signalisiert, dass eine Vernachlässigung der Liturgica bei der Rekonstruktion der zertrümmerten Kodizes des Weissen Klosters ein methodischer Fehler wäre mit notwendig schädlichen Folgen.

Schmerzlichste Lücke unserer Kenntnisse vom Gottesdienst im Weissen Kloster bleibt, dass wir bisher wenig Genaues wissen über die Struktur der einzelnen Feiern, so der Eucharistie, der Stundenliturgie am Morgen, am Abend und in der Nacht usw. Sie lässt sich

---

34. Für die Lektionare mit nichtevangelisch-neutestamentlichen Perikopen bleibt nützlich die Liste bei K. Schüssler, Epistularum Catholicarum Versio Sahidica, Diss. Münster (1969).

35. Nagel, Das Alte Testament 42f.

eben nicht allein aus Lektionaren und Euchologien erheben, sondern
erfordert auch Beachtung der in anderen Büchern verzeichneten Di-
akonen- und Kantorentexte. B. Laytons Londoner Katalog und seine
Besprechung durch H. Quecke lassen jetzt gleich mehrere derartiger
Kodizes erkennen, deren Edition reizvoll und ausserordentlich
nützlich sein müsste, etwa »Z 108, 1«,[36] »Z 108, 2«;[37] »Z 108, 3«[38]
mit ihren Komplementblättern und Parallelzeugen. Erinnert sei ferner
an die seit langem bekannte geschlossene Blattfolge mit wichtigen Di-
akonentexten im Paris. copt. 129.20 (van Haelst nr. 853 [= 854]), die
noch immer auf Bearbeitung warten.

V

Die liturgischen Traditionen Unterägyptens begründen die heutigen
Consuetudines der ganzen koptischen Kirche. Prägende Zentren waren
der Gottesdienst des Patriarchen und der sketischen Klöster, Konkur-
renten und zugleich Vermittler von Material die Feiern im Gegenpatri-
archat der Melchiten.
Die melchitische Markos-Liturgie, auch in Süditalien verbreitet,[39]
behandelt G. C. Cumings postum veröffentlichtes Buch. Es verbindet
eine Textausgabe, die man sich übersichtlicher, zuverlässiger und
vollständiger gewünscht hätte, mit einem Kommentar, der nicht
wenige Anregungen bietet für eine Gesamtdarstellung der Messfeier
im christlichen Ägypten, die eines Tages neben J. A. Jungmanns
»Missarum sollemnia« und R. Tafts »History of the Liturgy of St.
John Chrysostom« stehen mag.
Die erhaltenen liturgischen Bücher der unterägyptisch-koptischen
Tradition sind selten älter als das 13. Jh., die Umstände ihrer Redaktion nur teilweise bekannt. Hauptidiom ist vereinzelt das Griechische,
in der Regel jedoch das Bohairische. Noch zu klären bleibt, wann und

---

36. Layton nr. 65; vgl. van Haelst nr. 1045. 758-763. 995. 119.
37. Vgl. Layton nr. 68 mit Quecke, Rec. 239; ferner Schmitz / Mink Sa 342L.
38. Vgl. Layton nr. 67 mit Quecke, Rec. 239; ferner Schmitz / Mink Sa 342L.
39. Die beiden süditalienischen Liturgiehandschriften mit der Markos-Liturgie
(Messan. gr. 177 u. Vat. gr. 1970) untersucht eingehend A. Jacob.

wo die bohairische Version dieser Texte entstand, in welchem Umfang
sie auf griechischen Vorlagen beruhen, in welchem auf sahidischen.

Erschienen sind neuerdings eine Anzahl von Übersetzungen koptischer liturgischer Texte in westliche Sprachen, häufig veranlasst durch
Emigranten oder ihre Freunde oder den Wunsch beider Päpste, des
römischen wie des alexandrinischen. Hervorzuheben sind, aus freilich
unterschiedlichen Gründen, P. Bradshaws Auswahl von Ordinationstexten mit komparatistischer Einleitung sowie die moderne »Diakonis-
senweihe«, deren Verankerung in ägyptischer Tradition auch U. Zanettis Lesefrucht nicht beweisen kann.[40]

Schon in Louvain-la-Neuve war deutlich geworden, wie sehr eine
verbessere Kenntnis der »langweiligen« bohairischen liturgischen
Handschriften nötig ist. Heute zu melden sind einige Anmerkungen zu
den Käufen koptischer Manuskripte auf Zypern 1671 durch J. M.
Wansleben († 1679) sowie zu den überwiegend liturgischen Coptica
des französischen Kanzlers Séguier († 1672). Die Difnartexte zu
Pesyntheos veröffentlicht Gawdat Gabra und kündigt zugleich die
Edition der ältesten bekannten Difnar-Handschrift (1384/85, Anto-
nios-Kloster) an. Besondere Aufmerksamkeit dürfen wieder die
Manuskriptstudien Zanettis beanspruchen, der nach seiner grossen
Monographie von 1985 über Lektionare Unterägyptens jetzt die dort
gleichfalls langwährende Vielfalt regionaler Gebräuche des Stun-
dengebets und der Feier der Pascha-Woche aufzeigt.

Als Folgerungen ergeben sich daraus: 1) der Wunsch detaillierter
Beschreibungen auch der bohairischen Liturgica nach dem Vorbild der
vatikanischen Kataloge und der sich inzwischen häufenden Analysen
byzantinischer Euchologien;[41] 2) die Erkenntnis, dass anspruchsvolle
Editionen bohairischer liturgischer Texte nicht allein auf Grundlage
des ältesten oder vollständigsten Zeugen eines Buchtyps erfolgen

---

40. Vgl. A. G. Martimort, Les diaconesses. Essai historique (Rome 1982) 73-97;
zum heutigen Frauenamt s. auch ebd. 97 Anm. 111; M. P. Martin / Ch. van Nispen /
F. Sidarouss, Les nouveaux courants dans la communauté copte orthodoxe, in:
PrOrChr 40 (1990) 250.

41. Zuletzt A. A. Thiermeyer, Das Euchologion Ottoboni Gr. 434, Diss. Rom PIO
(1992).

können, sondern die Überlieferung und gottesdienstliche Nutzung möglichst umfassend zu dokumentieren haben.

Im Berichtszeitraum erschienen mehrere Handbücher und Lexika, die die gewordene Liturgie der koptischen Kirche gebührend zu berücksichtigen suchen, am ausführlichsten natürlich die unübersehbare »Coptic Encyclopedia». Daneben finden sich Untersuchungen zu Einzelfragen, so zu Werk und Wirken Patriarch Gabriels II., zur Datierung des 2. Teils des unterägyptischen Synaxarions (1317-1354), zur Segnung von Ikonen oder zur Evangeliar-Auflegung bei der Bischofsweihe. Weiterhin fehlen, nicht zuletzt bedingt durch unzureichende Aufbereitung der Quellen,[42] grosse liturgiehistorische Studien etwa zur Feier der Initiatio Christiana oder der Rekonziliation von Sündern und Apostaten.

Nicht nur Texte und Riten machen Liturgie aus, sondern auch Musik, Bilder, Gewänder und Geräte. Erfreulich daher, dass die Bibliographie auch einige einschlägige musikwissenschaftliche und kunsthistorische Arbeiten aufführen kann. Nicht zuletzt hier wird spürbar, dass liturgiehistorische Dokumentation die arabischen Schriften koptischer Theologen, wie Ibn Sabbaʿ und Ibn Kabar, einschliessen oder erst noch erschliessen muss.

»Der Weinberg ist gross ...«

F. J. Dölger Institut   Heinzgerd Brakmann
der Universität Bonn

---

42. Microfiches bislang schwer erreichbare Drucke koptischer liturgischer Bücher liefern: Microlibrary, Slangenburg Abbey, Abdijlaan 1, NL-7004 JL Doetinchem, Nederland, und Saint Shenouda The Archimandrite Coptic Society, 1701 S. Wooster St., Los Angeles, Cal. 90035, USA.

Bibliographie

Albertine, R., The Post Vatican consilium's (Coetus X) treatment of the epiclesis question in the context of select historical data (Alexandrian family of anaphoras) and the fragment of «Der Balyzeh», in: Ephemerides Liturgicae 102 (1988) 385ff.

Alcock, A., A document from the Coptic marriage service, in: Orientalia 57 (1988) 84-86 (P. Oxy. 5B/125A [1-2], ca. XI saec.). Anonymus, Das Ritual der [Kirch-] Weihe, in: St. Markus Jan./Febr./ März 1991, 15-31.

Arranz, M. / Parenti, S., Liturgia patristica orientale. Tracce per uno studio sistematico, in: A. Quacquarelli (ed.), Complementi interdisciplinari di patrologia (Roma: Città Nuova 1989) 605-655.

Arras, V., Quadraginta historiae monachorum = CSCO 505-6/Aeth. 85-6 (Lovanii: Peeters 1988).

Assfalg, J. / Krüger, P., Petit dictionnaire de l'Orient Chrétien (Turnhout: Brepols 1991).

Atiya, A. S. (ed.), The Coptic Encyclopedia 1/8 (Utah: Macmillan 1991).

Böcher, O., Art. Honig, in: Reallexikon für Antike und Christentum 16 (1992) 466-468 (Lit.: ib. 471-473).

Böll, V., Marienverehrung bei den Äthiopiern, in: Der Christl. Osten 45 (1990) 140f. 144f.

Böll, V., Some remarks about the andemta on the Qeddase Maryam, specifically the anaphora of Our Lady Mary from Hereyaqos of Behensa, in: Proceed. of the XIth Intern. Conference of Ethiopian Studies, Addis Ababa 1991 (im Druck).

Botte, B. / Gerhards, A., La Tradition Apostolique de saint Hippolyte. Essai de reconstitution. 5. verbesserte Auflage = Liturgiewissenschaftliche Quellen und Forschungen 39 (Münster: Aschendorff 1989).

Boud'hors, A., Manuscrits coptes «chypriotes» à la Bibliothèque nationale, in: Études coptes III. Troisième journée d'études. Musée du Louvre 23 mai 1986 = Cah. de la Bibl. copte 4 (Louvain/Paris: Peeters 1989) 11ff.

Bradshaw, P. F., Ordination Rites of the Ancient Church of East and West (New York: Pueblo 1990).

Bradshaw, P. F., Baptismal practice in the Alexandrian tradition, eastern or western, in: idem (ed.), Essays in early eastern initiation (Bramcote: Grove 1988) 5-17.

Brakmann, H., Neue Funde und Forschungen zur Liturgie der Kopten (1984-1988), in: Actes du IVe Congrès Intern. d'Études Coptes, Louvain-la-Neuve 1988.

Brakmann, H., Renaudots »Pontificale Seguierianum«, die »Fourmont«-Manuskripte in Leningrad und andere Coptica Coisliniana, in: Tesserae, Festschrift für Josef Engemann = Jahrbuch für Antike und Christentum ErgBd. 18 (Münster: Aschendorff 1991 [1992]) 406-415.

Brakmann, H., Der Gottesdienst in den östlichen Kirchen, in: Archiv für

Liturgiewissenschaft 30 (1988) 303-410 (Literaturbericht).

Brakmann, H., Muster bewegter Liturgie in kirchlicher Tradition, in: W. Meurer (ed.), Volk Gottes auf dem Weg (Mainz: Grünewald 1989) 25-51.

Brakmann, H., Art. Axomis (Aksum), in: Reallexikon für Antike und Christentum Suppl. 1, 5/6 (1992) 718-810.

Brakmann, H., Zur Evangeliar-Auflegung bei der Ordination koptischer Bischöfe, in: Εὐλόγημα, Studies in hon. of R. Taft = Analecta liturgica 17 (Roma: Benedictina - Ed. Abbazia S. Paolo 1993) (im Druck).

Brakmann, H., La »Mystagogia« de la liturgie alexandrine et copte, in: La mystagogie dans la pensée liturgique d'aujourd'hui et dans la liturgie ancienne. 39e Semaine d'études liturgiques de Saint-Serge, Paris 1992 = Bibl. Eph. Lit. Subs. (im Druck).

Brakmann, H. / Gerhards, A. (ed.), Prex Eucharistica. Ed. secunda + Supplementum (in Vorb.).

Brashear, W. , A Christian Amulet, in: Journal of Ancient Civilisations 3 (Changchun [China] 1988) 35-45 (P. Louvre E 7332bis; 7. Jh.).

Brashear, W. / Hoogendijk, F. A. J., Corpus Tabularum Lignearum Ceratarumque Aegyptiarum, in: Enchoria 17 (1990) 21-54.

Brashear, W. / Quecke, H., Ein Holzbrett mit zweisprachigen Hymnen auf Christus und Maria, in: Enchoria 17 (1990) 1/16 (Tafel K 1019).

Camplani, A., Sulla cronologia delle lettere festali di Atanasio, in: Augustinianum 21 (1987) 617-628 (zu: R. Lorenz, Der zehnte Osterfestbrief des Athanasius von Alexandrien [Berlin/New York 1986]).

Camplani, A., Le lettere festali di Atanasio di Alessandria. Studio storico-critico (Roma: Centro Italiano Microfiches 1989).

Camplani, A., In margine alla storia dei Meliziani, in: Augustinianum 30 (1990) 313-351.

Camplani, A., La Quaresima egiziana del VII secolo: Note di cronologia su Mon. Epiph. 77, Manchester Rylands Suppl. 47-48, P. Grenf. II 112, P. Berol. 10677, P. Köln 215 e un'omelia copta, in: Augustinianum 32 (1992) 423-432.

Carroll, Scott T., The Melitian schism. Coptic Christianity and the Egyptian church, Diss. Oxford, Ohio (1989).

Chaillot, Ch., Comment vit la femme copte aujourd'hui au sein de l'église, in: Le Monde Copte 16 (1989) 66-73 (Appendice [72f]: Prières de consécration des diaconesses coptes orthodoxes).

Colin, G., Le synaxaire éthiopien. État actuel de la question, in: Analecta Bollandiana 106 (1988) 273-317.

Colin, G., Le synaxaire éthiopien. Mois de maskaram, eqemt, ḥedār, terr = PO 43, 3; 44, 1. 3; 45, 1 (Turnhout: Brepols 1986/90).

Coombs, St., Thematic Correspondence in Iberogallic, Egyptian and Ethiopian Eucharistic Prayers, in: Ostkirchliche Studien 38 (1989) 281-310.

Coquin, R.-G., rec. U. Zanetti, Les lectionnaires coptes annuels, in: Orientalia 57 (1988) 103-105.

Coquin, R.-G., Saint Georges ou saint Jean-de-Sanhūt?, in: BullSocArchCopte 29 (1990) 23-26.

Coquin, R.-G., À propos des vêtements des moines égyptiens, in: BullSocArchCopte 31 (1992) 3-23.

Costin, V., Der Kult der koptischen Kirche und der Kult der orthodoxen Kirche im Lichte des gegenwärtigen Ökumenismus, in: Am Beginn des Theologischen Dialogs, Festschrift für Th. Piffl-Perčević = Pro Oriente 10 (Innsbruck: Tyrolia 1987) 298-306.

Cuming, G. C., The Liturgy of St Mark = OrChrAn 243 (Roma: PISO 1990).

Cuming, G. C., The shape of the Anaphora, in: Studia Patristica 20 (Leuven: Peeters 1989) 333-345.

Cyrille d'Alexandrie, Lettres festales (I-VI). Introduction générale par P. Évieux. Introduction critique, texte grec par W. H. Burns. Traduction et annotation par L. Arragon, M.-O. Boulnois, P. Évieux, M. Forrat, B. Meunier = Sources Chrétiennes 372 (Paris: Cerf 1991).

Devos, P., Les cinq premières lettres festales de s. Athanase d'Alexandrie. Un test, in: Analecta Bollandiana 110 (1992) 5-20 (zu: R. Lorenz, Der zehnte Osterfestbrief des Athanasius von Alexandrien [Berlin/New York 1986]).

Di Bitonto Kasser, A., Ostraca greci e copti a Deir el Gizāz: Aegyptus 70 (1990) 57-72 (Psalmi [Hermeniai?]; inno liturgico in greco).

Doresse, J., Deir el Gizāz, ou couvent de Samuel: Un monastère thébain oublié ... et même disparu, in: Aegyptus 69 (1989) 153-163. (p. 162 zu: R.-G. Coquin, Le synaxaire des coptes, in: AnalBoll 96 [1978] 351-365).

Dufrasne, M. D., Art. Sérapion de Thmuis, in: Dict. de Spiritualité 14 (1990) 647-652 (Résumé von M. D. Dufrasne, Les tendances ariennes et pneumatomaques de l'eucologe du Pseudo-Sérapion. 3 vol. Diss. theol. Louvain-la-Neuve [1981]).

Dyer, J., Monastic psalmody in the Middle Ages: RevBén 99 (1989) 41-74 (Lit.).

Ezra Gebremedhin, The Anaphora of St Cyril of Alexandria in the Liturgical Practice of the Ethiopian Orthodox Church. Observations on the Text and the Interpretation of the Ge'ez Version, in: On Both Sides of al-Mandab. Ethiopian, South-Arabic and Islamic Studies presented to O. Löfgren = Swedish research Inst. in Istanbul, Transactions 2 (Stockholm 1989) 7-11.

Fenwick, J. R. K., The Anaphoras of St. Basil and St. James. An investigation into their common origin = Orientalia Christiana Analecta 241 (Rome: PISO 1992).

Fenwick, J. R. K., The significance of similarities in the anaphoral intercession sequence in the Coptic anaphora of St Basil and other ancient liturgies, in: Studia Patristica 18, 2 (Kalamazoo/Leuven 1989) 355-362.

Finn, Th. M., Early Christian Baptism and the Catechumenate. Italy, North Africa, and Egypt = Message of the Fathers of the Church 6 (Collegeville: Lit. Press 1992).

Fitschen, K., Serapion von Thmuis. Echte und unechte Schriften sowie die Zeugnisse des Athanasius und anderer = Patristische Texte und Studien 37 (Berlin/New York: de Gruyter 1992).

Frend, W. H. C. / Dragas, G. / Kontoyiannis, Sp., Some further Greek liturgical fragments from Q'asr Ibrim, in: Jahrbuch für Antike und Christentum 35 (1992) (im Druck).

Frend, W. H. C., Fragments of a version of the Acta Georgii from Q'asr Ibrim, in: Jahrbuch für Antike und Christentum 32 (1989) 89-104.

Gascou, J., Un nouveau calendrier de saints égyptiens (P. Iand. inv. 318), in: Analecta Bollandiana 107 (1989) 384-392.

Gawdat Gabra, Bemerkungen zum Text des Difnars über Pesyntheus, Bischof von Koptos, in: Muséon 102 (1989) 5-18.

Geymonat, G., Un antico lezionario della chiesa di Alessandria, in: Laurea corona. Studies in hon. of Edward Coleiro (Amsterdam: Grüner 1987) 186-196. 2 Abb. (Gregory/Aland l 1601; van Haelst nr. 287).

Gramaglia, P. A., L'Ordo battesimale di Timoteo, Vescovo di Alessandria, unpubl. Diss. Roma: PISO (1968).

Grillmeier, A., Jesus der Christus im Glauben der Kirche 2, 4. Die Kirche von Alexandrien mit Nubien und Äthiopien (Freiburg/Basel/Wien: Herder 1990) (zu: T. Orlandi, Shenute. Contra Origenistas [Roma 1985]; A. Gerhards, Die griech. Gregoriosanaphora [Münster 1984]; H. Brakmann, Zu den Fragmenten einer griech. Basileios-Liturgie aus dem kopt. Makarios-Kloster, in: Oriens Christianus 66 [1982] 118-43).

Habtämicha'el Kindanä, L'Ufficio divino etiopico. Studio storico-critico con particolare riferimento alle ore cattedrali, Diss. Roma: PISO (1990).

Habtemicael Bahlebbi, The biblical-liturgical theology of the Pentecostal office of Gheez, Diss. Roma: Pont. Univ. Urbaniana (1989).

Hammerschmidt, E., Orientalische Liturgiewissenschaft und koptische Eucharistiefeier, in: Koptisch-Orthodoxes Zentrum/St. AntoniusKloster (ed.), Seminar-Vorträge (Waldsolms 1990) 53-63.

Hanna, O. / Hanna, S. Die koptische Liturgie des Hl. Basilios und des hl. Gregorios mit Abend- und Morgenweihrauch (Köln 1990).

Hasitzka, M., Koptische Totenklagen auf Papyrus, in: M. Capasso et al. (ed.), Miscellanea Papyrologica in occasione del bicentenario dell'edizione della Charta Borgiana 1 = Papyrol. Florent. 19 (Firenze: Ed. Gonnelli 1990) 297-303.

Hassab Alla, W., Évolution historique du rite et de la pratique du baptème dans l'église copte orthodoxe d'Alexandrie, in: Le Monde Copte 13 (1988) 26-33.

Holze, H., Könobitische Gebetspraxis und individuelle Gebetserfahrung in den pachomianischen Klöstern, in: Wort u. Dienst 21 (1991) 133-148.

Horn, J., Untersuchungen zu Frömmigkeit und Literatur des christlichen Ägypten: Das Martyrium des Viktor, Sohnes des Romanos (Einleitung in das koptische Literaturwerk/Kommentar zum »ersten Martyrium«, Diss. phil. Göttingen (1981 [publ. 1988]).

Innemée, K. C., Parallels between Nubian and Byzantine Liturgical vestments, in: Jahrbuch für Antike und Christentum 32 (1989) 181-185, 3 Abb. u. 3 Taf.

Innemée, K. C., Old Testament Elements in Nubian Costume, in: Nubian Letters 14 (1990) 13-18.

Innemée, K. C., Ecclesiastical Dress in the Medieval Near East = Studies in Textile and Costume History 1 (Leiden: Brill 1992).

Ioannidou, G., P. Berol. 21329: Theotokion und Osterhymnus, in: Zeitschrift für Papyrologie und Epigraphik 89 (1991) 39/43.

Jacob, A., La date, la patrie et le modèle d'un rouleau italo-grec (Messanensis gr. 177), in: Helikon 22-27 (1982/87 [1988]) 109/25.

Jacob, A., L'Euchologe de Sainte-Marie du Patir et ses sources, in: Atti del Congresso Internazionale su S. Nilo di Rossano, 28 sett. - 1 ott. 1986 (Rossano/Grottaferrata: Università Popolare Rossano - Amministrazione Comunale Rossano 1989) 75-118, 2 Taf.

Janeras, S., Le Vendredi-Saint dans la tradition liturgique byzantine. Structure et histoire de ses offices = Studia Anselmiana 99 = Analecta Liturgica 13 (Roma: Benedictina - Ed. Abbazia S. Paolo 1988 [1989]).

Johnson, D., The dossier of Aba Zenobius, in: Orientalia 58 (1989) 193-212.

Johnson, M. E., A Fresh Look at the Prayers of Sarapion of Thmuis, in: Studia Liturgica 22 (1992) 163-183.

Johnson, M. E., The Prayers of Sarapion of Thmuis, Diss. Univ. of Notre Dame (1992?).

Kabes, A. P., La spiritualité du mariage dans l'église copte et la nouvelle génération, Diss. Roma (1987).

Kannengiesser, Ch., Questions ouvertes sur Athanase d'Alexandrie, in: Vox Patrum 8 (1988) 689-705.

Kannengiesser, Ch., The homiletic festal letters of Athanasius, in: D. G. Hunter (ed.), Preaching in the patristic age. Studies in honor of W. J. Burghardt (New York: Paulist 1989) 73-100.

Kardong, T. G., The monastic practices of Pachomius and the Pachomians, in: Studia monastica 32 (1990) 59-78.

Khella, K., Die koptische Liturgie übersetzt und kommentiert (Hamburg 1989).

Kok, F., L'office pachômien: psallere, orare, legere, in: Ecclesia Orans 9 (1992) 69-95.

Kolb, A. Das Symbolum Nicaeno-Constantinopolitanum. Zwei neue Zeugnisse: Zeitschrift für Papyrologie und Epigraphik 79 (1989) 253-260 (O.Heid. inv. 419; Lond. copt. 155 frg. 2).

Krause, M., Ein Vorschlagsschreiben für einen Priester, in: R. Schulz/M. Görg (ed.), Lingua Restituta Orientalis, Festgabe für J. Assfalg = Ägypt. u. AT 20 (Wiesbaden: Harrassowitz 1990) 195-202 (P. Pierpont Morgan inv. 660.B.12 [ed. princ.: L.S.B. MacCoull, Coptic Marriage Contract: Actes du 15e Congr. intern. de Papyrologie 2 (Bruxelles 1979) 116-123]).

Langen, L., A mysterious altar-casket in Abu Sefein Church in Old-Cairo, in: BSAC 28 (1986/89) 75-79.

Lanne, E., L'initiation dans la tradition égyptienne, in: La mystagogie dans la pensée liturgique d'aujourd'hui et dans la liturgie ancienne. 39e Semaine d'études liturgiques de Saint-Serge, Paris 1992 = Bibl. Eph. Lit. Subs. (im Druck).

Lattke, M., Hymnus. Materialien zu einer Geschichte der antiken Hymnologie = Novum Testamentum et Orbis Antiquus 19 (Freiburg/ Schw.-Göttingen 1991).

Liturgie dell'Oriente Cristiano a Roma nell'Anno Mariano 1987-1988. Testi e studi (Città del Vaticano: Libr. Ed. Vaticana 1990) 586-685: »Preghiera dell'incenso in rito alessandrino-copto«.

MacCoull, L. S. B., Stud. Pal. XV 250ab: A Monophysite Trishagion for the Nile Flood, in: JournTheolStud NS 40 (1989) 129-135 (P. Vindob. G 39 789 olim K 9740; van Haelst nr. 1047).

MacCoull, L. S. B., More Coptic papyri from the Beinecke Collection, in: Archiv für Papyrusforschung 35 (1989) 25-35 (P. Yale inv. 2 106 [VII/VIII]: Hermeneia on the Psalms?).

MacCoull, L. S. B., The paschal letter of Alexander II, Patriarch of Alexandria. A Greek defense of Coptic theology under Arab rule, in: Dumbarton Oaks Pap. 44 (1990) 27-40 (zu: P. Berlin 10677; van Haelst nr. 621).

MacCoull, L. S. B., Further notes on P. Gr. Wess. Prag. 3: Greek Psalm antiphons in 11th cent. Egypt, in: Ephemerides Liturgicae 106 (1992) 162-170.

Maestri, G., Un contributo alla conoscenza dell'antica liturgia egiziana. Studio dell'Anafora del santo Evangelista Matteo, in: Memoriam sanctorum venerantes. Misc. in on. di M. V. Saxer = Studi di antichità cristiana 48 (Città del Vat.: Pont. Ist. di archeol. Crist. 1992) 525-537.

Maestri, G., Un contributo allo studio dell'antica liturgia egiziana: Analisi del frammento F Hyvernat, in: Qvaeritur inventvs colitvr. Misc. in on. di P. U. M. Fasola = Studi di antichità cristiana 40 (Città del Vat.: Pont. Ist. di archeol. Crist. 1989) 439-448.

Malaty, T. Y., Die Ikonostase in der koptischen Tradition, in: Hermeneia, Zeitschrift für Ostkirchliche Kunst 2 (1986) 208-214.

Martin, A., Topographie et liturgie. Le problème des «Paroisses» d'Alexandrie, in: Actes du 11e Congr. intern. d'Arch, chrét., 1986 2 (Rome 1989) 1133-1144. (cf. H. Brakmann, Synaxis katholikè in Alexandreia, in: JbAntChrist 30 [1987] 74/89).

Mazza, E., L'anafora eucaristica. Studi sulle origini = Bibl. Eph. Lit. Subs. 62 (Roma 1992).

Meinardus, O. F. A., The Eucharist in the historical experience of the Copts: Coptologia 1988, 53-74.

Messner, R., Prex Eucharistica. Zur Frühgeschichte der Basileios-Anaphora. Beobachtungen und Hypothesen, in: E. Renhart / A. Schnider (ed.), Sursum Corda. Variationen zu einem liturgischen Motiv. für Ph. Harnoncourt zum 60. Geburtstag (Graz: Akad. Dr.- u. Verl.-Anst./A. Schnider 1991) 121-129.

Müller, C. D. G., Gab es ein koptisches Theater?, in: BullSocArchCopte 29 (1990) 9-22.

Müller, C. D. G., Gabriel II. ibn Turaik, 70. Papst und Patriarch des Missionsbereichs des Heiligen Markos, in: Oriens Christianus 74 (1990) 168-186.

Nagel, P., Das Alte Testament im geistigen und geistlichen Leben der koptischen Kirche, in: Koptisch-Orthodoxes Zentrum/St. Antonius-Kloster (Ed.), Seminar-Vorträge (Waldsolms 1990) 29-51.

Nagel, P., Editionen koptischer Bibeltexte seit Till 1960, in: Archiv für Papyrusforschung 35 (1989) 43-100.

Nagel, P., Fragmente eines sahidischen Genesiskodex der Nationalbibliothek zu Paris (BN copt. 129.1 fol. 8-13), in: Zeitschrift für Ägypt. Sprache 116 (1989) 71-90.

Nagel, P., rec. A. Bouvarel-Boud'hors, Catalogue des fragments coptes 1. Fragments bibliques nouvellement identifiés (Paris 1987), in: Archiv für Papyrusforschung 36 (1990) 91f.

Neugebauer, O, Abu Shaker's »Chronography«. A treatise of the 13th century on chronological, calendrical, and astronomical matters, written by a Christian Arab, preserved in Ethiopic = Österr. Akad. der Wiss., philos.-hist. Kl., Sitzungsber. 498 (Wien: Verlag der Öst. Akad. d. Wiss. 1988) 198 S. 7 Taf.

Orlandi, T., La patrologia copta, in: A. Quacquarelli (ed.), Complementi interdisciplinari di patrologia (Roma 1989) 457-502 (Lit.).

Paprocki, H., Mistyczna. Anafory eucharystyczne chrzecijaskiego Wschodu (Warszawa: Inst. Wydawniczy Pax 1988).

Paprocki, H., Les liturgies eucharistiques coptes comme témoignage de la continuité de la tradition: Vox Patrum 9 (1989) 893-900.

Pelsmaekers, J., Het gebed in de teksten op koptische grafplaten. Bemerkingen en vragen, in: Bull. de l'Inst. Hist. Belge de Rome 59 (1989) 31-42.

Pezolt, S., Die Heilig-Geist-Bitte (Epiklese) in den alten Hochgebeten, in: Erbe u. Auftrag 67 (1991) 305ff.

Pickering, S. R., A baptism text in Greek and Old Nubian, in: Proceedings of the 18th Intern. Congress of Papyrology, Athens 1986 (Athens: Greek Pap. Soc. 1988) 2, 133 (P. Macquarie inv. 374).

Quecke, H., rec. B. Layton, Catalogue of Coptic literary manuscripts, in: Orientalia 57 (1988) 237-239.

Quecke, H. Ein sahidisches Fragment der Basiliusliturgie (Cod. Vat. copt. 103, 2), in: W. Nyssen (ed.), Simandron. Der Wachklopfer. Gedenkschrift für Klaus Gamber (1919-1989) = Koinonia-Oriens 30 (Köln: Luthe 1989) 137-147.

Quecke, H., Psalmverse als 'Hymnen' in der koptischen Liturgie? (im Druck).

Quecke, H., Eine koptische alphabetische Akrostichis, in: Orientalia 61 (1992) 1-9.

Robertson, M., The reliability of the oral tradition in preserving Coptic music 3. A comparison of four recordings of the confession of faith from the Liturgy of Saint Basil, in: BullSocArchCopte 28 (1986/89) 93-105.

Roca-Puig, R. P., L'epíclesi segona a l'Anàfora de Barcelona, P. Barc. Inv. n. 155a, lín. 18-27 (Barcelona 1988).

Roca-Puig, R. P., La imposició de les mans sobre els malalts. P. Barc. inv. 155b, lín. 19-26 i 156a, lín. 1-5. Colofò: P. Barc. inv. 156b (Barcelona 1989).

Roca-Puig, R. P., Oració desprès de la Comunió. P. Barc. inv. núm. 155b, lín. 1-18 (Barcelona 1990).

Roca-Puig, R. P., Exorcisme de l'Oli dels Malalts, P. Barc. inv. núm 156a, 6-25. 156b, 1-5 (Barcelona 1991).

Roca-Puig, R. P., Casta oblació, P. Barc. inv. núm. 157ab (Barcelona 1992).

Rose, A., La fête de Paques selon les lettres festales de saint Athanase, in: A. M. Triacca / A. Pistoia (ed.), La prédication liturgique et les commentaires de la liturgie. Conférences Saint-Serge. 38e Semaine d'Études liturgiques, Paris 1990 = Bibl. Eph. Li. Subs. 65 (Roma 1992) 193-203.

Samir Kh., rec. U. Zanetti, Les manuscrits de Dair Abū Maqār, in: BullSocArchCopte 28 (1986/89) 147-151.

Samir Kh., Ibn Tarīk ou ibn Turayk?, in: Muséon 101 (1988) 171-177.

Samir Kh., L'année liturgique copte: in: Proche-Orient Chrétien 39 (1989) 26-34.

Saxer, V., Les rites de l'initiation chrétienne du IIe au VIe siècle. Esquisse historique et signification d'après leurs principaux témoins = Centro Italiano di Studi sull'alto Medioevo 7 (Spoleto 1988).

Schmitz, F. J. / Mink, G., Liste der koptischen Handschriften des Neuen Testaments I. Die sahidischen Handschriften der Evangelien 2. Teil 2. Halbband = Arbeiten zur neutestamentlichen Textforschung 15 (Berlin/New York: de Gruyter 1991).

Schneider, R., Nouveaux témoins du texte éthiopien des Règles de l'église, in: Journal Asiatique 276 (1988) 71-96.

Schneiders, M., Acclamations in the eucharistic prayer, in: Ch. Caspers / M. Schneiders (ed.), Omnes circumadstantes. Contributions towards a history of the role of the people in the liturgy pres. to H. Wegman (Kampen: Kok 1990) 78-100.

Shelemay, K. K., Music, Ritual, and Falasha History (East Lansing: Michigan State Univ. Press 1989).

Searle, M. / Stevenson, K. W., Documents of the Marriage Liturgy (Collegeville:

Lit. Press 1992) 79-99: The Coptic Rite.

Sijpesteijn, P. J., New light on the ΦΙΛΟΠΟΝΟΙ, in: Aegyptus 69 (1989) 95-99.

Spinks, B. D., The Sanctus in the Eucharistic Prayer (Cambridge: Cambr. Univ. Press 1991).

Spinks, B. D., The Jerusalem liturgy of the catecheses mystagogicae: Syrian or Egyptian, in: Studia Patristica 18, 2 (Leuven: Peeters 1989) 391-395 (zu: G. Cuming, Egyptian Elements in the Jerusalem Liturgy, in: JournTheolStud NS 25 [1974] 117-124).

Taft, R. F., The interpolation of the Sanctus into the Anaphora: When and where? A review of the dossier, in: Orientalia Christiana Periodica 57 (1991) 281-308; 58 (1992) 83-121.

Taft, R. F., A History of the Liturgy of St. John Chrysostom. Vol. IV. The Diptychs = Orientalia Christiana Analecta 238 (Roma: PISO 1991) 76-94: »The diptychs in Egypt«.

Taft, R. F., »Holy Things for the Saints«. The ancient call to communion and its response, in: G. Austen (ed.), Fountain of Life. In memory of N. K. Rasmussen (Washington DC: The Pastoral Press 1991) 87-102.

Taft, R. F., Penance in contemporary scholarship, in: Studia Liturgica 18 (1988) 2-21.

Teteriatnikov, N., Upper-Story Chapels near the Sanctuary in Churches of the Christian East, in: Dumbarton Oaks Papers 42 (1988) 65-72.

Theodorou, E. D., Ἡ Εὐχαριστικὴ ἀναφορὰ τῆς μονῆς Der-Balyzeh. (Εἰσαγωγικὰ – Κείμενον – Σχόλια, in: Θεολογία 61 (1990) 380-389.

Treu, K., Carl Schmidt als Patristiker, in: P. Nagel (Hrsg.), Carl-Schmidt-Kolloquium an der Martin-Luther-Universität 1988 (Halle 1990) 41 (P. Vindob. G 19 934 Bl. 1a: Hymnus).

Treu, K., Christliche Papyri, in: Archiv für Papyrusforschung 34 (1988) 69-78; 35 (1989) 107-116 (p. 110: P. Vindob. G 26134 = Markos-Anaphora); 36 (1990) 95-98; 37 (1991) 93-98.

Van Esbroeck, M., La tradition copte de la fête de la dormition de la Vierge, in: Actes du IVe Congrès Intern. d'Études Coptes, Louvain-la-Neuve 1988.

Van Moorsel, P., Ein Thron für den Kelch, in: Tesserae. Festschrift für Josef Engemann = Jahrbuch für Antike und Christentum ErgBd. 18 (Münster: Aschendorff 1991 [1992]) 299-303, Taf. 39f.

Viaud, G., Les 24 Presbytres de l'Apocalypse dans la tradition copte, in: BullSocArchCopte 29 (1990) 123-145 (avec traduction de quelques textes liturgiques).

Vidman, L., Rotolo liturgico [Gr. I 27 + Ar. II 74 + Ar. III 193], in: R. Pintaudi / R. Dostálová / L. Vidman, Papyri Graecae Wessely Pragenses = Papyrologica Florentina 16 (Firenze 1988) 30-41.

Wahedd Hassab Alla, Discours pour la fête de la croix attribué à S. Cyrille d'Alex., in: Oriens Christianus 75 (1991) 166-197 (versio arab.).

Warns, R., Untersuchungen zum 2. Clemens-Brief, Diss. Marburg (1985 [publ. 1988/89]).

Zanetti, U., La prière copte de consécration d'une icône, in: Le Monde copte 19 (1991) 93-98.

Zanetti, U., Abū-l-Barakāt et les lectionnaires de Haute-Égypte, in: Actes du IVe Congrès Intern. d'Études Coptes, Louvain-la-Neuve 1988.

Zanetti, U., La distribution des psaumes dans l'horologion copte, in: Orientalia Christiana Periodica 56 (1990) 323-369.

Zanetti, U., Une seconde copie du livre de Marc ibn al-Qanbar sur la confession, in: Orientalia Christiana Periodica 55 (1989) 199f.

Zanetti, U., Y eut-il des diaconesses en Égypte?, in: Vetera Christianorum 27 (1990) 369-373.

Zanetti, U., Horologion copte et vêpres byzantines, in: Muséon 102 (1989) 237-254.

Zanetti, U., Is the Ethiopian Holy Week Service translated from Sahidic? Towards a study of the Gebra Ḥemāmāt, in: Proceedings of the XIth International Conference of Ethiopian Studies, Addis Ababa 1991 (im Druck).

Zanetti, U., Les icônes chez les théologiens de l'église copte, in: Le Monde copte 19 (1991) 77-91.

STEPHEN EMMEL

RECENT PROGRESS
IN COPTIC CODICOLOGY AND PALEOGRAPHY
(1988–1992)

In Rome twelve years ago, at the Second International Congress of Coptic Studies, Bentley Layton stated that "Coptic palaeography, in the narrow sense of the precise science of dating Coptic manuscripts according to the form of their script, does not yet exist," and that the lack of such a science places "an intolerable limitation upon the historical value of all our Coptic manuscripts." He pointed out, however, that in the current circumstances of our knowledge about dated manuscripts, "any attempt to establish a [chronological] typology of Coptic hand[writing] is hopelessly premature," raising the question of whether it is even reasonable to assume that such a typology is feasible, at least for literary scripts. As an auxiliary tool, or even as an outright substitute for a dated series of Coptic scripts, he outlined a vision of "a new Coptic paleography" according to which as much attention is to be paid to the more technological features of the manuscripts—that is, to features of codicology—as to the copyists' handwriting, because there is much more hope of discovering a chronological typology in the total technique of codex manufacture than in styles of handwriting alone. The major hindrance to pursuing the type of study that this point of view endorses is a lack of detailed data, systematically recorded from a large number of manuscripts.[1]

In response to this need, recent research has continued a useful trend toward collecting the kinds of data that are necessary for the establishment of Coptic paleography and codicology as a science. Lay-

---

1. Layton 1985 (the quotations are from p. 152).

ton's *Catalogue of Coptic Literary Manuscripts in the British Library*, which appeared in 1987, has set a new standard for Coptic codicological description, and its salutary influence can already be perceived in subsequent literature.

The newly published data are mostly found in descriptions of manuscripts accompanying editions of Coptic texts. It is encouraging to see the number of editors who have taken seriously the demanding task of describing their manuscripts, even though such descriptions are not usually the primary interest of the publication. The number of editions that include photographic facsimiles is also impressive. The scientific value of such descriptions and of good facsimiles cannot be overemphasized.

Prominent among recent Coptic manuscript publications are editions of four papyrus codexes, dated by paleographers between the third and the fifth centuries. To begin with, Bernd Jørg Diebner and Rodolphe Kasser (1989) have overseen the publication of the rest of the bilingual Greek-Coptic papyrus codex in the university library in Hamburg, the first part of which was published by Carl Schmidt and Wilhelm Schubart in 1936. This codex contains a Greek copy of the apocryphal Christian work known as the *Acts of Paul*, followed by Coptic versions of the Song of Solomon and Lamentations, and then Ecclesiastes in both Greek and Coptic.

Second, what had been known since the mid-1950s as Mississippi Coptic Codex I has now been published by a team of scholars as the Crosby-Schøyen Codex, under the general editorship of James E. Goehring (1990). This papyrus codex contains the second century sermon *On the Passover* by Melito of Sardis, followed by an excerpt from 2 Maccabees, then 1 Peter, Jonah, and the fragmentary beginning of an unidentified homily.

Third, Søren Giversen's facsimile publication of the Manichaean Psalm-Book (1986–88, vols. 3–4) has completed his four-volume facsimile edition of the Manichaean papyri belonging to the Chester Beatty Library in Dublin. This facsimile edition is the first publication of some of the manuscripts in this collection, whose terribly dilapidated condition poses severe problems for editors.

And also now published, by William Brashear, Wolf-Peter Funk, James M. Robinson, and Richard Smith (1990), is another papyrus codex in the Chester Beatty Library, Ac. 1390, a peculiar manuscript combining mathematical exercises in Greek with a lengthy excerpt from the middle of the Gospel of John in the Coptic dialect *L5*.

The descriptions of Chester Beatty Ac. 1390 and the Crosby-Schøyen Codex, written by Robinson, provide a thorough analysis of all the relevant features about which a papyrus codicologist wants to know. One of the most interesting insights into the structure of papyrus codexes finds confirmation here yet again: the sheets of the quires were cut from papyrus rolls. In the case of the single-quire Crosby-Schøyen Codex, four rolls were used, and each roll was made by gluing together two broad kollemata, sheets of papyrus between one and one-and-a-half meters in length. Because such remarkably broad papyrus sheets continue to be found only when codexes are reconstructed into the rolls from which they were manufactured, it remains likely that it was the development of the codex book-form that led to this technological innovation in the making of papyrus rolls.

The structure of the Hamburg codex, of which four consecutive quires survive out of an indeterminately larger number, had already been described by Schmidt and Schubart. But the new description by Diebner provides a useful revision on certain points, and the excellent photographic facsimiles included in the earlier edition have now been supplemented completely, even including some old photographs showing the papyrus leaves in a more complete state of preservation.[2] This is a codex of unusual linguistic interest, because the Coptic texts in it are written in dialect *F7*, a variety of Faiyumic that is otherwise

---

2.   The new codicological description does not attend to the reconstruction of the papyrus rolls out of which the sheets of the quires were cut, despite the fact that Hugo Ibscher (1940, x) noted the occurrence of two kolleseis in the codex (from the newly published plates it seems that kolleseis possibly occur on pp. 14 and 39) and claimed that fiber continuity is traceable across at least several of the sheets. I may also note in passing that the claim (Diebner & Kasser 1989, 16) that some leaves are palimpsest is doubtful: the relevant ink traces appear to be just offset ("blotting") from facing pages, clearly so in the margins of, e.g., pp. 33 and 35.

unattested. Furthermore, Kasser has argued that the remarkable ortho-
graphic peculiarities of the final section of the codex (Ecclesiastes in
F7) are best explained by positing an Old Coptic *Vorlage* of which this
part of the Hamburg codex is a revision. If so, and if—as it seems—
the copyists of the codex were more comfortable writing Greek than
Coptic, and also considering that this codex might date from as early
as the third century, all indications are that the Hamburg codex is an
artifact bringing us into contact with the earliest stage of development
in Coptic book production.

Leaving aside the Manichaean codexes for the moment, because
their very poor physical condition warrants discussing them in a different context, this survey of publications relating to papyrus codicology would be incomplete without mention of the continuing appearance of text editions of the Nag Hammadi Codices: four more volumes in the Coptic Gnostic Library series (Layton 1989; Hedrick
1990;[3] Parrott 1991;[4] Sieber 1991), thus bringing the American edition almost to completion, one more volume in the French language
series Bibliothèque copte de Nag Hammadi (Thomassen & Painchaud
1989), and two more volumes in the German series Texte und Untersuchungen (Kirchner 1989; Schenke 1989). Because Nag Hammadi
codicology has been well-known for some time, editors of Nag Hammadi texts can be content with more or less detailed recapitulations

---

3.   This edition makes remarkably few explicit references to the relevant additions
and corrections in *The Facsimile Edition of the Nag Hammadi Codices: Introduction*
(Leiden: E.J. Brill, 1984) given that the study especially of NHC XI–XIII is so
greatly aided by the improvements published there (pp. 124–30, pls. 2*a, 13*–24*,
27*–28*).

4.   Despite my admiration for the pioneering codicological work on NHC III by
Frederik Wisse (1975), I am surprised that his essay, which is wrong on certain
important points, is cited (Parrott 1991, 18–19) to the exclusion of the complete and
updated codicological description that appeared earlier in the Coptic Gnostic Library
series itself (Emmel 1984, 19–27). This omission is somewhat mitigated by a reference to *Facsimile Edition: Introduction*, chaps. 3–6, where the corrected codicological reconstruction is presupposed (but here the presentation concerns the Nag
Hammadi codexes generally, and no codex is completely described as an individual
entity).

where codex structure is concerned. But concerning features of orthography and punctuation in the texts, the recent editions include many new and useful observations. Regarding these same kinds of paleographical data in other manuscripts, it is especially Wolf-Peter Funk's essay (Brashear et al. 1990, 61–82) on the spelling and orthography of the Chester Beatty codex Ac. 1390 that shows that a minute and linguistically informed analysis of a copyist's product can teach us much about his practice (see also Kasser's study of the Coptic sections of the Hamburg codex [in Diebner & Kasser 1989]).

In the realm of Coptic parchment codexes, one codicological and paleographical essay stands out as a model of thoroughness and exactitude: Hans-Martin Schenke's description (1991) of the Glazier Codex in the Pierpont Morgan Library. This small-format parchment codex, assigned to the fifth century and containing the first half of the so-called "western text" of the Acts of the Apostles in the Mesokemic dialect, survives in an amazing state of preservation: not only is the entire bookblock intact, with only minor damage at some of the edges of some leaves, but the original cover made of wooden boards and leather also survives, still partly attached to the bookblock.

The codicological interest of the Glazier Codex is great largely because the codex is so well-preserved. Complete Coptic codexes are the exception, at least from before a relatively recent period. As a rule, Coptologists are confronted by badly damaged books and masses of fragments. Well-preserved manuscripts provide invaluable glimpses of the codicological order that lies beneath the chaotic welter of fragments. A large collection of such well-preserved manuscripts, with a single provenance and dating from a relatively early period—many of them with dated colophons from the ninth and tenth centuries—is the Hamouli library, a group of about fifty parchment codexes now mostly also in the Pierpont Morgan Library, and not so well known codicologically as they deserve to be. A full descriptive catalog of the Morgan Library's Coptic collection, which includes other manuscripts besides the Hamouli codexes and the Glazier Codex, has been prepared by Leo Depuydt, using the descriptive method that was established by Layton for his British Library catalog. The Morgan catalog is currently in press (Louvain: Peeters) and is expected to include a separate album of photographic plates.

The Glazier Codex, the Hamouli codexes, and relatively well-preserved papyrus codexes like the Crosby-Schøyen Codex and some of the Nag Hammadi codexes make it possible to formulate empirically based hypotheses about the construction of codexes that are poorly preserved. The Manichaean papyri that are now divided between Berlin and Dublin are examples of damaged codexes in need of working hypotheses on which to base the beginnings of codicological reconstructions. To some extent, relevant hypotheses were already formulated by the two Ibschers in the course of conserving the papyrus leaves, but the recently published facsimile edition of the Dublin part of the collection makes it clear to what extent the conservators' hypotheses mark only the beginning of the work of reconstruction. The published photographs make clear also how difficult this work is likely to be: words could hardly describe the sorry state of these ancient manuscripts, and at first sight it seems almost miraculous that so much has been learned from them already (thanks to the editions of H.J. Polotsky, Alexander Böhlig, and C.R.C. Allberry). Giversen, editor of the facsimile edition, has stated repeatedly his belief that only a philological restoration of the manuscripts' text will make it possible to establish with certainty the order of the pages, and thereby perhaps also to reconstruct the codexes as such.

But in a series of cogent observations based on the first two volumes of Giversen's facsimile edition, Wolf-Peter Funk (1990) has demonstrated the kind of progress that can be hoped for when philology and codicology together, combined in a rigorous method, are applied to the task of rescuing the Manichaean codexes, both as technological products and as texts. Funk's preliminary results make one optimistic that more success might be forthcoming in this enterprise than one dares hope at first glimpse of the problem. And his work also underscores the obvious need for collaboration in this enterprise, not simply because more pairs of eyes will see more data and significant connections among them, but also because the papyri are not all in one place. One more or less immediate fruit of the facsimile publication of the Dublin Manichaica was the unambiguous identification of an isolated leaf in that collection as a part of the Manichaean *Acta* codex, the bulk of which is in Berlin (Funk 1990, 539). With the publication of Giversen's facsimile edition, part of the stated purpose of which was to elicit constructive observations such as Funk has supplied, one hopes that we are now going to see continuing fundamental progress in the study of the Coptic Manichaean corpus. Progress will not be easy or quick: another recent contribution in this area, Paul Mirecki's study (1988) of the chapter titles extant in the Manichaean *Synaxeis* codex in Berlin, is an example of the kind of painstaking systematic collection of data that will contribute fundamentally to the eventual reconstruction of the Manichaean codexes (see also Krause 1991). When philology and codicology are made to work together, both will profit.

For Coptologists, then, codicology is interesting and important not just because the history of Coptic book production is interesting and important. On the development and proper application of codicology as a science also depends the reconstruction of Coptic literature. This statement is especially true with regard to the largest Coptic library of which we know, the library of the so-called White Monastery near Sohag in Upper Egypt, where Shenoute, one of Coptic Egypt's greatest writers, held sway from the middle of the fourth century to the middle of the fifth. As is well known, the decaying contents of this large library—the remains of hundreds of parchment codexes containing a wealth of Coptic literature—were dispersed piecemeal to collectors between the end of the eighteenth century and the beginning of the present one. No single codex from the White Monastery survives intact, and so far as we know at present no single White Monastery codex survives completely, with all its leaves preserved, however widely scattered. Thus, as with the Manichaean codexes, White Monastery codicology is a venture in reconstruction, with our knowledge of a large body of Coptic literature at stake. Progress in discovering codicological relationships among the extant White Monastery fragments has been steady ever since the beginning of the nineteenth century, and recent years have been no exception.[5]

The amount of accumulated data concerning codicological relationships among dismembered fragments of White Monastery codexes has
now grown so large that it is difficult to keep track of, and hence the
importance of the steps taken by Tito Orlandi during the last few years
to disseminate his computer database for Coptic manuscripts. This
database is one of the main products of the research project directed
by him, the Corpus dei Manoscritti Copti Letterari, and it is a rich
source of information about manuscripts from the White Monastery.
However, the database is a work-in-progress, and the purpose of dis-
seminating it is to foster collaboration on its enhancement, through
both augmentation and correction. At present, things could hardly be
otherwise with such a tool. For while the reconstruction of the White
Monastery codexes is still in progress—and probably it will be in
progress for many years to come—the results remain to a great extent
necessarily preliminary, in need of periodic reevaluation in the light of
subsequent discoveries and observations.

One can tell from the publications that researchers in the field of
White Monastery library reconstruction share a methodological orien-
tation that is basically uniform, largely based on the science of codicology in general—that is, codicology that is not specifically Coptological—with its detailed attention to quire structure, page format,
decoration, and so on. But the presuppositions and methods of this ori-
entation, particularly as they apply to the reconstruction of the White
Monastery library, have nowhere been explicitly set forth. The time is
rapidly approaching when significant further progress in this field will
depend on the publication of a kind of manual of codicology concerned specifically with the White Monastery library. I hope that my
own current work on the White Monastery codexes of Shenoute's

---

5.   So many specific contributions have been made in this domain by so many
scholars, that space does not permit more than a list of the most important
publications: Boud'hors 1988; Camplani 1989; Coquin 1988b, 1989a, 1991; Devos
1988; Elanskaja 1988, 1989, 1991a; Emmel 1989, 1990a, 1990b; Johnson 1989;
Lucchesi 1988a, 1988b, 1988c, 1988d, 1989a, 1989b; Nagel 1988, 1989a, 1989b;
Orlandi 1988; Quecke 1988b; Schmitz & Mink 1986–91; Schüssler 1990a; Sheridan
1990; Wisse 1990, 1991; Zanetti 1988.

works might contribute to the preparation of such a manual. For I have tried to systematize and articulate explicitly the applicable codicological presuppositions and methods, and the reconstructed corpus of nearly one hundred codexes can serve as the nucleus of a database of White Monastery codexes from which empirically sound codicological and paleographical generalizations can be drawn.[6]

In his plenary report on Coptic literature at the Fourth International Congress of Coptic Studies four years ago, Orlandi advocated a point of view concerning Coptic manuscripts that gives primary attention to ancient groupings, which he called "bibliological units," rather than focusing primarily on the components of the accidental groupings in the modern collections. In accord with this viewpoint is the focus on the Coptic Manichaean codexes as a discrete ancient group of books (Robinson 1992; cf. Giversen 1988), or on the White Monastery codexes as a discrete ancient library. The present geographical disbursement of such groups is but an accident, or rather, an obstacle to be overcome by scientific methods. Recent research has made progress also in the reconstruction of other ancient groups of manuscripts.

James M. Robinson (1990a, 1990b; cf. Kasser 1988) has published his findings concerning the provenance of the "Dishna Papers," a designation roughly synonymous with the older and more familiar name, "Bodmer Papyri." The latter name refers to the modern collection that contains a majority of the relevant manuscripts, the Bodmer Library in Geneva. The designation "Dishna Papers," specifying the Upper Egyptian town that was closely involved in the discovery and dispersal of the manuscripts, refers to the components of what is thought to be an ancient collection, whatever its exact contents are eventually determined to be, and without reference to the various modern collections into which it has been dispersed. In compiling an inventory of forty-seven manuscripts that seem to have been discovered together near Dishna in 1952, Robinson chose to include some items "only

---

6.   I refer to my forthcoming dissertation, "Shenoute's Literary Corpus" (Ph.D. diss., Yale University, in progress), on which see my paper, "Shenoute's Literary Corpus: A Codicological Reconstruction," elsewhere in these *Acts* (vol. 2, pt. 1). [My dissertation was completed May 1993.]

with hesitation," while also acknowledging the likelihood that other manuscripts will someday be added to his list. The exercise in cross-examination and further detection thus called for is of no small significance, because according to Robinson's reconstruction there is reason to believe that the Dishna Papers are the remnants of the library of a Pachomian monastery.

The possible identification of a Pachomian monastic library is also the focus of a recent essay by Clemens Scholten (1988). On the basis of a broad assemblage of historical data, including, inter alia, information about the manufacture and use of books in early Egyptian monasticism, Scholten has addressed the disputed question of a possible Pachomian monastic provenance for the Nag Hammadi Codices. Whereas such a provenance at first seemed assured by the contents of the cartonnage removed from the codexes' covers, it was thrown into doubt when the relevant documents were finally published in detail. Scholten argues that the most plausible historical reconstruction, taking into consideration all the relevant evidence, places the codexes in a monastic milieu. And given the region, only a Pachomian monastery is likely to have been involved. This thesis still cannot be regarded as proved, but Scholten's essay shows the desirability of pursuing the discussion in a broad historical context.[7]

Two other Coptic "bibliological units" have received recent attention. I myself have compiled a conservative inventory of about 450 codexes that are known to have come from the Monastery of Bishoi in the Wadi Natrun, but that are now scattered among ten different collections (Emmel 1990c).[8] Anne Boud'hors (1989) has investigated a group of Coptic manuscripts in the Bibliothèque nationale in Paris that were acquired on the island of Cyprus by Johann Wansleben in 1671, and she has demonstrated that at least some of these manuscripts were

---

7.   As one note of detail, the suggestion (p. 163 n. 156) that NHC I A/B might have been placed in antiquity at the end of the codex is extremely unlikely. There is no doubt that structurally this leaf was the first in the codex, and the pattern of deterioration that it shares with pp. 1/2 indicates that it was in its structurally correct position, and hence most probably still bound in that position, when the damage occurred, which was after the codex was inscribed.

in fact produced on Cyprus for the Coptic community there during the centuries just prior to Wansleben's visit. Her essay underscores nicely the fact that even though the groupings of manuscripts in modern museums and libraries are accidental, they are not necessarily also irrational; they may well provide important clues as to the composition of ancient collections of manuscripts. Thus the modern history of Coptic manuscripts is of interest to Coptic codicologists, just as are the manuscripts themselves. And in this connection, an article by Agnès Bresson (1988) sheds further light on another famous seventeenth-century enthusiast of Coptic studies and collector of Coptic manuscripts, Claude Fabri de Peiresc.

Concluding this survey of recent publications are two reference works. First, Franz-Jürgen Schmitz and Gerd Mink (1986–91) have completed the first part of their *Liste der koptischen Handschriften des Neuen Testaments*, a descriptive catalog of manuscripts of the gospels, many of them reconstructed from scattered fragments. Sixty-seven pages of indexes make this book particularly useful. Second, Alla I. Elanskaja (1991a) has published a catalog of the Coptic literary manuscripts in the library of the Puškin State Museum of Fine Arts in Moscow, with brief descriptions of close to a hundred codicological entities (including many White Monastery fragments), text editions of previously unpublished items, and seventy photographic plates. Until the appearance of Elanskaja's book, this collection constituted a large piece of codicological and textual terra incognita, which has now been mapped at least preliminarily.

In his article on paleography in *The Coptic Encyclopedia* (1991), Rodolphe Kasser wrote that "all Coptologists recognize this one fact: Coptic paleography is still a new field" (vol. 8, p. 176). The second half of this statement is echoed repeatedly in publications of Coptic manuscripts, either as a justification for not offering an opinion as to the date of an undated manuscript, or as a caveat accompanying an

---

8. To be added to my list, as no. 25a, is Paris, Bibliothèque nationale Copte 91 (Horner's Bohairic Apocalypse manuscript H). [Please note also that W. H. P. Hatch did in fact publish his apocryphal Acts fragment from the Monastery of Macarius (pace Emmel 1990c, 160), as his contribution to the Crum Festschrift (*Coptic Studies in Honor of Walter Ewing Crum* [Boston 1950] 305–17).]

opinion ventured. A reliable means of dating undated Coptic manuscripts is still beyond our grasp, but dedicated and competent scholars are patiently laying the groundwork on which our successors may someday achieve the goal that we can still only envision.

References and Select Bibliography

Beaux, Nathalie
1989, Pour une paléographie du papyrus Chester Beatty 2018. In Rosenstiehl 1989, 46–49.
Boud'hors, Anne
1988, Fragments du Nouveau Testament fayoumique à la Bibliothèque nationale. *Langues orientales anciennes: Philologie et linguistique* 1:95–116.
1989, Manuscrits coptes "chypriotes" à la Bibliothèque nationale. In Rosenstiehl 1989, 11–20.
Brashear, William; Funk, Wolf-Peter; Robinson, James M.; and Smith, Richard
1990, *The Chester Beatty Codex Ac. 1390: Mathematical School Exercises in Greek and John 10:7–13:38 in Subachmimic.* Chester Beatty Monographs, vol. 13. Louvain: Peeters.
Bresson, Agnès
1988, Peiresc et les études coptes: Prolégomènes au déchiffrement des hiéroglyphes. *XVIIe siècle* 40:41–50.
Bryder, Peter
1988, (ed.) *Manichaean Studies: Proceedings of the First International Conference on Manichaeism, August 5–9, 1987, Department of History of Religions, Lund University, Sweden.* Lund Studies in African and Asian Religions, vol. 1. Lund: Plus Ultra.
Camplani, Alberto
1989, *Le lettere festali di Atanasio di Alessandria.* Rome: CIM.
Coquin, René-Georges
1988a, (ed.) *Mélanges Antoine Guillaumont: Contributions à l'étude des christianismes orienteaux.* Cahiers d'orientalisme, vol. 20. Geneva: Patrick Cramer.
1988b, La "Règle" de Moïse d'Abydos. In Coquin 1988, 103–10.
1989a, Complément aux "Miracles de saint Georges" (MS. I.F.A.O., copte 30). *Bulletin de la Société d'archéologie copte* 28 (1986–1989): 51–73, pl. facing p. 51.
1989b, Deux fragments fayoumiques du fonds copte, IFAO 28 et 29. In Rosenstiehl 1989, 21–31.
1991, Fragments d'une chronique, relatifs à un patriarche d'Alexandrie, sans doute Théodose (535–566 A.D.. *Bulletin de la Société d'archéologie copte* 30:1–24, pl. facing p. 1.

Coquin, René-Georges, and G. Godron

1990, Un encomion copte sur Marie-Madeleine attribué à Cyrille de Jérusalem. *Bulletin de l'Institut français de archéologie orientale* 90:169–212.

Devos, Paul

1988, Jean de Lycopolis revisité: Nouveaux feuillets du "codex B." *Analecta Bollandiana* 106:183–200.

Diebner, Bernd Jørg, and Rodolphe Kasser

1989, (eds.) *Hamburger Papyrus bil. 1: Die alttestamentlichen Texte des Papyrus bilinguis 1 der Staats- und Universitätsbibliothek Hamburg, Canticum canticorum (Coptice), Lamentationes Ieremiae (Coptice), Ecclesiastes (Graece et Coptice)*. Cahiers d'orientalisme, vol. 18. Geneva: Patrick Cramer.

Elanskaja, Alla I.

1988, *Passio Pauli* in the Coptic MS. GMII I.1.b.686. In Coquin 1988, 19–37.

1989, A Fragment of "Ancoratus" in Coptic (the MS. I.1.b.668 of the Pushkin Museum of Fine Arts). *Bulletin de la Société d'archéologie copte* 28 (1986–1989): 5–10, followed by pls. 3–4.

1991a, *Coptic Literary Texts of the Pushkin State Fine Arts Museum in Moscow.* Studia Aegyptiaca, vol. 13. Budapest: Chair d'égyptologie de l'Université Loránd Eötvös.

1991b, A Fayyumic Text of Psalm 118, 50–52, 62–67, 74–77 (the MS. I.1.b.637 of the Pushkin Museum of Fine Arts). *Bulletin de la Société d'archéologie copte* 30:25–28, followed by pls. 1–3.

Emmel, Stephen

1984, (ed.) *Nag Hammadi Codex III,5: The Dialogue of the Savior*. The Coptic Gnostic Library; Nag Hammadi Studies, vol. 26. Leiden: E.J. Brill.

1989, Fragments of White Monastery Manuscripts Acquired by the Beinecke Rare Book and Manuscript Library (Yale University). International Association for Coptic Studies, *Newsletter*, no. 26:3–4.

1990a, [Note on the Beinecke Library's acquisition of three Coptic manuscript fragments from the White Monastery]. *Yale University Library Gazette* 64 (1989): 174–75.

1990b, More Fragments of White Monastery Manuscripts Acquired by the Beinecke Rare Book and Manuscript Library (Yale University). International Association for Coptic Studies, *Newsletter*, no. 27 (April 1990): 3; no. 28 (November 1990): 9 (corrigendum).

1990c, Reconstructing a Dismembered Egyptian Library. In *Gnosticism and the Early Christian World: In Honor of James M. Robinson*, edited by James E. Goehring et al., 145–61 (with bibliography on pp. 162–84, passim). Forum Fascicles, vol. 2. Sonoma, CA: Polebridge Press.

1990d, Coptic Biblical Texts in the Beinecke Library. *Journal of Coptic Studies* 1:13–28, pls. 1–4.

Funk, Wolf-Peter

1988, Der Anfang des Johannesevangeliums auf Faijumisch. *Archiv für Papyrus-forschung und verwandte Gebiete* 34:33–42, pl. 14.

1990, Zur Faksimileausgabe der koptischen Manichaica in der Chester-Beatty-Sammlung, I. *Orientalia* 59:524–41. [Review of Giversen 1986–88, vols. 1–2.]

Gardner, Iain

1988, *Coptic Theological Papyri II: Edition, Commentary, Translation, with an Appendix: The Docetic Jesus.* 2 vols. Mitteilungen aus der Papyrussammlung der Österreichischen Nationalbibliothek (Papyrus Erzherzog Rainer), 2d ser., vol. 21. Vienna: Verlag Brüder Hollinek.

Giversen, Søren

1986–88, *The Manichaean Coptic Papyri in the Chester Beatty Library: Facsimile Edition.* 4 vols. Cahiers d'orientalisme, vols. 14–17. Geneva: Patrick Cramer.

1988, The Manichaean Texts from the Chester Beatty Collection. In Bryder 1988, 265–72.

Goehring, James E.

1990, (ed.) *The Crosby-Schøyen Codex MS 193 in the Schøyen Collection.* Corpus Scriptorum Christianorum Orientalium, vol. 521 (Subs. 85). Louvain: Peeters.

Hedrick, Charles W.

1990, (ed.) *Nag Hammadi Codices XI, XII, XIII.* The Coptic Gnostic Library; Nag Hammadi Studies, vol. 28. Leiden etc.: E.J. Brill.

Ibscher, Hugo

1940, Die Handschrift. In *Kephalaia*, by H.J. Polotsky and Alexander Böhlig, v–xiv. Manichäische Handschriften der Staatlichen Museen Berlin, vol. 1. Stuttgart: Verlag von W. Kohlhammer.

Johnson, David W.

1989, The Dossier of Aba Zenobius. *Orientalia* 58:193–212.

Kasser, Rodolphe

1988, Status quaestionis 1988 sulla presunta origine dei cosiddetti Papiri Bodmer. *Aegyptus* 68:191–94.

Kirchner, Dankwart

1989, *Epistula Jacobi Apocrypha: Die zweite Schrift aus Nag-Hammadi-Codex I.* Texte und Untersuchungen, vol. 136. Berlin: Akademie-Verlag.

Krause, Martin

1991, Zum Aufbau des koptisch-manichäischen Psalmenbuches. In *Manichaica Selecta: Studies Presented to Professor Julien Ries on the Occasion of His Seventieth Birthday,* edited by Aloïs van Tongerloo and Søren Giversen, 177–90. Manichaean Studies, vol. 1. Louvain: Peeters.

Layton, Bentley

1985, Towards a New Coptic Palaeography. In *Acts of the Second International Congress of Coptic Studies: Roma, 22–26 September 1980,* edited by Tito Orlandi and Frederik Wisse, 149–58. Rome: Centro Italiano Microfiches.

1987, *Catalogue of Coptic Literary Manuscripts in the British Library Acquired since the Year 1906*. London: British Library.

1989, (ed.) *Nag Hammadi Codex II,2–7 together with XIII,2*, Brit. Lib. Or. 4926(1), and P. Oxy. 1, 654, 655*. 2 vols. The Coptic Gnostic Library; Nag Hammadi Studies, vols. 20–21. Leiden etc.: E.J. Brill.

Lucchesi, Enzo

1988a, Chénouté a-t-il écrit en grec? In Coquin 1988, 201–10.

1988b, Le recueil copte des lettres d'Ignace d'Antioche: Nouvelle glanure (Paris, *B. N.* 131.8, 87 + Leiden, *Insinger* 90). *Vigiliae Christianae* 42:313–17.

1988c, Additamentum ad Martyrium S. Thomae Apostoli Coptice. *Analecta Bollandiana* 106:319–22.

1988d, "Martyre" de Zacharie et protévangile de Jacques. *Muséon* 101:65–76.

1989a, Review of *The Life of Samuel of Kalamun by Isaac the Presbyter*, by Anthony Alcock (Warminster: Aris and Phillips, 1983). *Bibliotheca Orientalis* 46:89–96.

1989b, Le *Pasteur* d'Hermas en copte: Perspective nouvelle. *Vigiliae Christianae* 43:393–96.

Mirecki, Paul Allan

1988, The Coptic Manichaean Synaxeis Codex: Descriptive Catalogue of Synaxis Chapter Titles. In Bryder 1988, 135–45.

Nagel, Peter

1988, Textumfang und Textabfolge der sahidischen Version des Buches Exodus. In Scholz & Stempel 1988, 181–89.

1989a, Fragmente eines sahidischen Genesiskodex der Nationalbibliothek zu Paris (BN copte 129.1 fol. 8–13). *Zeitschrift für ägyptische Sprache und Altertumskunde* 116:71–90.

1989b, Editionen koptischer Bibeltexte seit Till 1960. *Archiv für Papyrusforschung und verwandte Gebiete* 35:43–100.

Orlandi, Tito

1988, *Paolo di Tamma, opere: Introduzione, testo, traduzione e concordanze*. Rome: Centro Italiano Microfiches.

Parrott, Douglas

1991, *Nag Hammadi Codices III,3–4 and V,1 with Papyrus Berolinensis 8502,3 and Oxyrhynchus Papyrus 1081: Eugnostos and The Sophia of Jesus Christ*. The Coptic Gnostic Library; Nag Hammadi Studies, vol. 27. Leiden etc.: E.J. Brill.

Quecke, Hans

1988a, Zur sahidischen Psalmenzählung. In Scholz & Stempel 1988, 205–9.

1988b, Review of Layton 1987. *Orientalia* 57:237–39.

1989, Auszüge aus Evagrius' "Mönchsspiegel" in koptischer Übersetzung. *Orientalia* 58:453–63, pl. 70.

1992, Eine koptische alphabetische Akrostichis. *Orientalia* 61:1–9.

Robinson, James M.

1990a, The First Christian Monastic Library. In *Coptic Sudies: Acts of the Third International Congress of Coptic Studies, Warsaw, 20–25 August, 1984*, edited by Włodzimierz Godlewski, 371–78. Warsaw: Państwowe Wydawnictwo Naukowe.

1990b, *The Pachomian Monastic Library at the Chester Beatty Library and the bibliothèque Bodmer*. Occasional Papers of the Institute for Antiquity and Christianity, vol. 19. Claremont, CA: Institute for Antiquity and Christianity.

1992, The Fate of the Manichaean Codices of Medinet Madi 1929–1989. In *Studia Manichaica: II. Internationaler Kongreß zum Manichäismus, 6.–10. August 1989, St. Augustin/Bonn*, edited by Gernot Wießner and Hans-Joachim Klimkeit, 19–62. Studies in Oriental Religions, vol. 23. Wiesbaden: Otto Harrassowitz.

Rosenstiehl, Jean-Marc

1989, (ed.) *Études coptes III: Troisième journée d'études, musée du Louvre, 23 mai 1986*. Cahiers de la bibliothèque copte, vol. 4. Louvain and Paris: Peeters.

Schenke, Hans-Martin

1989, *Das Thomas-Buch (Nag-Hammadi-Codex II,7)*. Texte und Untersuchungen, vol. 138. Berlin: Akademie-Verlag.

1990, Review of Layton 1987. *Orientalistische Literaturzeitung* 85:153–58.

1991, *Apostelgeschichte 1,1–15,3 im mittelägyptischen Dialekt des koptischen (Codex Glazier)*. Texte und Untersuchungen, vol. 137. Berlin: Akademie-Verlag.

Schmidt, Carl, and Wilhelm Schubart

1936, ΠΡΑΞΕΙΣ ΠΑΥΛΟΥ: *Acta Pauli nach dem Papyrus der Hamburger Staats- und Universitäts-Bibliothek*. Veröffentlichungen aus der Hamburger Staats- und Universitäts-Bibliothek, vol. 2. Glückstadt and Hamburg: Verlag von J.J. Augustin.

Schmitz, Franz-Jürgen, and Gerd Mink

1986–91, *Liste der koptischen Handschriften des Neuen Testaments*. Pt. 1, *Die sahidischen Handschriften der Evangelien*. 2 vols. (vol. 2 in two parts). Arbeiten zur neutestamentlichen Textforschung, vols. 8, 13, 15. Berlin and New York: Walter de Gruyter.

Scholten, Clemens

1988, Die Nag-Hammadi-Texte als Buchbesitz der Pachomianer. *Jahrbuch für Antike und Christentum* 31:144–72.

Scholz, Piotr O., and Reinhard Stempel

1988, (eds.) *Nubia et Oriens Christianus: Festschrift für C. Detlef G. Müller zum 60. Geburtstag*. Bibliotheca Nubica, vol. 1. Cologne: Verlag Jürgen Dinter.

Schüssler, Karlheinz

1990a, Review of *Catalogue des fragments coptes*, vol. 1, *Fragments bibliques nouvellement identifiés*, by Anne Bouvarel-Boud'hors (Paris: Bibliothèque nationale, 1987). *Enchoria* 17:167–68.

1990b, Review of Schmitz & Mink 1986–1991, vol. 2.1. *Enchoria* 17:175–76.

Sheridan, Mark J.

1990, The Homilies of Rufus of Shotep on the Gospels of Matthew and Luke. Ph.D. diss., Catholic University of America. Ann Arbor: University Microfilms International. [A revised version of this work is about to be published in Rome (Centro Italiano Microfiches) under the auspices of the Corpus dei Manoscritti Copti Letterari.]

Sieber, John H.

1991, (ed.) *Nag Hammadi Codex VIII*. The Coptic Gnostic Library; Nag Hammadi Studies, vol. 31. Leiden etc.: E.J. Brill.

Thomassen, Einar, and Louis Painchaud

1989, *Le Traité tripartite (NH I, 5)*. Bibliothèque copte de Nag Hammadi, section "textes," vol. 19. Québec: Presses de l'Université Laval.

van Regemorter, Berthe

1992, *Binding Structures in the Middle Ages: A Selection of Studies*. Translated and annotated by Jane Greenfield. Studia Bibliothecae Wittockianae, vol. 3. Brussels and London: Bibliotheca Wittockiana and Maggs Bros.

Wisse, Frederik

1975, Nag Hammadi Codex III: Codicological Introduction. In *Essays on the Nag Hammadi Texts in Honour of Pahor Labib*, edited by Martin Krause, 225–38. Nag Hammadi Studies, vol. 6. Leiden: E.J. Brill.

1990, Pseudo-Liberius, *Oratio consolatoria de morte Athanasii. Muséon* 103:43–65.

1991, The Naples Fragments of Shenoute's "De certamine contra diabolum." *Oriens Christianus* 75:123–40.

Zanetti, Ugo

1988, Review of Layton 1987. *Analecta Bollandiana* 106:171–81.

GAWDAT GABRA

CHRISTIAN ARABIC LITERATURE OF THE COPTS: NOTES ON THE STATE OF RESEARCH, 1988-1992[1]

The appearance of the eagerly awaited Coptic *Encyclopedia* represents the most important "publishing event" since the last congress of Coptic Studies in Louvain-La Neuve (1988). In the Encyclopedia, "Coptology" is defined as:

"a scientific discipline in Oriental studies that investigates the language and culture of Egypt and Nubia in the widest sense: literature, religion, history, archaeology, and art. Its range extends from late antiquity to the Middle Ages, or even down to the present."

In the same entry ("Coptology") we read:

"We thus come to the period that extends from the ARAB CONQUEST OF EGYPT down to the present. Here there are connections with Arabic studies and with the study of Islam. The Coptic language gradually lost its significance as a colloquial and literary language and was replaced, except as the language of the church, by Arabic. The Copts translated their literary works into Arabic, and prepared Coptic-Arabic word lists, the *scalae*, and grammatical summaries, in order to preserve the knowledge of their language. Part of the Coptic literature is preserved only in Arabic translation."[2]

---

1.   I would like to thank the Catholic University of America for enabling me to attend this Congress.
2.   M. Krause, in: *The Coptic Encyclopedia*, Aziz S. Atiya, ed., vol. 2, New York 1991, pp. 616f.

The Coptic Encyclopedia contains 2500 entries. For the preparation of almost twenty percent of them (i.e., about 500 entries) a reading knowledge of Arabic was essential. (I have included in this tally neither those entries related to the time of Napoleon in Egypt and later, nor the geographical sites, nor the entries which begin with the Arabic word for monastery dayr.) The 500 articles in question were written by only 22 of the 267 contributors to the Encyclopedia, and, indeed, three of those 22 authors—Samir Khalil, René-Georges Coquin and Aziz Atiya—were responsible for most of the 500 entries. This general survey shows clearly that there is a serious problem.

Moreover, although an important proportion of the Christian Arabic literature of the Copts represents translations of Coptic texts, only a very few scholars are able to read both languages. There is no doubt that many interesting contributions to this field have been published in the last four years in addition to the Coptic Encyclopedia. The most important among them are those of Johannes Den Heijer[3] and Bishop Samuel al-Syriany.[4] But the current situation in Coptic Arabic studies as signalled above is very disappointing. The main tool for the scholar specializing in Christian Arabic literature remains the seminal work of Georg Graf,[5] published almost half a century ago. Its five volumes show the richness of the corpus of Coptic-Arabic literature. Despite the shortcomings and errors of Graf's work, it continues to be the indispensable reference tool in the field.

It is well known that most of the Christian Arabic literature of the Copts is still unpublished. A considerable part of the Arabic manuscripts of the Copts is preserved in the Coptic Museum in Cairo,[6] in the old Coptic patriarchate,[7] in many Coptic monasteries through-

---

3.   *Mawhub Ibn Mansur Ibn Mufarrig et l'historiographie Copto-arabe. Étude sur la composition de l'Histoire des Patriarches d'Alexandrie*, CSCO, vol. 513, Subsidia 83, Louvain 1989.

4.   Abu al Makaram, *History of the Churches and Monasteries in Lower Egypt in the 13th Century*, Cairo 1992.

5.   *Geschichte der christlichen-arabischen Literatur*, 5 vols., Vatican City, 1944-53.

7.   Idem, *Catalogue. ..*, vol. II, Cairo 1942.

out Egypt, and in Coptic churches. Only a few catalogues have been compiled for the manuscripts of the Coptic churches and monasteries.[8] Thus it is not an exaggeration to state that Coptic Arabic studies are considerably neglected.

I would like to make three proposals intended to further studies in the field of the Christian Arabic literature of the Copts.

In view of the trend toward ever-increasing emphasis on the scientific disciplines at the expense of the humanities, it is perhaps problematic to recommend Coptic-Arabic literature as a field or study to the student just entering the university. However, wherever Coptic studies are taught, students who have chosen the field should be encouraged to learn Arabic.

Secondly, it should be emphasized that Coptic-Arabic literature is especially important for the study of Coptic hagiography and monasticism. Specific projects in these two fields to edit and translate texts would be very welcome. It is certainly not always necessary to publish a complete text; in many cases, the publication of only some important paragraphs of a text, with translation and commentary, has also proved very useful.[9]

Thirdly, the preparation of catalogues of Coptic-Arabic manuscripts preserved in libraries, museums, churches and monasteries is vital to further research in this field. Such catalogues should include information on the provenance, if known, like the compilation of Gérard Troupeau[10] concerning the Christian Arabic manuscripts in the Biblio-

6.   M. Simaika, *Catalogue of the Coptic and Arabic Manuscripts in the Coptic Museum, the Patriarchate, the Principal Churches of Cairo and Alexandria and the Monasteries of Egypt,* vol. I, Cairo 1939.

8.   A. Khater and O. H. E. Burmester, *Catalogue of the Coptic and Christian Arabic Manuscripts preserved in the Cloister of Saint Menas at Cairo,* Cairo 1967; Khater and Burmester, *Catalogue of the Coptic and Christian Arabic Manuscripts preserved in the Library of the Church of All-Holy Virgin Mary Known as Qasriat ar-Rihan at Old Cairo,* Cairo 1973; Khater and Burmester, *Catalogue of the Coptic and Christian Arabic Manuscripts Preserved in the Library of the Church of Saints Sergius and Bacchus Known as Abu Sargah at Old Cairo,* Cairo 1977; U. Zanetti, *Les manuscripts de Dair Abu Maqar: Inventaire* (Cahiers d'Orientalisme 11), Geneva 1986.

thèque Nationale, Paris. The provenance is essential for determining whether a particular Arabic text was used in the Coptic church or outside Egypt. Unfortunately, there are no catalogues for a considerable number of Christian Arabic manuscripts preserved in Egypt. I believe that this situation could be improved through patient attempts to encourage monks to prepare catalogues of the Coptic-Arabic manuscripts in the many monasteries and churches of Egypt.

I hope these three suggestions will help to promote research in the field of Christian-Arabic literature of the Copts which will in turn further studies of Coptic literature. As noted above, a significant proportion of Coptic literature is preserved only in Arabic translation. Finally, I would like to point out that there has been much less progress in this field than in other areas of Coptology, such as in Coptic language and literature per se, or in Coptic art. Much more concerted effort is needed in this very rich and promising area.

---

9.   See G. Gabra, "Zu einem arabischen Bericht über Pesyntheus, einem Heiligen aus Hermonthis im 4.-5. Jhr., *BSAC* 25 (1983), 53-60; idem, "Patape (Bidaba), Märtyrer und Bischof von Koptos (ca. 244 - ca. 312): Ein Vorbericht uber sein arabisches Enkomium," in: *Coptic Studies. Acts of the Third International Congress of Coptic Studies*, Warsaw, 20-25 August 1984, W. Godlewski, ed., Warsaw 1990, 119-125; idem, "Zur Vita des Bane (Abu Fana), eines Heiligen des 4./5. Jhr., *BSAC* 19 (1990), 27-42.
10.   *Catalogue des manuscrits arabes I: Manuscrits chrétiens*, 2 vols., Paris 1972-74.

WLODZIMIERZ GODLEWSKI

COPTIC ARCHAEOLOGY

There is no need to convince anyone of the importance of the developments in research on the Coptic period in Egypt made since the IV Congress of Coptic Studies in Louvain-La-Neuve in 1988.

These have nothing to do with spectacular excavations this time. Rather they are the result of several important studies being published, some of which were years in the coming. Once out, they have had a tremendous impact upon research, leading to a re-evaluation of many opinions and emphasizing with new force all the uncertainties and evident gaps in our knowledge.

The Coptic Encyclopedia, published in 1991, is certainly a breakthrough event. A joint effort of almost all the known scholars in the field, gathered around the Late Professor Aziz S.Atiya, it has been edited as far as Coptic archaeology is concerned by Peter Grossmann and the Late Pierre Du Bourguet. In many cases, it is probably the fullest review of research in Coptic archaeology, often incorporating the latest findings made just before the book went to print. This is largely due to Peter Grossmann, who has put his extensive store of knowledge of recent discoveries (up to 1987) in two recent reviews of the latest archaeological work in Egypt: in the *Actes du XI Congrès International d'Archéologie Chretienne*, and the *Acts of the IV Congress of Coptic Studies*.

An important contribution was made by the acts of the last congress in Louvain-La-Neuve and the long-delayed acts of the previous congress of Coptic Studies in Warsaw.

Another important study by Peter Grossmann was his monumental publication of Abu Mena, reviewing the German mission's excavations over the years.

The *International Directory of Institutions holding Collections of Coptic Antiquities outside of Egypt*, edited by Stephen Emmel, is worth a note for the sake of methodology. One should also mention two interesting general studies: *Coptic Art and Culture*, edited by Hans Honelink and published by the Netherlands Institute for Archaeology and Arabic Studies in Cairo, and *Guide to Ancient Coptic Churches and Monasteries in Egypt*, edited by bishop Samuel al-Syrany and Badii Habib, published by the Coptic Institute in Cairo.

A few words of general commentary are in order before going into details of recent archaeological developments.

Abou Mena, a center of ancient Christian pilgrimages, remains the most important site presently investigated in Egypt. The German mission's study program covers topics ranging from a historical overview of the site's topography in the Byzantine and Arab periods to the functionality of pilgrims' houses (*hospitia*) and the workshop and dwelling areas where the famous ampullae, terracottas and pottery as well as wine were produced. Considering that large-scale excavations in Alexandria are all but impossible inside the thriving modern city, Abu Mena appears all the more important as a site where the Hellenistic-Byzantine trends may be traced in the architecture and painting of Coptic Egypt.

Another site of comparable importance is Antinoe, second only to Alexandria as a center of Classical Greek art in Egypt and particularly significant for understanding the various phenomena taking place in Upper Egypt. It is being excavated by an Italian mission, but unfortunately the work is limited now and not fully reported. The value of the funerary paintings from the Antinoe cemeteries cannot be underestimated for any studies of the iconography and wall painting styles of Coptic Egypt in the early period.

The focus point of Coptic archaeology are excavations on monastic sites. Since progressing irrigation works have left little more that could be done in terms of excavations at Kellia, the Coptic Institute and the IFAO in Cairo have come up with the initiative to excavate in Wadi an Natrun, outside the present monasteries. Promising results have been achieved over the last four years at Abu Fana (Austrian mission) and at Naqlun (Polish expedition), two other monastic sites. New important and extensive excavations have started on the Sinai, with a German mission and an Egyptian one working at Wadi Faryan and on the neighbouring sites of Gebel Takhna and Deir el Banat as well as inside the monastery of St. Catherine. Significant archaeological discoveries have been made by an Egyptian mission at Ouyoum Mousa, while another Egyptian mission together with a Japanese one have been excavating at Al Tur.

Australian research at Ismant el Gharab in the Dahla oasis has provided important archaeological and textual material for the study of the Christianization of the oasis. The Egyptian mission's excavations at the site of a large and wealthy Roman town at Marina are insufficiently published as regards the Byzantine period, making it difficult to judge the role it played in the times just before Amr's conquest of Egypt.

It should be remembered that Coptic evidence from many important Pharaonic or Graeco-Roman sites is usually not published until the final reports which come years after the original discovery. Furthermore, a lack of preliminary reports bars scholars from knowledge of the discoveries which Egyptian archaeologists make every year, whether as a result of planned excavations or rescue work.

The following is a summary of the most important results of excavations in the past four years (1988-1992) and those whose scientific importance has been fully comprehended.

Starting with architecture, the German mission's advanced studies on the buildings and urbanization of the pilgrimage center at Abu Mena come to mind foremost. Conducted on an impressive scale, the excavations have led to a whole, vast urban complex, together with squares and streets, being cleared around the Great Basilica and the Funerary Basilica. Thnaks to this Abu Mena is now the best known urban complex of the Justinian period, not only in Egypt but also in the Byzantine Emire in general. The historical stratification of the settlement and the singling out of late habitations and domestic architecture have also provided grounds for some interesting studies of the early medieval spatial structure of the complex.

Studies on the early as well as medieval church architecture have
also been progressing thanks to Peter Grossmann's work. A recent catalogue including plans of newly discovered buildings as well as
checked plans of existing structures has gone a long way in changing
what is known of church establishments of Egypt and their development over the centuries. At the same time, the discoveries of very early basilicas of the 4th century at Faw el Qibli and new complexes on
the Sinai have had a tremendous impact upon an understanding of the
formative epoch in church architecture in Egypt. Other new churches
have been uncovered recently at Marsa Matruh, Abu Sir, Ashmunein
(Hermopolis Magna) and Medinet Maadi in the Fayum.

New discoveries of monastic architecture have increased our
knowledge of the diversity of erem forms. Their plans and complexity
are largely dependent not only on the period when particular structures
were built, but also on topography and the material used in their construction. The rockcut erems in Naqlun are particularly interesting, re-
calling as they do some early structures from Kellia. The underground
erems at Esna and Adaima also deserve mention.

Excavation of a large church at Abu Fana has brought to light a
monumental complex identified as a tarabeza which has provided important evidence for verifying the interpretation of various structures
discovered at Bawit and Saqqara at the begining of our century.

Recent years have also brought a marked increase in our knowledge of secular architecture, whether in crowded districts as in
Alexandria (habitations with complex function, featuring living quarters on the upper floor above workshops and a shop opening of the
portico of a street) or in less organized country settlements full of spa-
cious villas as in Abu Mena and Marina.

New evidence concerning military outposts includes the American
discoveries at Abu Shacar on the Red Sea coast. The Byzantine fort
dug there has turned out to follow typical Roman military architecture
from the Eastern Desert, which finds analogies in fortifications of
Nothern Africa. An Egyptian expedition working in Nag al-Hagar
near Aswan has also uncovered a Roman military complex which was

used into the Byzantine Period to judge by the church found inside the fort.

The last four years have been exceptionally rich in discoveries of wall paintings from Egypt. To start with there was the discovery of murals in the funerary chapel at Abu Mena which turned out to be very important for studies on early Coptic painting. Renewed studies of the Kom al-Akhbariya murals have shown the dependence of these paintings on exellent Byzantine painting traditions. Of equal importance are discoveries of murals in the funerary chapels at Antinoe. A valuable addition for this period are the hermitage paintings from Kellia, presently in the hands of restorers, and the recently uncovered decoration of the walls of the great hall at Abu Fana which is so close to the decoration of Room 6 at Bawit.

The Annunciation composition from the western conch of the Deir es-Suriani church at Wadi an- Natrun, dated to the mid-tenth century is quite exceptional in both artistic and iconographic terms.

Newly discovered medieval paintings of the 13th century from the Deir el-Baramus monastery church at Wadi en Natrun should also be mentioned here as well as the compositions uncovered under layers of later plaster in the Archangel Gabriel Church at Naqlun where they are dated to the second half of the 12th century. In terms of style, they represent very diverse groups, enriching considerably our knowledge of medieval painting in Egypt. Beside repeated scenes from the Old Testament, there appear theological compositions such as the apse murals: Ascension to Heaven at Deir el-Baramus and Mother of God enthroned between archangels at Naqlun, as well as typical representations of the warrior saints, including a representation of the completely unknown St. Pitchosh at Naqlun.

There can be no doubt that our increased knowledge of wall paintings and entire programs of wall decoration in monastic churches in Coptic Egypt is a very valuable addition to the study of art of the late Middle Ages spread throughout the eastern oikumene and the former Byzantine koine.

Discoveries of pottery over the last four years include valuable evidence on the production of local workshops in the Nile Valley. This concerns both ceramics in the Late Roman traditions and domestic wares such as kitchen pottery, amphorae and small water containers as well as early glazed pottery.

The considerable advances in the study of Coptic and Early Arab pottery made in this period are largely due to Pascal Ballet and Joseph Engemann (early 7th-8th century glazed pottery from Abu Mena); David M. Bailey's increasingly exact distinguishing of Middle Egyptian workshops at Ashmunein deserves mention as well. A very interesting group of handmade pottery was found at Naqlun; it was presumably made at the monastery and reflects metal vase traditions in the unusual applied and openwork decoration and in the shapes which include incense burners, chalices and small containers.

Another aspect of pottery studies in recent years is the relation between Egyptian pottery and products from Palestine, especially in the 7th and 8th centuries.

Progress in studies of the Late Roman and Byzantine pottery in Egypt depends not only on publishing new material from excavations, but also on preparing specific programs for the study of pottery production centres in Egypt at the time (at such sites in Middle and Upper Egypt as Antinoopolis, Hermopolis Magna, Zawyet el-Maletin, Medamud, Esna, Edfu and Aswan). The work carried out by the IFAO in cooperation with the Ceramologic Lab in Lyon and the Coptic Museum in Cairo is particularly helpful in the proper recognition of the main centers of pottery production and its distribution. As far as chronology and typology are concerned, new material from Egyptian sites dated to the Early Roman period (e..g. Marina, Tell el-Haraby where a kiln was discovered by an EAO mission, Mons Claudianus and Ismant el Kharab) has in many cases constituted an important contribution.

In the field of studies on metal artifacts, D. Benazeth's work on objects in various collections has added considerably to present knowledge. Following her publication of bronzes from the French excavations at Tod and a catalogue of the Louvre collection, there is now a preliminary report on the collection of the Coptic Museum.

Finally, a significant achievement of the last four years of research in the field, even though usually discussed without the archaeological context, are the Greek, Coptic and Arabic texts and documents found at Naqlun in the Fayum, Ismant al-Gharab in Dahla and Tehna el Gebel and Akoris in the Nile Valley.

There are two other archaeological projects which are mainly connected with studies of the economy of the Coptic Period in Egypt. At Dush (anc.Kysis) in the Kharga Oasis, A French expedition from the IFAO has uncovered the irrigation system made up of deep pits and an extensive complex of tunnels called qanat, known from Greek texts as well. The other project is a combined French and Egyptian expedition to the Eastern Desert which has carried out important research on the geological milieu of the gold and copper mines as well as the dwellings and archaeological material. Some of the investigated mines had been used in the Late Roman and Coptic Periods.

Archaeological activity 1988-1992

ALEXANDRIA-Kom el Dikka

Polish Mission (Center of Mediterranean Archaeology of Warsaw University)

Earlier research on the habitations lining the eastern side of street R4, south of the entrance to the Baths, was continued. The two large houses G and H discovered here were built on top of a thick levelling layer of debris, coming from the destruction of the Early Roman villa architecture of this district at the turn of the 3rd century to judge by available numismatic and archeological evidence. Houses G and H were in use from the 4th to the 7th century, during which time they underwent a number of renovations and functional changes. Glass slag in large quantities as well as remains of furnaces suggest the existence of a glass workshop. This and other evidence suggests the houses had served as workshops and shops opening onto the street, with living quarters located on the upper floor. A deep well was discovered in room G.13. The houses were apparently abandoned in the middle of

the 7th century and were largely taken apart for building material in
the 8th-10th cent.

ABU MENA

German mission (DAIK), Egyptian mission (EAO)

In recent years continued research on one of the greatest centers of
pilgrimage in Egypt concetrated upon a reconstruction of the topography and plan of the town in the Byzantine period (4th-7th century) and
later. It should be emphasized that Abu Mena is the only town in
Egypt from this period to be known in such detail as regards plan,
with all the various churches and pilgrims' inns of all kinds (hospitia)
being located in respect to the network of streets and to other structures such as baths, workshops, administrative centers, villas and
townhouses with domestic workareas and wine presses.

In Medieval times (7th-9th century), presumably after the Persian
invasion, there were many changes to the architecture of the town with
the new houses, 3 or 4, being built on a regular plan especially in the
western districts. There is no doubt that the houses also served as
workshops.

East of the Great Basilica the mission discovered the the ruins of a
building which went back to the formative stages of the cult of Menas
in Abu Mena (2nd-3rd century). A small funerary chapel was found to
contain ornamental paintings imitating marble revettment.

Coptic finds include an abundance of coins, pottery (including early
glazed forms), terracottas and bone and ivory products.

ABUSIR (Taposiris Magna)

German expedition (DAIK)

In the course of an archaeological survey carried out within the
area of the town, a small church of the early Christian period was uncovered. The building is a three-aisled basilica with two facing apses
at the eastern and western ends.

KARM EL-SHUWAILHY

German expedition (DAIK), Egyptian expedition (EAO)

An archaeological survey on the northwest outskirts of Abu Mena uncovered a settlement consisting of houses decorated with wall paintings and the remains of wine presses.

EL AMRYA-TEIBA

Egyptian expedition (EAO)

During excavations of the Roman settlement a few rooms belonging to a monastic complex of the Coptic period were uncovered. Paintings on the walls of this complex include Christian symbols such as crosses, fish and floral motifs.

MARSA MATRUH

American expedition (Museum of Pennsylvania University- Donald White)

In 1987 the expedition uncovered a poorly preserved small basilican church (22.0 x 16.25 m) of 5th century date. A small apse with an altar and sanctuary ocupies the eastern part of the nave, while the western end is composed of three rooms.

KELLIA

French mission (IFAO); Swiss mission (University of Geneva); Egyptian mission (EAO)

Fieldwork has been limited by progressing irrigation works which have raised the ground water table. The 1988-1989 excavations of the Swiss mission were concentrated in the areas of the two most secluded erem complexes in the southeastern part: Qoucour Hegeila and Qoucour Ereima.

Of the several complexes investigated so far at Qoucour Hegeila, the extensive complex of erems 39 and 40 is doubtless of greatest importance, connected as it is with a sanctuary of martyrs' cult.

The large erem 39 at Qoucour Ereima was discovered in 1989 but fieldwork was interrupted. In progress are recording and conservation activities, concerning mostly murals. These are carried out by a French team headed by Michel Wuttmann who has had valuable experience with the paintings from erem 195 at Qoucour al Ruba yat, uncovered in the years 1986-88. The murals have been studied by Margarite Rassart Debergh.

The Swiss team has established the chronology for Hermitage 14 at Qoucour Izeila, while the Egyptian mission excavated the erems at Qoucour el Abiad, discovering some new paintings.

WADI EN NATRUN

Expeditions from the Copt. Inst. in Cairo, the IFAO in Cairo, the EAO

The Coptic Institute and French expeditions have undertaken study of the erems in Wadi Natrun. At Deir el Baramus work is proceeding on the conservation of murals in the haikal and on the walls of the aisles. Matt Immerzeel is researching the 13th century church painting repertory which consists of mainly scenes from the New Testament: Pentacost, Baptism of Christ, Miracle of Cana, Entry into Jerusalem. Theological subjects such as Maiestas Domini appear beside symbolic compositions connected with the eucharist Sacrifice of Abraham or Melhizedeh as Old Testament typology.

At Deir es Suriani the wonderful painting in the western conch of the church's apse was brought to light upon the removal of a later scene of the Ascension of Christ. The newly discovered painting shows the Annunciation in the presence of the prophets Moses, Ezechiel, Daniel and Isaiah. The painting is dated to the mid-10 century and is undoubtedly one of the best artistically of those preserved in Egypt.

NAQLUN (Nekloni)

Polish expedition (Center of Mediterranean Archaeology of Warsaw University in Cairo-W.Godlewski)

During four seasons of continued excavations at this monastic site erems 25 and 89 were uncovered, yielding interesting finds of objects of daily life, fragments of textiles, pottery, glass, coins and documents in Greek, Coptic and Arabic from the 6th to the 13th century.

On the kom excavations revealed several rooms of the monastic complex with evidence that the upper floor had been decorated with paintings. Small fragments of the murals were found as well as stucco grills from the windows which had circular and cross-shaped openings paned with glass. The most important find here was a casket with in-laid decoration and gilding, probably of Sicilian origin and dating to the 12th century. Inside it there were five books in Arabic and several documents of the Mameluk period, all muslim in character.

Renovation inside the Church of Archangel Gabriel revealed murals under layers of later plain plaster. Three compositions: enthroned Virgin between Archangels, St Pitchosh mounted on a horse and a saintly monk have already been cleaned and fully restored by the expedition's conservators.

MEDINET MAADI (Fayum)

Italian expedition (University of Pisa-E. Bresciani)

On the site occupied till the end of the 9th century seven churches and a small chapel have been investigated, but the main objective of the expedition in recent years was mapping the settlement. Professor Walter Ferri has continued a systematic topographical study of the area, gathering important evidence on the development of the town in the Roman and Byzantine periods.

ABU HAWEL (Fayum)

Egyptian Expedition (EAO-Akram Eduard)

Close to 350 tombs of the Coptic period were uncovered at this cemetery site. Some of the skeletons were found with jewelry and pectoral crosses.

TEHNA el-GEBEL (Akoris)

Japanese expedition-Prof. Bun-ei Tsunda

Clearing of the rock temples of Nero and Hathor continued with the dromos; west of the main extrance of the chapel of Hathor some papyri documents in Coptic were found, most probably belonging to monastic archives of the 7th century. Some Greek ostraca were also found.

ANTINOOPOLIS

Italian expedition (Institute of Papyrology-G. Vitelli, University of Florence)

All of the new funeral chapels uncovered in the Northern Necropolis could be dated to the 5th-6th century. The square chapels are domed, and are decorated with paintings. The archaeological material includes painted pottery, terracotta figurines of orants and horses, glass, wooden and metal objects as well as coins and fragments of papyri and parchment.

ASHMUNEIN (Hermopolis Magna)

German expedition (DAIK)

Excavations in the South Church revealed a basilican structure with three aisles and a baptistery to the south. The building could be dated to the 5th century.

FAW QIBLI

American expedition (University of California, Santa Cruz), German expedition (DAIK)

In 1989 the team tried to establish the plan of the earliest church on the site. Traces of that structure were uncovered in several trial-pits. The earliest 40 m long basilica with two rows of columns on either side of the nave could be dated to the times of Pachomius (ca

330-346). Remains of earlier constructions were also uncovered but their function has not been identified satisfactorily as yet.

THEBES - Nobles' Necropole

German expedition (DAIK-H. Guksch and E. Eisermann)

In the vestibule of tomb TT.85 layers of Coptic date were recorded and dated to the 6-7th century. This is the latest period in the tomb's functioning.

Searching for evidence of Christian occupation in the Valley of the Queens, a French team has concentrated fieldwork on Deir er-Rumi and the pharaonic tombs. The material discovered covers a period from the 5th to the 8th century.

TOD

French expedition (Dep. of Egyptian Antiquities of the Louvre)

Work on this site was concluded in 1989 with the last season being devoted to a study of the pottery from the northwestern part of the area of the chapel of Tothmes III, dated to a period from the 2nd cent. B.C to the 6th cent. AD. Earlier investigations of the site yielded a great deal of Coptic material, mainly pottery and bronzes.

NAG EL HAGAR

Egyptian expedition (EAO)

An extensive fortress of the Roman period contained habitations and a church in ruins.

ISMANT el-GHABAR (Dakhlah) anc. Kellis

Canadian expedition (Society for the Study of Egyptian Antiquities and Royal Ontario Museum, Toronto)

The archaeological works continued in the residential section in Area A with the complete clearing of house 2, and were extended into Area B.

The extensive collection of textual matter-ostraca, papyri and wooden boards-was dated to the 3rd-4th century. The papyri included fragments of contracts and letters written in Greek and in Coptic (Sub-Akhmimic dialect). Two intact "books" written in Greek: one on nine boards, the other on eight, were found in the kitchen of the villa. One is a schoolboy's copy of the three Cyprian orations of Isocrates the Orator, the second is a record of agricultural transactions by the owner of the house.

In Area B a large administrative building was excavated; it was provided with a colonnaded hall and walls and ceiling covered with paintings. One of the documents found here was a record of the sale of a house in Akhmim.

The archaeological and textual material from these excavations is of great importance for a study of the life in the oasis and particularly its christianization.

DUSH, anc. Kysis (Kharga)

French expedition (IFAO-M. Redde)

The temple-fortress which the French team continued to excavate was most probably important in collecting crops and taxes in the oasis. Christian traces are rather insignificant, although the site was occupied into the 5th century to judge by coins and pottery. There is no doubt that the house between the two temples was still used in the 5th century by Christians; it is at this time that a sigma - banquet bed, well known from Syria and Asia Minor, was installed. This is the first time that a bed of this kind was recorded in Egypt.

A system of irrigation canals known as qanats, mentioned in Greek texts, was discovered; it consisted of deep pits and a complex of tunels sunk 7 m in the ground and ca.0.6 m in diameter.

ABU SHA'AR (Red Sea coast)

American expedition (University of Delaware-S.E. Sidebotham)

The excavations which started in 1987 have concetrated on the Abu

Shacar fort. It is small, enclosing a rectangular area 77.5 x 64 m, with square and rectangular towers and two gates, from the north and west. The interior follows a plan typical of Roman Eastern Desert military buildings, known also from North Africa. The central E-W building with an apse on its east side could be the principia or the church.

Ceramic and numismatic evidence would point to the site being occupied from the 5th to the 7th century with some evidence of earlier occupation in the region dated to the 3rd - 4th century.

A survey uncovered some other instalations like a hydreuma contemporary to the fort at Abu Shacar The hydreuma has double outer walls enclosing an area 46 x 53 m, one entrance on the nortwest side flanked by a semi-circular tower. Inside there is a large waterproofed cistern 11.2 x 12 m and a storage room.

EASTERN DESERT - gold and copper mines

French-Egyptian joint expedition

The expedition investigated the geological milieu of the mines as well as the habitations and archaeological material. Evidence from some sites explored at el Urf Mongul south, Um Balad and Wadi Dara would indicate that the mines could have been worked in Late Roman and Byzantine times.

WAYUM MUSA or Ouyoum Mousa (Sinai)

Egyptian expedition (EAO)

Newly identified site of Late Roman and Early Islamic periods. A pottery and glass workshop was discovered in one of the trenches, along with considerable quantities of plates, figurines, pots with painted decoration. Coins help date the site to the Roman and Coptic periods. Inside the second trial-pit a small foundry was identified together with containers for grain, a place for baking bread and some constructions dated to the Islamic Period.

WADI FAYRAN or Pharan (Sinai)

German expedition (DAIK) in cooperation with the St Catharine Monastery-P. Grossmann

A basilical episcopal church continued to be uncovered. The building has a narthex and tripartite pastophories connected by a passage in back of the apse. On the cemetery pre-Christian tombs with funeral chambers in three levels were excavated. The oldest Christian tombs were of a traditional form: a domed mausoleum with underground funeral chamber.

At the nearby Gebel Takhuna two other churches were excavated, while at Deir el Banat, also close to Wadi Fayran, a site which was most probably a Roman military post was identified.

Al-TUR (Sinai)

Japanese and Egyptian (EAO) expedition-Mutsuo Kawatoko.

The expedition completed a general survey of the site. The monastery building was found to be well preserved, with only the roof being destroyed. Documents uncovered last year in structures to the west of the kom, near the harbor, were dated to the 14-19th century.

News and Bibliography

I. Preliminary announcements

Archaeologische Anzeiger 1989, Heft 4; 1990, Heft 4; 1991, Heft 4.
BIFAO 89, 1990: P. Posener-Krieger, Travaux de l'IFAO au cours de l'annee 1988-1989; 90, 1991: N. Grimal, Travaux de l'IFAO en 1989-1990.
Bulletin de liaison du GIECE, Le Caire IFAO, XIII, 1989; XIV, 1990; XV, 1991.
Bulletin d'information archaeologique IFAO, Le Caire, 1, 1990; 2, 1991; 3, 1991.
Canadian Mediterranean Institute Bulletin, Cairo.
Egyptian Archaeology. The Bulletin of the Egyptian Society 1, Summer 1991.
Orientalia 59:3, 1990; 60:3, 1991; 61:3, 1992.
Polish Archaeology in the Mediterranean I, 1988-1989, Warsaw 1990; II, 1989-1990, Warsaw 1991; III, 1991, Warsaw 1992.

II.Journals:

Bulletin de la Societe d'Archeologie Copte, Le Caire, XXX, 1990.
Journal of Coptic Archeology I, 1991; II, 1992
Bulletin de la Societe Archeologique d'Alexandrie, Alexandrie, 44, 1991.
Nubica, Koln, I/II 1990.

III. Main publications:

The Coptic Encyclopedia, ed. Aziz S. Atiya, vol. 1-7, 1991
Coptic Art and Culture, ed. H. Honelink, Cairo 1990.
Coptic Studies. Acts of the 3rd International Congress of Coptic Studies, Warszawa 20-25 August 1984, ed. W. Godlewski, Warsaw 1991.
Actes du IV Congres Copte, Louvain-la-Neuve, 5-10 septembre 1988, I.Art et Archaologie, ed. M. Rassart-Debergh et J. Ries, Louvain-la-Neuve 1992
Coptic and Nubian Pottery. Part I. International Workshop, Nieborow August 29-31, 1988, Occasional Paper. National Museum in Warsaw, 1, 1990, ed. W. Godlewski.
Cahiers de la ceramique egyptienne, Le Caire IFAO, 2, 1991, ed. P. Ballet
An International Directory of Institutions holding Collections of Coptic Antiquities outside of Egypt, ed. S. Emmel, Roma 1990.
Guide to Ancient Coptic Churches and Monasteries in Upper Egypt, ed. Samuel al-Syrany, Badii Habib, Cairo 1990

BAILEY D. M
1990 The Local Late Roman Red Slip Ware of Hermopolis Magna, 4-26.
1990 Late Roman Pottery in the Nile Valley. A Discusion, Occas. Paper. Nat. Mus.Warsaw, 1:27-28.
1991 Hermopolis Magna. Buildings of the Roman Period, London
1991 Islamic Glazed Pottery from Ashmunein. A Preliminary Note, CCE 2: 205-219
BALLET P.
1992 Lampes du Musee Copte (Vieux - Caire). Breve presentation, Actes du IV Congres Copte, I:124-126
BALLET P., MAHMOUD F., VICHY M. et PICON M.
1991 Artisant de la ceramique dans l'Egypte romaine tardive et byzantine. Prospections d'ateliers de potiers de Minia a Assouan, CCE 2:129-144
BENAZETH D.
1991 Tod. Les objects de metal, San Antonio
1992 Catalogue General du Musee Copte. Les objects de metal, BSAC XXX:49-51
1992 Catalogue des objects de metal du premier millenaire apres J.C. Musee du Louvre, Paris
1992 Objects de metal de la section copte du Musee du Louvre, Actes du IV Con-

gres Copte, I:63-68

BARANSKI M.

1990 Preserving the Christian Basilica of el-Ashmunein, BIFAO 90:41-49

BUSCHHAUSEN H.

1988 Die Ausgrabungen von Dayr Abu Fana in Mittelagypten im Jahre 1987, Jb OB 38:353-362

1989 Die Ausgraubungen von Dayr Abu Fana in Mittelagypten im Jahr 1988, Jb OB 39:241-257

1991 Die Ausgraubungen von Dayr Abu Fana in Mittelagypten im Jahr 1989, Agypten und Levante II:121-146.

DOBROWOLSKI J.

1990 Naqlun - Deir al Malak Ghubra'il: The Existing Monastic Complex, Nubica I/II:161-170

ENGEMANN J.

1989 Des Ende der Wallfahrten nach Abu Mina und die Datierung fruher islamischer glasierter Keramik in Agypten, JbAC 32:161-177 1990 Die Spatbesidlung von Abu Mena, JbAC 33:240-241.

1990 Early Islamic glazed Pottery of the Eight Century A.D. from the Excavations at Abu Mena, Occasi.Pap. Nat. Mus. Warsaw I:63-70

GODLEWSKI W.

1990 Coptic Pottery from Deir el Naqlun (Fayum), Occas.Pap. Nat. Mus. Warsaw I:49-62

1992 Deir el Naqlun. Quelques observations historiques, Actes du IV Congres Copte, I:178-186

GODLEWSKI W., HERBICH T., WIPSZYCKA E.

1990 Deir el Naqlun (Nekloni) 1986-1987. First Preliminary Report, Nubica I/II:172-207

GORECKI T.

1990 Coptic Painted Amphorae from Tell Atrib, Occas.Pap., Nat. Mus. Warsaw, I:34-48

GRIGGS W.,

1992 General Archaeological and Historical Report of 1987 and 1988 Season at Fag el Gamous, Actes du IVe Congres Copte, I:195-202

GROSSMANN P.

1989 Abu Mina I. Die Gruftkirche und die Gruft, Mainz am Rhein

1989 Neue Fruhchristliche Funde aus Agypten, Actes du XIe Congre International d'Archeologie chretienne, II:1843-1908

1991 Spatantike Baudenkmaler im Gebiet von Dair al-Gabrawi, JbAC 18:170-180

1992 New Discoveries in the Field of Christian Archaeology in Egypt, Actes du IVe Congres Copte, I:143-157

in press A new church at Taposiris Magna-Abusir, BSAC

GROSSMANN P., BAILEY D.M.

in press Report on the excavations in the South Church at Hermopolis Ashmunayn in spring 1991, BSAC

GROSSMANN P., HOLZLE W., JARITZ H., KOSCIUK J.

1991 Abu Mena, 12 Vorlaufiger Bericht. Kampagnen 1984-1986, AA, 3:457-456

GROSSMANN P., KOSCIUK J.

1991 Report on the Excavation at Abu Mina in Autumn 1989, BSAC XXX:65-75

GROSSMANN P., LEASE G.

1990 Faw Qibli-1989. Preliminary Report, GM 114:9-12

GROSSMANN P., REICHERT A.

1992 Report on the Season in Fayran (March 1990), GM 128:7-20

GUIDOBALDI A.G.

1990 I capitelli della basilica giustinianea della Theotokos oggi di S. Caterina sul Monte Sinai, Milton 2:265-314

HOPE, C.A.

1988 Three Seasons of excavations at Ismant el-Kharab in Dakhleh Oasis, Egypt, Mediterranean Archaeology I:160-178

1991 The Dakhleh Oasis Project: Ismant el-Kharab 1988-1990:159-176

HULIN, L.

1989 Marsa Matruh 1987: Preliminary Ceramic Report, JARCE 26:115-126

KISS, Z.

1989 Alexandrie V. Les ampoules de saint Menas decouvertes a Kom el Dikka (1961-1981), Varsovie

KOSCIUK J.

1992 Some early Medieval Houses in Abu Mina, Actes du IVe Congres Copte, I:158-167

KUBIAK W.

1990 Roman-type pottery in Medieval Egypt, Occas.Pap., Nat.Mus. Warsaw I:77-82

LECUYOT, G.

1989 Deir Roumi. Monastere Copte de la Valle des Reines, Dossiers histoire et archeologie no 136:60-63

MAHMOUD A. M. , GROSSMANN P.

1991 On the recently excavated monastic building in Dayr Anba Shinuda. Archaeological Report, BSAC XXX:53-64

1991 MARINA EL ALAMEIN. Archaeological Background and Conservation Problems I, Warsaw

VAN MOORSEL P

1989 Forerunners of the Lord. Saints of the Old Testament in Medieval Coptic Church Decoration, Cah.Arch. 37:119-133

1991 Deir es Sourian Revisited. Nubian Letters 17:1-16

1992 Treasures from Baramous. With some remarks on a Melchizedek Scene, Actes du IVe Congres Copte, UI:171-177

NAUERTH, C

1992 Die Publikation der Grabungsfunde von Karara und el-Hibe Methoden und Moglichkeiten der Aufarbeitung, Actes du IVe Congres Copte, I:203-215

PIERRAT, G.

1991 Essai de classification de la ceramique de Tod de la fin du VIIe siecle au debut du XIIIe siecles ap.J.C., CCE 2:149-204

1990 Poteries trouvees dans les fouilles de Tod. 1984-1986. VIIe-XIVe siecles apres J.C., Occas.Pap., Nat. Mus. Warsaw, I:29-33

1992 Peintres potiers d'Assouan du IXe au XIIe siecle ap. J.C. La Revue du Louvre et du Musees de France 4:30-37

REDDE, M.

1990 Quinze annees de recherches francaises a Douch. Vers un premier bilan, BIFAO 90:281-301

RENNER-VOLBACH, D.

1988 Die koptischen Textilien im Museo Missionario Etnologico der Vatikanischer Museen, Wiesbaden

RUTSCHOWSCAYA, M-H.

1990 Tissus Coptes, Paris

SEVERIN, H.-G.

1989 Kapitelle mit einem Blattkranz aus Hinterlegten Olblattzweigen, JbAC 32:151-160

SHARPE, J.L.

Dakhleh Oasis Project: The Kellis Codices:192-197

SIDEBOTHAM, S.E.

1991 Romische Strassen in der Agyptischen Wuste, Antike Welt 3:177-189

SIDEBOTHAM, S.E., RILEY, J.A., HAMROUSH, H.A., BARAKAT, H.

1989 Fieldwork on the Red Sea Coast: Season 1987, JARCE 26:127-166

STERNBERG, Th.

1988 Der Vermeitliche ursprung der Westlichen Diakonien in Agypten und die Conlations des Johannes Cassian, JbAC 31:173-209

TAWAB, M. A., CASTEL, G., POUIT, G., BALLET, P.

1990 Archeo-geologie des anciennes mines de cuivre at d'or des regions el Urf (Mongul-sud et Dara-ouest), BIFAO 90:259-364

WALTERS C.C.

1989 Christian paintings from Tebtunis, JEA 75:191-208

WHITCOMB, D.

1989 Coptic Glazed Ceramics from the Excavations at Aqaba, Jorda, JARCE 26:167-182

WHITE D.
1989 1987 Excavations on Bates's Island, Marsa Matruh: Second Preliminary Report, JARCE 26:87-114.
ZITTERKOPF, R.E., SIDEBOTHAM , S.E.
1989 Stations and towers on the Quseir-Nile Road, JEA 75:155-190.

IV. Exhibition Catalogues

Les Kellia. Ermitages coptes en Basse-Egypte. Musee d'art et d'histoire, Geneve 12 octobre 1989 - 7 janvier 1990, Geneve 1989
E. Dauterman Magire, H.P. Maguire, M.J. Duncan-Flowers, Art and Holy Powers in the Early Christian House. Krannert Art Museum of the University of Illinois at Urbana, 25 August - 10 October 1989, Kelsey Museum of Archaeology of the University of Michigan in Ann Arbor, 27 October 1989 - 29 April 1990, llinois 1989
L'Egypte en Perigord. Dans les pas de Jean Cledat. Catalogue raisonne de exposition Musee du Perigord 16 mai - 15 septembre 1991, Paris 1991

MARTIN KRAUSE

REPORT ON RESEARCH
IN COPTIC PAPYROLOGY AND EPIGRAPHY

Die Fortschritte auf dem Gebiete der koptischen Papyrologie, die seit dem letzten Kongreß 1988 in Louvain-la-Neuve[1] erzielt worden sind, zeigen sich schon darin, daß die Sektion vergrößert worden ist. Nachdem Herr Kollege Emmel[2] bereits über die koptische Kodikologie und Paläographie, Teile der Papyrologie, referiert hat, berichte ich über die koptische Papyrologie, wobei ich die Zaubertexte mit einschließe, und über die koptische Epigraphik - über Inschriften und Grabsteine. Im Laufe meines Berichtes werde ich Ihnen Beispiele nennen, die zeigen, daß Schreibübungen auf Ostraka und Papyri, ebenso auf den Wänden von Klöstern, nachweisbar sind und daß Grabinschriften - offenbar als Muster - auf Ostraka nachweisbar sind, ebenso finden sich Grabinschriften als Graffiti in Klöstern. Obwohl Texte in ihrem Inhalt sowohl innerhalb der Papyrologie als auch der Epigraphik nachweisbar sind, werden beide Disziplinen wissenschaftlich in den Altertumswissenschaften getrennt als Unterabteilungen der Hilfswissenschaften geführt.

Bereits in Louvain hatte ich auf die große Anzahl griechischer Papyri aus der byzantinischen Zeit Ägyptens hingewiesen,[3] die wegen ihres Umfangs und ihrer Bedeutung für die Koptologie ebenfalls als Primärquellen verdienten, hier vorgestellt zu werden. Neben der

---

1. M. Krause, Publikationen koptischer nichtliterarischer Texte der Jahre 1984-1988 in: Actes du IVe congrès copte, Louvain-la-Neuve 5-lo septembre 1988, edites par M. Rassart-Debergh et J. Ries, II, Louvain-la-Neuve 1992, 89-103.
2. St. Emmel, Report on Research in Coptic Codicology and Palaeography.
3. Krause, aO. 94.

Vielzahl griechischer Ostraka, die Herr Kollege Grossmann in Abu Mena[4] freigelegt hat, sei nur noch auf einen einzigen Papyrus, P. Oxyr. LVIII 3959[5] hingewiesen, der Frau Kollegin Ruth Altheim-Stiehl[6] den Nachweis eines neuen Terminus ante quem für die Ankunft der persischen Truppen in Oxyrhynchus geliefert hat: bereits am 12. Januar 620 sind sie dort nachweisbar. Weitere Beispiele wird uns heute Nachmittag Herr Kollege van Minnen[7] in seinem Referat nennen. Unserem Kollegen Gerald Browne[8] verdanken wir den 2. und 3. Band Old Nubian Texts from Qasr Ibrim. Die Urkunden und Briefe sind von großer Wichtigkeit für die nubische Geschichte. Ein Beispiel soll genügen: Urkunde 37[9] zeigt, daß im Jahre 1155, als Menas Bischof von Ibrim[10] war, in Kurte der bisher nicht bekannte Darme Bischof von Kurte war. Er erweitert also unsere Kenntnis der Bischöfe dieser Diözese.

Ich empfehle, daß Herr Kollege Browne als Herausgeber der wichtigen altnubischen Texte, auf deren Erscheinen wir seit Jahren warten, auf dem nächsten Kongreß über das in altnubischer Sprache überlieferte Textgut berichtet. Wie ich kürzlich in London hörte, sollen nun auch die in den Grabungen der Egypt Exploration Society gefundenen koptischen Texte bald herausgegeben werden, so daß unsere Kenntnis Nubiens in christlicher Zeit bald erweitert wird.

---

4.   Sie sollen von Frau G. Robinson-Fantoni veröffentlicht werden.
5.   The Oxyrhynchus Papyri, Vol. LVIII, edited with translations and notes by J. R. Rea, London 1991, 116-118.
6.   R. Altheim-Stiehl, The Sasanians in Egypt - Some Evidence of Historical Interest in: BSAC 31, 1992, 87-96, 96 und dieselbe, Zur zeitlichen Bestimmung der sāsānidischen Eroberung Ägyptens. Ein neuer terminus ante quem für Oxyrhynchos ist nachzutragen in: ΜΟΥΣΙΚΟΣ ΑΝΗΡ, Festschrift für Max Wegner zum 90. Geburtstag, hrsg. von O. Brehm u. S. Klie, Bonn 1992, 5-8.
7.   P. v. Minnen, Coptology and Papyrology
8.   G. Browne, Old Nubian Texts from Qasr Ibrim, Vol. II, London 1989, Vol. III, London 1991.
9.   Browne, aO. III 54.
10. M. Krause, Zur Kirchengeschichte Nubiens in: Nubian Culture Past and Present. Main Papers presented at the Sixth International Conference for Nubian Studies in Uppsala, 11-16 August 1986, edited by T. Hägg (= Kungl. Vitterhets Historie och Antikvitets Akademien, Konferenser 17), 293-308, 298.

Nach langen Vorarbeiten[11] ist mit der Vorlage des "International Directory of Institutions holding Collections of Coptic Antiquities outside of Egypt", dessen Redaktion wir unserem Kollegen Stephen Emmel[12] verdanken, ein großer Schritt getan worden, koptisches Quellenmaterial, auch die papyrologischen Quellen, zu erfassen. Die 1976 von Arthur Schiller veröffentlichte "Checklist of Coptic Documents and Letters"[13] war ja bereits bei ihrem Erscheinen nicht vollständig.[14] Leider hat das Directory gegenüber dem mir vorgelegenem Manuskript durch Auslassungen im Druck an Wert verloren: nicht nur die Namen der für die koptischen Quellen verantwortlichen Leiter der Sammlungen sind weggelassen worden, sondern auch Angaben, wer mit der Publikation der koptischen Bestände betraut worden ist. Ich beschränke mich auf die Angaben zu den Papyri: bei der Beinecke Rare Book and Manuscript Library in New Haven war vermerkt: "Several of the papyri are assigned for publication to Leslie MacCoull". Bei der hiesigen Catholic University of America konnte man lesen: "The papyri have been assigned for publication to Leslie MacCoull." Beim Kelsey Museum of Archaeology der University of Ann Arbor war vermerkt: "the papyri will be published by G.M. Browne." Ob diese Angaben noch zutreffend sind, entzieht sich meiner Kenntnis.

Für die Coptic Encyclopaedia hatte ich in einem langen Artikel "Papyrus Collections" von 46 DIN A4 Seiten eine nach Ländern geordnete Liste von Sammlungen mit koptischen papyrologischen Beständen zusammengestellt. Sie enthielt außer detaillierten Angaben über den Umfang der Bestände auch ein Verzeichnis der Publikationen dieser Bestände, soweit sie vollständig oder in Teilen publiziert worden sind. Er sollte auch den Artikel von A. Schiller up to date bringen.

---

11. M. Krause, Die Disziplin Koptologie in: The Future of Coptic Studies, edited by R. McL. Wilson, Leiden 1978 (= Coptic Studies Vol. 1), 1-22, 18 f.
12. An International Directory of Institutions Holding Collections of Coptic Antiquities Outside of Egypt, edited by St. Emmel, Roma 1990.
13. A. A. Schiller, A Checklist of Coptic Documents and Letters in: BASP 13, 1976, 99-123.
14. Krause, aO. 19 u. A.109.

Diese Übersicht ist von einer mir nicht bekannten Person des Verlags MacMillan völlig umgearbeitet und auf 8 Druckseiten[15] verkürzt worden: die Literatur zu den einzelnen Sammlungen wurde dabei an das Ende des Gesamtartikels gesetzt. Der Artikel ist dadurch für einen Spezialisten wertlos geworden und vermittelt selbst dem Laien nur einen ungefähren Eindruck vom Umfang der Bestände.

Aus drei selbständigen Artikeln: Inscriptions, Building Inscriptions und Tomb Inscriptions wurde ebenfalls von einer mir unbekannten Person ein einziger Artikel "Inscriptions"[16] gemacht und gedruckt, so daß Angaben am Beginn des Lemmas, die sich speziell auf eine der 3 Gruppen bezogen, nun als Aussage für alle Inschriftengruppen erscheinen!

Somit ist - die Beispiele ließen sich leider vermehren - aus einer wissenschaftlichen leider eine populärwissenschaftliche Enzyklopädie entstanden!

Erfreulicher ist, daß im Rahmen des Catalogue général des Koptischen Museums Kairo, über dessen Fortschritt Herr Dr. Gawdat Gabra[17] gestern berichtet hat, und dessen erste Bände bereits im Manuskript vorliegen, auch die papyrologischen Bestände des Museums erfaßt werden. Kent Brown wird mit Gawdat Gabra einen Katalog der großen Sammlung der koptischen Ostraka vorlegen. Frau Sofia Schaten hat gestern über die Bearbeitung der Grabsteine berichtet.[18] Das Egyptian Department des British Museum London hat inzwischen auch die koptologischen Quellen einschließlich der großen Ostrakasammlung auf einem Computer erfaßt; dasselbe haben unsere Kollegen im Louvre getan. Unsere Kollegin Leslie MacCoull[19] hat innerhalb ihrer Arbeiten dankenswerterweise die koptologischen

---

15. M. Krause, Papyrus Collections in: The Coptic Encyclopedia, Aziz S. Atiya Editor in Chief, New York 1991, Vol. 6, 1890-1896, Lit. 1896-1898.
16. M. Krause, Inscriptions in: The Coptic Encyclopedia aO., Vol. 4, 1290-1299.
17. Gawdat Gabra, The Project "Catalogue général du Musée Copte": Progress of the work until 1991.
18. S. Schaten, Zur Bearbeitung der Grabsteine mit Inschriften im Rahmen des Projektes "Catalogue général du Musée Copte": Die Grabsteine des Apa Moyses-Klosters in Abydos.

Bestände weiterer Sammlungen in Ägypten, Amerika und Europa vorgestellt und wird heute Nachmittag auch die der Bayerischen Staatsbibliothek in München vor uns ausbreiten.[20] Sie findet erfreulicherweise jetzt Mitarbeiter in jüngeren Kolleginnen und Kollegen:

Frau Sarah Clackson[21] aus Cambridge wird heute über "The Michaelides Collection in the Cambridge University and British Libraries" referieren und Herr Terry Wilfong[22] über die Bestände im Oriental Museum Chicago berichten.

Einen Schritt weiter wird Herr Paul Allen Mirecki[23] gehen, der uns mitteilen wird, welche koptischen Texte in Band IV der Berliner Koptischen Urkunden veröffentlicht werden. Es handelt sich wie in Bd. 3 (herausgegeben von Herrn Kollegen Satzinger)[24] um Texte, die teils durch ihn, teils durch den Restaurator in der *Westberliner* Papyrussammlung für die Publikation restauriert wurden. Die Ostberliner Bestände werden bekanntlich seit mehreren Jahrzehnten von meinem Berliner Lehrer, Fritz Hintze,[25] bearbeitet. Die erfreuliche Vereinigung Deutschlands wird hoffentlich auch auf die Publikation der Ostberliner koptologischen Bestände beschleunigend wirken.

Auf dem letzten Kongreß hatte ich den Abschluß der Ostberliner

---

19. L. S. B. MacCoull, The Teshlot papyri and the survival of documentary Sahidic in: OCP 55, 1989, 201-206; dies., Missing pieces of the Dioscorus archive in: CdE 65, 1990, 107-110.

20. L. S. B. MacCoull, Coptic documentary papyri in the Bayerische Staatsbibliothek, Munich.

21. S. Clackson, The Michaelides Collection in the Cambridge University and British Libraries.

22. T. Wilfong, Coptic texts in the Oriental Museum (Chicago): A preliminary survey.

23. P. A. Mirecki, BKU IV: A preview.

24. Ägyptische Urkunden aus den Staatlichen Museen Berlin, Koptische Urkunden III. Band 1.2. Heft, Berlin 1967/68, bearbeitet von H. Satzinger.

25. Er hat bisher nur einzelne Texte publiziert, zuletzt die koptischen Steuerquittungsostraka der Berliner Papyrus-Sammlung in: Mitteilungen aus der Ägyptischen Sammlung Bd. VIII (= Festschrift zum 150jährigen Bestehen des Berliner Ägyptischen Museums), Berlin 1975, 271-284.

Zaubertexte durch Walter Beltz[26] melden können. Bei einer in der Zwischenzeit vorgenommenen Überprüfung dieser Publikation anhand von Fotos wurden leider so gravierende Fehler bei der Textabschrift und Texttrennung festgestellt, die sich auf die Übersetzung und Interpretation auswirken mußten, daß der Direktor der Sammlung, Herr Kollege Karl Heinz Priese, einer Neuedition dieser Texte durch meine beiden Schüler, Siegfried Richter und Gregor Wurst, seine Zustimmung erteilt hat. Ein Beispiel werden Sie in dem im Druck befindlichen nächsten Band des "Archivs für Papyrusforschung" finden.[27] Herrn Kollegen J. van der Vliet verdanken wir eine minutiöse Untersuchung von Wörtern und Eigennamen in koptischen magischen Texten.[28]

Die Wiedervereinigung Deutschlands eröffnete auch mir den Zugang zu den maschinengeschriebenen Exemplaren meiner Leipziger und Berliner Dissertationen. Da der Verlag Brill die Aufnahme von Dissertationen in die Reihe der 'Coptic Studies' abgelehnt hat, haben wir in Münster eine neue Reihe "Arbeiten zum spätantiken und koptischen Ägypten" begründet,in der bereits zwei computergeschriebene Dissertationen erschienen sind,[29] der 1. Band wird hier noch vorgestellt werden. Als Bd. 3 erscheint die Leipziger Arbeit,[30] die unter einem neuen Titel[31] erscheinen wird. Wegen der Neufunde von Urkunden zum meletianischen Mönchtum, die von Bärbel Kramer und

---

26. Vgl. A.1, S. 89 A.1.

27. S. Richter u. G. Wurst, P. Berol. 10587 - Neue Edition in: Archiv für Papyrusforschung 13, 1993, 39-45.

28. J. van der Vliet, Varia magica coptica in: Aegyptus 71, 1991, 217-242.

29. Bd. 1: C. Wietheger, Das Jeremias-Kloster zu Saqqara unter besonderer Berücksichtigung der Inschriften, Altenberge 1992; Bd. 2: K. Urbaniak-Walczak, Die "conceptio per aurem". Untersuchungen zum Marienbild unter besonderer Berücksichtigung der Malereien in El-Bagawat, Altenberge 1992.

30. Der Titel der Dissertation lautet: Untersuchungen zum ägyptischen Mönchtum. Unveröffentlichte koptische Urkunden aus dem Apa Apollon Kloster zu Bawit, Leipzig 1957.

31. Die Verkaufsurkunden von Klosterteilen des Apa-Apollon-Klosters von Bawit (BM Or 6201-6204 u. 6206) herausgegeben, übersetzt und untersucht von Martin Krause.

John Shelton 1987[32] herausgegeben worden sind und zu denen inzwischen weitere neue Fragmente, die die Urkunden joinen, gekommen sind, verzichte ich auf den Abdruck von Kapitel 5, das sich mit den Verkaufsurkunden der beiden meletianischen Klöster (SB 5174 und 5175) befaßt.[33] Der jetzt ausgelassene Teil soll nach der Neuveröffentlichung der Trierer und Heidelberger Texte durch Bärbel Kramer unter Einschluß des neuen Textmaterials veröffentlicht werden. Die Veröffentlichung der großen Bawit-Urkunden wird dafür erweitert um ein Kapitel über die Sprache der Urkunden und umfangreiche Indices.

Inzwischen ist es auch gelungen, weitere Texte aus den französischen Grabungen in Bawit, deren Existenz zwar bekannt, deren Aufbewahrungsort aber unbekannt war,[34] aufzuspüren. Die in Frankreich aufbewahrten Texte werden von unserer französischen Kollegin Anne Boud'Hors ediert. Durch Vermittlung meines Schülers Gawdat Gabra habe ich von den im Museum von Ismaelija aufbewahrten 26 Briefen und Urkunden, in der Mehrzahl nur unvollständig erhalten, für eine Publikation geeignete Fotos erhalten. Die Texte stammen aus dem Apollon-Kloster von Bawit, sind dem 7. bis 9. Jh. zuzuweisen und werden hoffentlich helfen, die bisher bekannten Urkunden den verschiedenen bisher bekannten Apa-Apollon-Klöstern zuzuweisen.

Fast 40 Jahre waren seit der Ausgrabung des koptischen Klosters Deir el Gizaz (7 km südwestlich von Nagada) vergangen, bei der Jean Doresse[35] auch koptische und griechische Ostraka gefunden hatte, als Anna di Bitonto Kasser,[36] eine ausgewiesene griechische Papyrologin,

---

32. Das Archiv des Nepheros und verwandte Texte hrsg. von B. Kramer u. J. C. Shelton mit zwei koptischen Beiträgen von G. M. Browne, Mainz 1987 (= Aegyptiaca Treverensia, Trierer Studien zum griechisch-römischen Ägypten Bd. 4).
33. S. 136-174 der Dissertation.
34. E. Gaillard, Les archives de l'égyptologue Jean Clédat retrouvés in: La revue du Louvre Juin 1988, Nr. 3, 195-202; vgl. auch das Referat von D. Bénazeth u. M.-H. Rutschowscaya, Archives de Jean Clédat données au Louvre auf diesem Kongreß.
35. J. Doresse, Deir el Gizaz, ou couvent de Samuel: Un monastère thébaine oublié...et meme disparu in: Aegyptus 69, 1989, 153-163.

sich erfreulicherweise auch der koptischen Papyrologie zuwandte und die Ostraka in drei Aufsätzen veröffentlichte. Es handelt sich neben Bibel- und liturgischen Texten um Briefe und Schreibübungen.

Diese Schreibübungen sind auch aufgenommen worden in die zweibändige Untersuchung von Frau Monika Hasitzka, Neue Texte und Dokumentation zum koptischen Unterricht herausgegeben unter Mitarbeit von Hermann Harrauer, Wien 1990.[37] Die Arbeit ergänzt die Untersuchungen von H. Harrauer und Peter Sijpesteijn,[38] Neue Texte aus dem antiken Unterricht, Wien 1985 (= MPER XV), nach deren Vorbild sie angelegt ist. Sie basiert auf 332 Ostraka und Papyri aus vielen Museen und Inschriften aus Klöstern Ägyptens und behandelt einzelne Buchstaben, das Alphabet, Syllabare, Wörter und Wortteile, Namen, Formelteile, Briefformulare, Urkundenteile, Briefe, eine Gruppe betitelt "religiöse Texte", Wörterlisten, Zahlen, Bruchzahlen und Multiplikationen.

Das Buch wird *das* Standardwerk über den koptischen Unterricht, wenn es auch einige Mängel aufweist: Es geht nicht der Frage nach, welche Texte, die aus Klöstern stammen, als Texte aus *Klosterschulen* zu interpretieren sind. Thebanische Texte aus dem 7. Jh. werden zuweilen (Nr. 145) erst ins 8./9. Jh. datiert. Manche echte Briefe (vor allem die von Hall edierten) werden als Schreibübungen interpretiert. Nr. 221 ist kein Mustertext, sondern ein Kolophon (Nr. 63 von Lantschoot)![39] Bei der Übersetzung "religiöser Texte" merkt man der Verfasserin an, daß sie nicht als Theologin ausgebildet ist.

---

36. A. di Bitonto Kasser, Ostraca scolastici copti a Deir el Gizāz in: Aegyptus 68, 1988, 167-175; dies., Deir Apa Samuele: localizzazione e storia di un monastero della regione tebana in: Aegyptus 69, 1989, 165-177; dies., Ostraca greci e copti a Deir el Gizāz in: Aegyptus 70, 1990, 57-72.

37. M. Hasitzka, Neue Texte und Dokumentation zum koptischen Unterricht herausgegeben unter Mitwirkung von H. Harrauer, Wien 1990, 2 Bde. (= Mitteilungen aus der Papyrussammlung der Österreichischen Nationalbibliothek [= MPER] , N.S. XVIII) als Nr. 6, 72, 82, 290 a und 305 a.

38. H. Harrauer u. P. J. Sijpesteijn, Neue Texte aus dem antiken Unterricht, Wien 1985 (= MPER XV).

39. A. van Lantschoot, Recueil des colophons des manuscrits chrétiens d'Égypte. I Les colophons coptes des manuscrits sahidiques, Louvain 1929, 106-107.

Eine weitere Monographie ist das Buch unserer Kollegin Leslie
S.B. MacCoull, Dioscorus of Aphrodito.[40] Der im 6. Jh. (circa von
520 bis 585) lebende Jurist und Dichter schrieb sowohl in griechischer
als auch in koptischer Sprache, versuchte Christentum und Heidentum
miteinander zu verbinden. Diese Monographie, nach Keenan "an elo-
quent book, written with passion and pique",[41] sollte zur Pflichtlektüre
aller Koptologen gehören. Für die koptische Papyrologie sind vor
allem die juristischen Papyri wichtig, vor allem die Protokolle der
Anhörungsverfahren: der unveröffentlichte unvollständige P. Maspero
III 67 353, den uns die Autorin S. 41 ff. nach der Kopie von Charles
Kuentz aus dem Crum-Nachlaß im Griffith Institute mitteilt.[42] Wir
selbst bereiten die Veröffentlichung von P. Berol. 11349 vor, eines
ebenfalls unveröffentlichten Protokolls eines Anhörungsverfahrens,
dessen Inhalt S. 22 f. kurz mitgeteilt wird. Zusammen mit dem von A.
Schiller veröffentlichten P. Budge[43] haben wir reiches Material für das
Schiedsverfahren in der 2. Hälfte des 6. Jhs. bis zur 1. Hälfte des 7.
Jhs.

Bei der Interpretation von Pierpont Morgan 662 B 12 weichen die
Meinungen von Frau Kollegin MacCoull und mir leider voneinander
ab. Auf dem 15. internationalen Papyrologenkongreß hatte sie[44]

---

40. L. S. B. MacCoull, Dioscorus of Aphrodito. His Work and his World, Berkeley
1988 (= Transformation of the Classical Heritage XVI); vgl. auch ihren Artikel in:
The Coptic Encyclopedia Vol. 3, 1991, 916 und die Rezension von J. M. Keenan in:
BASP 25, 1988, 173-178.
41. Keenan, aO. 173.
42. Group V.4: copies of 6th century Aphrodito papyri (Coptic) some sent by
Lacau. Meine Kopie weicht an einigen Stellen von dem auf S. 41 f. publizierten Text
ab und sollte überprüft werden.
43. A. A. Schiller, The Budge Papyrus of Columbia University in: JARCE 7, 1968,
79-118; vgl. jetzt noch die beiden Artikel von Sch. Allam zu diesem Papyrus:
Glossen zu einem schiedsrichterlichen Verfahren (kopt. p.Budge + griech. p.BM
2017) in: MDIK 47, 1991, 1-9 und Observations on civil jurisdiction in late
byzantine and early arabic Egypt in: Life in a Multi-Cultural Society. Egypt from
Cambyses to Constantine and Beyond edited by Janet H. Johnson, Chicago 1992 (=
The Oriental Institute of the University of Chicago, Studies in ancient oriental
civilisation No 51), 1-8.

bekanntlich diese Urkunde als "Heiratsvertrag" bezeichnet. In den Zeilen 4 bis 6 werden zwar auch Ehefragen, genauer gesagt werden Ehehindernisse, zu nahe Verwandtschaftsgrade, aufgeführt. Diese Ehehindernisse werden schon in Rundschreiben des Bischofs Abraham von Hermonthis um 600 ebenso wie in den Kanones der koptischen Kirche genannt. Dagegen fehlen in dieser Urkunde die für die koptischen Eheverträge charakteristischen güterrechtlichen Vereinbarungen und Scheidungsstrafen. Im Zentrum des Papyrus stehen vielmehr Aussagen, die die Amtsführung eines Klerikers betreffen, wie wir sie aus den Ordinationstexten desselben Bischofs kennen (Darbringung der Eucharistie nur einmal pro Tag auf demselben Altar in nüchternem Zustand). Darüber hinaus enthält die Urkunde, die als ψήφισμα bezeichnet wird, weitere interessante Verpflichtungen: kein Verkehr mit Wandermönchen ⲘⲞⲚⲀⲬⲞⲤ ⲚⲤⲀⲢⲀⲔⲰⲦⲈ usw. Daher sah ich mich gezwungen, sie als "ein Vorschlagsschreiben für einen Priester" zu bezeichnen und habe sie 1990 unter diesem Titel neu interpretiert.[45]

Eine Einführung in das Gebiet Theben-West im 7. und 8. Jahrhundert hat Terry Wilfong[46] 1989 vorgelegt. Man ist erfreut, daß ein bisher unbekannter Wissenschaftler sich diesem umfangreichen Gebiet zuwendet und er in Fußnoten[47] mehrere Arbeiten über das schriftliche und archäologische Material ankündigt, von denen zwei nützliche Konkordanzen[48] und ein Aufsatz[49] bisher erschienen sind. Zunächst[50]

---

44. L. S. B. MacCoull, Coptic Marriage-Contract in: Actes du XVe congrès international de papyrologie, Bd. II, Brüssel 1979, 116-123.

45. M. Krause, Ein Vorschlagsschreiben für einen Priester in: Lingua restituta Orientalis. Festgabe für Julius Aßfalg, Wiesbaden 1990, hrsgb. von R. Schulz u. M. Görg (= Ägypten und Altes Testament 20), 195-202.

46. T. Wilfong, Western Thebes in the Seventh and Eighth Centuries: A Bibliographic Survey of Jême and its Surroundings in: BASP 26, 1989, 89-145.

47. T. Wilfong, aO. Anmerkungen 9, 19, 21, 25 , 27 u. 33.

48. T. Wilfong, Cross-Index of Coptic ostraca from the Cairo Catalogue (CGC) published in Crum's Coptic Ostraca, Chicago 1988 (mir bisher nicht zugänglich) = Wilfong, aO. A. 25; ders., A concordance of published Coptic and Greek ostraca from the Oriental Institute's excavations at Medinet Habu in: Enchoria 17, 1990, 155-160 = Wilfong, aO. A.27.

wird Jeme und das archäologische und inschriftliche Material behandelt, anschließend[51] die Klöster von Theben-West. Die Bibliographie[52] schließt den Artikel ab. Sie nennt die bereits in den einzelnen Sektionen genannten Arbeiten in alphabetischer Abfolge. Die nützliche Arbeit wird leider durch eine Reihe fehlerhafter Aussagen im Wert gemindert, von denen nur 3 genannt seien. Auf S. 106, wo zu Recht darauf verwiesen wird, daß in Theben-West magische Texte in Demotisch, griechischer und koptischer Sprache gefunden wurden, wird der Carnarvon Papyrus als bisher unpubliziert bezeichnet.[53] Zunächst hält man diese Aussage für einen Druckfehler, da allgemein bekannt sein dürfte, daß dieser Papyrus bereits seit 1931 von Angelicus Kropp herausgegeben[54] und in Bd. II übersetzt und kommentiert worden ist.[55] Jedoch auf S. 125 wiederholt Terry Wilfong unter Dēr al Bakhit seine Aussage.[56] Unter dem Titel "Pisentius Archive"[57] wird auch die Dissertation von Herrn Gawdat[58] genannt. Wilfong schreibt: "Hagiographical accounts of Pisentius' life exist in Coptic, Arabic and Ethiopic in several versions; reference to most are collected in Gawdat Gabra's dissertation, *to which can be added fragments of the Sahidic Life in Vienna published by Till, and the fragments in the British Library described by Bentley Layton*".[59] Heißt das, Gawdat habe die

---

49. T. Wilfong, The archive of a family of moneylenders from Jeme in: BASP 27, 1990, 169-181.
50. Wilfong, aO. (A.46) 96-118.
51. Wilfong, aO. 118-133.
52. Wilfong, aO. 133-144.
53. Wilfong, aO. 106: "the lenghthy, but still unpublished Carnarvon Papyrus (Cairo JdE 45o6o) from Deir el Bakhit."
54. A. Kropp, Ausgewählte koptische Zaubertexte, Bd. I, Brüssel 1931, 50-54.
55. Kropp, aO. Bd. II, Brüssel 1931, 31-40.
56. Wilfong, aO. 125: "The still unpublished magical papyrus Cairo JdE 45060, found by Carnavon."
57. Wilfong, aO. 113-115.
58. Gawdat Gabra Abdel Sayed, Untersuchungen zu den Texten über Pesyntheus Bischof von Koptos (569-632), Bonn 1984 (= Habelts Dissertationsdrucke Reihe Ägyptologie Heft 4)
59. Wilfong, aO. 114.

Wiener und Londoner Texte in seiner Dissertation nicht behandelt? Wilfong übersieht, daß Gawdat auf Seite 7 der Dissertation den Wiener Text als Text W und den Londoner Text als S^1 bezeichnet und mehrfach in der Arbeit behandelt. Gawdats Dissertation ist 1984 erschienen. Daher konnte er beim Londoner Text nicht vermerken, daß unser Kollege Bentley Layton[60] einige Jahre später diesen Text in seinem Katalog behandeln würde.

Unter der Rubrik "Translations and Synthesis of the Jeme Texts"[61] liest man "Whether or not the proposed posthumous edition of Kahle's writings on the subject by Martin Krause will materialize is unknown".[62]

Diese indirekte Frage ist deshalb verwunderlich, weil sie bereits seit nunmehr 18 Jahren von Fritz Hintze beantwortet worden ist. 1974 hat er das von Paul E. Kahle hinterlassene Manuskript unter Kahles Namen mit dem Titel "Zu den koptischen Steuerquittungen"[63] herausgegeben. In einer Vorbemerkung schreibt F. Hintze, daß ihm durch meine Vermittlung Kahles Material übergeben worden sei.[64] Diese Publikation zitiert T. Wilfong in seinem Aufsatz.[65] Hat er sie nicht gelesen? Terry Wilfong schreibt weiter: "Martin Krause himself has completed an extensive study of the Bishop Abraham of Armant, who

---

60. B. Layton, Catalogue of Coptic literary manuscripts in the British Library acquired since the year 1906, London 1987, 204 f. (= Nr. 167,2).
61. Wilfong, aO. 115-118.
62. Wilfong, aO. 117.
63. P.E. Kahle, Zu den koptischen Steuerquittungen in: Festschrift zum 150jährigen Bestehen des Berliner Ägyptischen Museums (= Mitteilungen aus der Ägyptischen Sammlung Bd. 8), Berlin 1975, 283-285.
64. Kahle, aO. 283: "Nach dem Tode von Paul E. Kahle wurde mir durch Vermittlung von Martin Krause dessen Material an Abschriften und Listen zu den koptischen Steuerquittungen übergeben, da ich damals ebenfalls Material für die koptischen Steuerquittungen gesammelt hatte. Die geplante Publikation konnte aber leider – ebenso wie die beabsichtigte Publikation aller koptischen Ostraka der Berliner Sammlung – noch nicht fertiggestellt werden, da die langjährige Feldarbeit im Sudan und andere Verpflichtungen es mir unmöglich machten, die dafür notwendige Zeit aufzubringen."
65. Wilfong, aO. 118.

lived for an number of years in western Thebes, but this work was published privately, and is not widely available".[66]

Bei dieser Arbeit handelt es sich um eine 1956 von der Philosophischen Fakultät der Humboldt-Universität in Berlin angenommene Dissertation, von der zwar einige Kopien in deutschen Universitätsbibliotheken vorhanden sind, die von verschiedenen Kollegen gelesen und zitiert[67] wurden, die aber bisher noch nicht publiziert ist. Die 114 im Jahre 1956 behandelten Texte sind in der Zwischenzeit auf ca. 200 Urkunden und Briefe angewachsen. In der Festschrift für Fritz Hintze[68] habe ich die Kirchenvisitationsurkunden des Bischofs Abraham von Hermonthis behandelt. Es handelt sich um ein vollständig erhaltenes Ostrakon in Tübingen und ein bruchstückhaft erhaltenes 2. Exemplar, das mir bisher nur aus den Burton-Fotos bekannt ist. Darin werden Kleriker aufgefordert, Kirchen zu visitieren und auf eventuelle Vernachlässigungen beim Lampendienst, beim Gottesdienst, Abendmahl, Fasten zu achten und die festgestellten Verstöße dem Bischof mitzuteilen. Der Beauftragte kann beim Ungehorsam die Kleriker aus dem Klerus ausschließen, wird selbst vom Bischof mit Strafe bedroht, falls er die Visitation nicht durchführt.

Sicher gibt es in öffentlichen oder Privatsammlungen weitere bisher unbekannte Texte aus dieser Bischofskorrespondenz - von 26 unveröffentlichten im British Museum habe ich erst kürzlich Fotos gemacht - dennoch soll die Arbeit über diesen Bischof zum Abschluß gebracht und in den "Arbeiten zum spätantiken und koptischen Ägypten" gedruckt werden.

---

66. Wilfong, aO. 117.

67. Genannt seien nur: E. Wipszycka, Les ressources et les activités économiques des églises en Égypte du IVe au VIIIe siècle, Brüssel 1972, 11 A.2 u.ö.; C. D. G. Müller, Die koptische Kirche zwischen Chalkedon und dem Arabereinmarsch in: Zeitschrift für Kirchengeschichte 1964, 271-308, vor allem 283-292; und St. Timm, Das christlich-koptische Ägypten in arabischer Zeit Teil 1 (A-C), Wiesbaden 1984, 162 u. A. 38, 168 u.ö.

68. M. Krause, Die Kirchenvisitationsurkunden. Ein neues Formular in der Korrespondenz des Bischofs Abraham von Hermonthis in: Meroitica 12, Berlin 1990, 225-236.

In thebanischen Urkunden des 7. und 8. Jahrhunderts fällt auf, welche Rolle Frauen als Pfandleiher und Geldverleiher spielen. Dieses Thema, das Frau B. Hogervorst[69] im Rahmen einer Dissertation untersuchen will, wird von T. Wilfong[70] in einem Aufsatz gestreift. Er behandelt 30 koptische Ostraka, die in Haus 34 von Djeme gefunden wurden und kann sie als ein Familienarchiv von Geldverleihern identifizieren. Über 5 Generationen sind Mitglieder dieser Familie, unter ihnen die bekannte Koloje, in ihrer Tätigkeit verfolgt worden.

Auf dem Carl-Schmidt-Kolloquium in Halle vom 27.-29. April 1988 habe ich ein Referat über "Carl Schmidts Beiträge zum ägyptischen Mönchtum auf Grund koptischer Urkunden"[71] gehalten, das 1990 von Peter Nagel in dem Kongreßband herausgegeben worden ist. Carl Schmidt hatte bekanntlich zwei Urkunden, die dasselbe Menas-Kloster von Sbeht betreffen, veröffentlicht, einen Arbeitsvertrag[72] und einen Vertrag zwischen dem δίκαιον des Menas-Klosters, vertreten durch eine Person, die das Amt des Klostervorstehers übernommen hatte, und dem Konvent der Mönche, in dem genau die Rechte und Pflichten des neuen Abtes genannt werden.[73] Während in der Literatur Zustimmung zum Arbeitsvertrag festzustellen ist, ist die Beurteilung des ägyptischen Mönchtums im 9. Jh. durch C. Schmidt nicht aufrecht zu halten. C. Schmidt hatte geurteilt: "Unser Papyrus... legt ein beredtes Zeugnis ab für den Niedergang des ägyptischen Mönchtums; besonders die finanziellen Verhältnisse müssen katastrophal gewesen sein, wenn die Würde eines Klostervorstehers für 53 Goldholokotinen verschachert werden konnte."[74] Von einem "Verschachern" kann keine

---

69. B. Hogervorst, Het fenomeen van de pandjesbaas in Djeme (Over wrouwen schulden en het belenen van bezittingen in de 7 de en 8ste eeuw).

70. T. Wilfong, The Archive of a familiy of moneylenders from Jême in: BASP 27, 1990, 169-181.

71. M. Krause, Carl Schmidts Beiträge zum ägyptischen Mönchtum auf Grund koptischer Urkunden in: Carl-Schmidt-Kolloquium an der Martin-Luther-Universität Halle-Wittenberg 1988, hrsg. von P. Nagel (= Martin-Luther-Universität Halle-Wittenberg, Wiss. Beiträge 1990/23), Halle 1990, 119-127.

72. C. Schmidt, Ein koptischer Werkvertrag in: ZÄS 67, 1931, 102-106.

73. C. Schmidt, Das Kloster des Apa Mena in: ZÄS 68, 1932, 60-68.

Rede sein, vielmehr hatte die Geldnot im Mönchtum wegen der
Zahlung des Kopfgeldes die Mönche in eine solche schwierige Lage
gebracht, daß – wie auch andere Urkunden, vor allem die Urkunden
aus Bawit[75] zeigen – neue Wege beschritten werden mußten, um das
Mönchtum im 9. Jh. noch zu erhalten. Hengstenberg[76] hatte von
einem Einzug des Gelddenkens im Mönchtum gesprochen.

Aus einem Klosterarchiv stammen koptische Briefe, die japanische
Wissenschaftler 1988 in Akoris gefunden und bereits 1989 in einem
Vorbericht publiziert hatten. Jacques Jarry befaßt sich in einem Aufsatz wieder mit ihnen, weil sie im Vorbericht, der in Eile entstanden
sei, mit einer großen Anzahl Ungenauigkeiten veröffentlicht worden
seien.[77] Nach den Jahreszahlen datieren sie um die Wende vom 6. zum
7. Jh. und sind wichtig für die Dogmengeschichte, weil sie häretische,
aphthardoketische Ansichten wiedergeben. Einen weiteren Brief aus
diesem Archiv veröffentlichte er 1992.[78]

Die bisher genannten Texte waren fast ausschließlich im sahidischen Dialekt geschrieben. Nun sind auch Briefe in anderen Dialekten
zu nennen. Es handelt sich einmal um 2 Briefe, die Hans-Martin
Schenke[79] publiziert hat. Bentley Layton[80] hatte diesen Text als Nr.
191 in seinem Katalog unter den fajumischen Handschriften als

74. Schmidt, aO. 68.
75. BM Or 6201-4 und 6206, vgl. dazu vorläufig M. Krause, Zur Möglichkeit von
Besitz im apotaktischen Mönchtum Ägyptens in: Acts of the Second International
Congress of Coptic Studies, Roma, 22-26 September 1980, edited by T. Orlandi and
F. Wisse, Rom 1985, 121-133.
76. W. Hengstenberg, Bemerkungen zur Entwicklungsgeschichte des ägyptischen
Mönchtums in: Bulletin de l'Institut Archéologique Bulgare 9, 1935,355-362.
77. J. Jarry, Inscriptions a intérêt théologique et historique d'Akoris in: BSAC 30,
1991, 105-111.
78. J. Jarry, Pêche interdite a la fin du VIIe siècle in: BSAC 31, 1992, 83-86.
79. H.-M. Schenke, Ein Brief als Textzeuge für den mittelägyptischen Dialekt des
Koptischen (P.Mich.Inv. 525) in: JCS 1, 1990, 59-72 und ders., "Mittelägyptische
Nachlese" II. Ein Brief im mittelägyptischen Dialekt des Koptischen (P.Bl Or
11173(2)) in: ZÄS 119, 1992, 43-60.
80. B. Layton, Catalogue of Coptic Literary Manuscripts in the British Library
acquired since the Year 1906, London 1987, 239 (Or. 11173 (2)).

wahrscheinlich liturgisches Fragment klassifiziert und auf Taf. 25,3 abgebildet. Schenke schreibt: "Es ist aber wiederum nur diese mysteriöse Katalognotiz nebst dem dortigen kurzen Textbeispiel und dem Faksimile-Ausschnitt, was meine zufällig auf das Mittelägyptische programmierten Augen neugierig machte, mich diese Spur aufnehmen ließ ünd schließlich zur intensiven Beschäftigung mit dem Dokument geführt hat."[81] Das Ergebnis ist die Klassifizierung des Briefes als M 5 nach Rodolphe Kassers neuer Nomenklatur.[82] Ebenfalls für die koptische Dialektforschung wichtig ist ein Brief in Gothenburg/Schweden, den Torgny Säve-Söderbergh 1991,[83] beraten von H.-M. Schenke, herausgegeben hat. Der aus dem 8. Jh. stammende Brief im fajjumischen Dialekt bedarf auch nach Meinung des Herausgebers noch weiterer Untersuchung.

Aus neuen Ausgrabungen stammen Briefe im Dialekt L, früher Subachmimisch genannt, die in der Oase Dahleh in dem antiken Kellis, dem heutigen Ismant el-Gharab, in einem Haus gefunden wurden. Die bisher durchgeführten Grabungen des Royal Ontario Museum in Verbindung mit australischen Wissenschaftlern[84] haben reiche Textfunde,[85] vor allem in Haus 2, gezeigt, von denen die manichäischen Textfunde[86] in Koptisch und Syrisch großes Aufsehen erregt haben. Nicht minder wichtig sind die ca. 40 auf Papyrus geschriebenen Briefe wegen ihrer Länge - es sind die längsten bisher bekannten Briefe -, wegen ihres Alters (4. Jh.) - vergleichbar etwa mit den Briefen des meletianischen Archivs - und wegen ihres Dialektes. Herr Kollege A. Alcock, der mit ihrer Publikation betraut wurde, hat am 14. Juli 1992 über sie auf dem Third International Symposium of

---

81. Schenke, ZÄS 119, 1992, 44.
82. Schenke, aO. 49.
83. T. Säve-Söderbergh, Papyrus Thorburn in: Orientalia Suecana 40, 1991, 228-235.
84. Vgl. die Grabungsberichte von C. A. Hope in: JJSEA 15, 1985, 114-125 und 16, 1986, 74-96 und C. A. Hope in: Med Arch I, 1988, 160-178.
85. In Vorbereitung befinden sich die Editionen von griechischen Papyri durch R. G. Jenkins u. K. J. McKay, The Kellis Isocrates (T. L. Kellis 2) und R. G. Jenkins u. G. Wagner, The Kellis Agricultural Account Book (T. L. Kellis 3).
86. Die Publikation wird vorbereitet von I. Gardner.

Manichaean Studies in London referiert.[87] Ein kurzer Bericht wird heute von Herrn Kollegen Funk verlesen werden. Es ist mit einer baldigen Publikation, die als Bd. 4 "Texts from three houses in Kellis" angekündigt ist, zu rechnen.

Kurz verweise ich auf einige Publikationen, die sich mit koptischen Inschriften befassen. Es handelt sich einmal um die Beischrift auf dem Kreuz der Theodote aus dem Ostberliner Museum, das in den Wirren des letzten Krieges verschollen ist. Aus dem Nachlaß von Jules Leroy haben unsere Kollegen Paul van Moorsel und R.-G. Coquin das aus dem 6.-7. Jh. stammende Kreuz mit Beischrift publiziert.[88]

Hishmat Messiha hat kürzlich einen Vorbericht über seinen Beitrag im Catalogue général du Musée Copte publiziert. Er gibt auch die griechischen Inschriften, allerdings ohne Übersetzung, wieder.[89] Man vermißt den Hinweis auf die Arbeit von J. Maspero, der die Inschrift übersetzt und besprochen hat.[90]

In der Festschrift für Antoine Guillaumont habe ich mich mit den Inschriften auf den Türsturzbalken des Apa-Apollon-Klosters von Bawit beschäftigt.[91] Auf ihnen werden u.a. die Triade von Bawit: Apollo, Anup und Phib oder einzelne von ihnen angerufen und sie nennen die Namen und Titel noch lebender Mönche und Klosterfunktionäre (u.a. Äbte, δευτεράριος Verwalter, χαρτουλάριος) des 7./8. Jhs., die in diesen Gebäuden wohnten. Gleichzeitig füllen sie Lücken unserer Kenntnis der Klosterfunktionäre dieses großen Klosters im 7./B. Jh.

Durch Herrn Kollegen Severin hatte ich alte Fotos der Eremitensiedlung von Esna erhalten, die um die Jahrhundertwende aufgenom-

---

87. In den Akten des 3rd international Symposium of Manichaean Studies London werden die neuesten Berichte über die Grabung und ihre Funde publiziert.

88. R.-G. Coquin, J. Leroy (†) und P. van Moorsel, Le croix, dite de Théodote, du Musée de Berlin-Est in: BIFAO 89, 1989, 73-80.

89. H. Mesiha, Portable altars. Luxor treasure (1893) in: BSAC 31, 1992, 129-134.

90. J. Maspero, Sur quelques objets coptes du Musée du Caire in: BIFAO 10, 1910, 173-176.

91. M. Krause, Die Inschriften auf den Türsturzbalken des Apa-Apollon-Klosters von Bawit in: Mélanges Antoine Guillaumont. Contributions à l'étude des christianismes orientaux (= Cahiers d'orientalisme XX), Genf 1988, 111-120.

men worden waren und die sowohl die Malereien als auch die Inschriften in einem weit besseren Erhaltungszustand zeigen als unsere französischen Kollegen Sauneron und Coquin sie vorgefunden haben. Diese Inschriften habe ich 1990[92] veröffentlicht.

Im Jahre 1987 hatte Ibrahim Kamel koptische Grabsteine aus dem Koptischen Museum veröffentlicht.[93] Diese Publikation, die nicht Teil des von Gawdat Gabra herausgegebenen Catalogue général du Musée Copte ist, ist nicht ohne Rezensionen zu benutzen. Bisher liegen Besprechungen von Sofia Schaten[94] und Wolfgang Brunsch[95] vor. Wir erwarten die Publikation des Referates unseres Kollegen Kent Brown, der am Donnerstag über "An Easter Calender on Limestone in the Coptic Museum" gesprochen hat.

Ihre Arbeit über die Grabsteine hat Frau Sofia Schaten gestern kurz vorgestellt. 1991 hat sie einen Grabstein eines Vorlesers namens Phoibamon publiziert.[96] Dieser Grabstein, den Herr Kollege Grossmann in der Kirche von Deir el Barsa, 4 km südlich von Deir Abu Hennis, fotografiert hat, gehört zur Gruppe der Grabsteine mit Totenklage, die aus dieser Gegend stammen.

Zum Abschluß verweise ich auf die Münsteraner Dissertation von Cäcilia Wietheger über das Jeremias-Kloster zu Saqqara unter besonderer Berücksichtigung der Inschriften.[97] Nach der Behandlung der Architektur, der Skulptur, der Wandmalereien und der übrigen Funde werden ab S. 82 die im Kloster gefundenen schriftlichen Quellen,

---

92. M. Krause, Verlorene Inschriften und Beischriften der Eremitensiedlungen 3 und 4 bei Esna in: Festschrift Jürgen von Beckerath zum 70. Geburtstag am 19. Februar 1990 (= Hildesheimer ägyptologische Beiträge 30), Hildesheim 1990, 147-170.
93. Ibrahim Kamel, Coptic Funerary Stelae with the collaboration of Girgis Daoud Girgis, Kairo 1987 (= Catalogue général des antiquités du Musée Copte Nos. 1-253).
94. S. Schaten, Bemerkungen zu einer Neuerscheinung: Ibrahim Kamel, Girgis Daoud Girgis, Catalogue général des antiquités du Musée Copte Nos. 1-253 Funerary Stelae in: Göttinger Miszellen 119, 1990, 115-117.
95. W. Brunsch, Bemerkungen zu koptischen und griechischen Inschriften aus Kairo in: Orientalia 60, 1991, 92-108.
96. S. Schaten, Der Grabstein des Phoibamon in: BSAC 30, 1991, 113-120.
97. Vgl. A. 29.

Manuskripte, Urkunden und Ostraka und ab S. 89 die Inschriften behandelt. Erstmalig wird auch der Versuch einer Paläographie koptischer Inschriften (S. 104-124) unternommen. Die 500 Grabinschriften, darunter eine Anzahl unveröffentlichter, werden dann in sieben Formulare gegliedert und untersucht. Ein interessantes Ergebnis ist, daß viele Sterbedaten im Monat Parmute (27.3. – 25.4.) liegen wie bereits in griechisch-römischer Zeit. Die fortgeschrittene Zeit verbietet mir, die Fülle der Ergebnisse dieser Arbeit hier vorzutragen. Das Buch sei Ihrer Lektüre empfohlen.

Überblickt man die Arbeiten des Zeitraumes von 1988 – 1992 auf dem Gebiet der Papyrologie und vergleicht man sie mit denen der Jahre 1984-1988, dann ergibt sich erfreulicherweise ein Fortschritt, der sich sowohl in der Anzahl der Arbeiten als auch der Kolleginnen und Kollegen zeigt, die jetzt auf diesem Gebiete mitarbeiten. Das ist auch nötig, weil der Umfang des unveröffentlichten Materials sehr groß ist und fortlaufend neue Texte gefunden werden. Außer den Texten in Dahleh sei nur daran erinnert, daß die rege Grabungstätigkeit z.B. in Theben-West eine Vielzahl koptischer Ostraka erbracht hat,[98] deren Publikation noch aussteht. Die Anzahl der Neufunde übertrifft den Umfang der veröffentlichten Quellen bei weitem, so daß wir mit unserer Arbeit immer mehr in Rückstand geraten. Daher müssen wir versuchen, noch mehr Mitarbeiter zu gewinnen und die Anzahl der Planstellen für Koptologen an den Papyrussammlungen zu vermehren.

---

98. Stellvertretend für die aller thebanischen koptischen Ostrakafunde seien die Funde des Heidelberger Ägyptologischen Instituts in den thebanischen Gräbern genannt.

BENTLEY LAYTON[1]

FOUR YEARS OF PROGRESS IN COPTIC LINGUISTICS
(1988–1992)

It is a real pleasure to report on the last four years of progress in Coptic linguistics, for these have been outstanding years, and more than one masterpiece has seen the light of day. The second volume of Polotsky's *Foundations of Clause Structure* [*Grundlagen, Zweite Hälfte*], Shisha-Halevy's proper noun syntax [*The Proper Noun*] and his chrestomathy [*Coptic Grammatical Chrestomathy*], Funk's monograph on nominal sentences ["Formen und Funktionen"], volume 8 of the *Coptic Encyclopedia* (mostly on linguistics)—surely all these works will make a permanent impression on our field. Furthermore, three new journals will now provide a home for Coptic linguistics: *Journal of Coptic Studies; Langues orientales anciennes, Philologie et linguistique;* and *Lingua Aegyptiaca, Journal of Egyptian Language Studies.* (The first volume of *The Journal of Coptic Studies* was dedicated to the distinguished grammarian Elanskaya, Ernštedt's student and successor in St. Petersburg. Is it too much to hope that a collection of essays on Coptic grammar by these two scholars might be translated into a West European language? I see this as urgently needed.) Other short works, some of considerable importance, are listed in the bibliography to this report. I sincerely regret that my assigned limit does not allow me to summarize all of these interesting works.

Finally, in the years covered by my report we have experienced a drastic loss in the death of Polotsky, professor at the Hebrew University in Jerusalem, whose scientific and pedagogical genius shaped two generations of Coptic linguistics.

---

1.   Yale University.

Following the lead of my predecessor at Louvain-la-Neuve, I will organize this report by topic; I shall also bear in mind that my audience consists mainly of non-linguists. There are three areas where especially striking progress has been made, namely: (1) the overall description of syntactic structure; (2) dialectology; and (3) noun syntax.

1. Systematic Descriptions of Coptic Syntax

I shall begin with the *overall descriptions of syntax*. First, I must mention Shisha-Halevy's chrestomathy of Sahidic. This book is organized progressively by grammatical phenomenon, covering all the basic structures, as it guides the students to evolve their own general-linguistic description. Quite different in presentation is the second volume of Polotsky's *Grundlagen des koptischen Satzbaus*. *Grundlagen* was the fruit of more than twenty years of constant labor. My predecessor at Louvain-la-Neuve [Wolf-Peter Funk in the proceedings of the Louvain congress] correctly called it Polotsky's *summa gramaticae,* though it is by no means the "sum" of Polotsky's vast and detailed knowledge. This slender pair of volumes is deliberately limited—as the title suggests—to a basic, or even reductionist, presentation of main-clause predication types, the "causative conjugation," and the relative, second-tense, cleft-sentence, and circumstantial conversions. The level of description is broad, by and large restricted to sentence pattern analysis and paradigms of sentence components. Volume 2 contains an interesting theory of the Tripartite and Bipartite Conjugation Patterns, followed by a classic exposition of the Circumstantial Conversion according to its degree of relationship to the main clause. The orderliness and clarity of this book are especially admirable, and its standard of reliability, the truth factor, is unmatched in any systematic presentation since Stern. It is richly filled with striking examples, mostly Sahidic and Bohairic contrasted with Greek.

This is not the time, and I am not the person, to state objectively whether Polotsky leaves behind an international Jerusalem school of Coptic linguistics, and if so what its essential characteristics have been or will be. Polotsky's last work does not clarify this question, clothing itself so unexpectedly in the language and thought of nineteenth and early twentieth-century European linguistics. On the one hand, Polotsky's deliberate silence, at the end, about many pertinent questions in contemporary linguistics may puzzle some readers, while on the other hand those opposed to Chomsky's kind of structuralism may view with suspicion Polotsky's system of clause transposition, which aligns three types of clause conversion with three main word classes—but which he chooses to identify as a descriptive mode of the early nineteenth century. In the meantime, Polotsky's disciples continued from his path and gave the impression of moving in a different direction, making ever fuller use of modern European concepts of structuralism and relocating Coptic grammatical studies in the general linguistics arena of the late twentieth century. I shall return to their work in a few minutes. Thus one was left with the final impression of a gap that had suddenly opened up between the later Polotsky and those whom he had earlier trained, at least in style of thought and point of reference, and perhaps in method, too. This impression is part illusion, and part reality. *Grundlagen* is a rich, provocative, and reliable parting gift to students of the Coptic language, taking its place alongside Stern's *Koptische Grammatik* as a monument of grammatical knowledge.

2. Coptic Dialectology

Second, I come to the topic of *dialectology*. The completion of the *Coptic Encyclopedia* is an arrival point in study of the dialects, after several decades of gradual progress, especially in phonology and morphology, but also in theorization, the latter sometimes brilliant in character (as, for example, the work of W.-P. Funk).

Now, Coptic dialectology is destined to be an uncertain field, since Coptic is a dead language known only from incomplete and unrepresentative written data. Of course, dialectology, in the sense of sociolinguistics, must involve field work to study the life and speech habits of living speakers. But since this cannot be carried out for Coptic, scholars can only classify written texts, and speak of the character of each textual set as if attesting a dialect. Almost no social or social-historical data about varieties of Coptic speech exist as evidence. To make matters worse, the varieties of speech represented in our manuscripts (if indeed that is what they represent) cannot be externally linked to the geography of Egypt, with only a few exceptions. The sociolinguistics and dialect geography of Coptic are therefore destined to be essentially hypothetical at best.

Bearing this in mind, I will divide Coptic dialect studies into three problem areas: the description of individual dialects, the conceptual distinction of dialects from one another, and the reconstruction of a developmental and social history of the dialects.

First, the notation, grammar, and lexicon of each dialect. Here I will mention a long and meticulous chapter by Kasser on the phonology and morphology of Faiyumic in Diebner and Kasser, *Hamburger Papyrus Bilinguis 1;* more new work by Schenke, of excellent quality, on Middle Egyptian, including an edition of the Glazier Codex of Acts with analytical preface and editions of other Middle Egyptian manuscripts (the rise to scientific prominence of this dialect is due almost entirely to Schenke's persistence and care); and, in the *Coptic Encyclopedia,* useful articles describing each of the major dialects, written by known specialists: Sahidic and Bohairic by Shisha-Halevy; Middle Egyptian by Schenke; Faiyumic and Dialect P by Kasser; Achmimic, L6, and L4 by Nagel (L6 and L4 are curiously lumped together here as one dialect, in contradiction of Funk's separation of the L dialects). A glance at these solid and helpful encyclopedia articles will show that Coptic dialectology still means little more than notation, phonology, and the conjugation morphs. Dialectal syntaxes are virtually untouched in the *Encyclopedia,* except in the articles on our best-known dialects, Sahidic and Bohairic, where syntactics is quite nicely covered. Furthermore, Coptic lexicography (dialectal or other), as the synchronic description of lexeme systems taken as a whole, continues to be dead—or more exactly, not yet born.

Second, as a conceptual problem, how many dialects should be distinguished, and what principles can be used to draw the lines. Funk, following the lead of Fritz Hintze, has demonstrated how to answer this question in his revolutionary articles of the mid and late-80s, by using "various 'clustering' techniques supplied by modern numerical taxonomy" in order to classify dialects by degree of closeness to one another, at one and the same level of descriptive detail. In his *Coptic Encyclopedia* article on "Coptic Dialects, Morphology of" Funk concludes that there are eight dialects at descriptive parity, and he displays their group affinities in various possible ways: L6 (Nag Hammadi Subachmimic), L4 (Manichean Subachmimic), Achmimic, Sahidic, Dialect P, Middle Egyptian, Faiyumic, Bohairic. At least to me, this article seems to have the greatest theoretical decisiveness of any in the volume; like Funk's other articles published elsewhere, its results seem both reliable and meaningful.

Third, the hypothetical reconstruction of when and where the dialects were spoken, their sociological status, and their influences upon one another, as aspects of Coptic linguistic history. In principle, this enterprise ought to belong to reconstructive comparative linguistics, using methods analogous to those of Indo-European or Semitic comparatism, but adapted to the structure and context of Egyptian. In this problem area, abstract dialect geography is the most respectable topic, but even here no definite results can be obtained for lack of hard geographical evidence, as Kasser correctly stresses in his *Coptic Encyclopedia* article on "Geography, Dialectal." Thus the reconstruction of an actual history or social description of the dialects seems to be hopeless, blocked by the lack of data. Some of the remaining pages of volume 8 of the *Encyclopedia* are occupied by definitional articles also by Kasser, in which particular general-linguistics concepts are illustrated, as it were, from Coptic—topics such as cryptophoneme, immigrant dialect, mesodialect, metadialect, etc. Minor dialects and some other points of dialectology and etymology are also covered.

3. Nominal Syntax

Leaving the topic of dialectology, I come third and finally to *noun syntax*. Once again, it is the Coptic noun that elicits the most innovative and theoretically problematical results. I refer again to full-length monographic treatments by Funk ("Forms and Functions of the Interlocutive Nominal Sentence in the Coptic Dialects") and Shisha-Halevy (*The Proper Name: Structural Prolegomena to Its Syntax—A Case Study in Coptic*), as well as pertinent articles by Polotsky ("Zur koptischen Determination," "'Article' and 'Determinative Pronoun' in Coptic"), and by myself ("The Coptic Determinator Syntagm and Its Constituents").

I shall speak of nominal syntax as existing on two levels: on the one hand, nexal syntax (for example, the pattern of juncture between a subject and a nominal predicate, or the constituent paradigms of a nominal sentence pattern) and on the other hand, lower-order syntax (including the relation of article and noun, constructions relating one noun to another at low-level syntax, subdivisions of the noun word class, actualizations of the noun lexeme, questions of cross reference, and so forth). At present we are relatively well informed about the basic facts of nexal syntax of the noun; whereas, our knowledge of lower-order noun syntax is more provisional and spotty, it lacks a satisfactory general theory, and many questions remain controversial and incompletely formulated. Nevertheless, great progress is being made. In the final analysis, it is impossible to describe nexal nominal syntax without a full descriptive and theoretical basis in lower-order syntax, and until this can be achieved I see this area of Coptic linguistics as existing in a state of crisis.

The basic facts of nexal syntax, prosody, and morphology of the Nominal Sentence patterns were reliably codified for the first time by Polotsky in volume 1 of *Grundlagen* (though formulated even earlier). This part of *Grundlagen* was substantially completed in the early 1970s; and its publication was delayed first by the demise of a publishing house. Its contents, however, have been known directly and indirectly for many years, and they are one of the tacit foundations on which additional progress has been made by many of us in the past twenty years.

Now, Funk's monograph on the interlocutive pattern takes Polotsky's analysis forward in two important ways (I base my remarks on part one, the only part that has appeared so far). First, it describes the interlocutive pattern across all the dialects. The evidence is especially complete as regards the morphology of the subject pronouns (ang-, ntk-, etc.); and much less complete in the dialectal survey of predicate types. Morphologically, Funk's results confirm previous groupings of the dialects by phonology and grammar. In the predicate, the most striking dialectal peculiarity appears in Bohairic, where the nominal sentence predicate paradigm includes *bare* ebol xen-, without the indefinite article, as a predicate; for example, nteten-l ebol xen-paikosmos "you are from this world;" and even a form with prosodic disruption of nexus such as nthok I hōk I ebol xen-nenmathētēs mpairōmi "you, too, (nthok hōk) are from (ebol xen-) the disciples of this man," where the Verstärker hōk interrupts the nexus. This feature of Bohairic syntax, so contrary to our Sahidic based theory of the Nominal Sentence, calls for additional explanation.

The second important advance of this monograph lies in its serious attention to the subclassification of predicate types, which are here distinguished partly by commutation table of the nuclear article, partly by phrasal syntax of the predicate as a whole, and partly by predictable semantic behavior of subclasses of the main predicate noun. This is an extremely worthwhile project, and the main impediment lying before it, is our systematic ignorance about subclasses of the noun according to syntactic affinity. A well known example of such a subclass is the set of kinship terms, whose affinity to possessive and non-possessive articles sets it apart: this is not just a question of anthropological semantics, but also one of grammatical categories. Needless to say, the decisive information about such subclasses will not be provided by a study on the interlocutive nominal sentence, and so we must not look to this monograph to provide systematic results.

And this brings me to the question of the lower-order syntax of the noun. In this area, we already have a superb foundation on which to build, namely Shisha-Halevy's *Coptic Grammatical Categories*, which was described at the preceding congress. In one way or another, this brilliant tour de force, despite a presentation that I personally find obscure, raises most of the fundamental issues of lower-order nominal syntax that need to be considered in the coming decade. It also launches the study of high-order Textgrammatik of the Coptic noun, an essential project. I venture to predict that *Categories* will accompany Coptic linguistics into the next millennium as our most valuable and challenging resource. This rich and deeply provocative book is now complemented by an equally fine sequel, ostensibly on the proper name, but actually exploring a vast array of nominal-syntax phenomena that bestow striking insight into the very deep issue of noun determination. Indeed, the *Proper Name* must be read as volume two of *Categories*. The author's perspective is once again modern European structuralism and post-structuralism, but now even more explicitly drawing Coptic into the domain of modern general linguistics, and making Coptic into a "general linguistics" language rather than an adjunct of Egyptology.

The book is equally valuable for theoretical insight and for a vast amount of detailed syntactic description. Shisha-Halevy conceptualizes the properness of a proper noun not as an inherent property of a lexeme. Rather, he describes a spectrum or graded scale of syntax that ranges from proper name to common noun with many intermediate points along the way. Any element of language can appear on this spectrum, and indeed, at more than one point on the spectrum; furthermore, its degree of properness is always flexible. It is obvious that any given word "habitually" resides at one specific degree of properness; for example, the unique place-name hierousalēm "Jerusalem" is habitually high on the scale and nobe "a sin" is habitually low; but all items can be promoted or demoted by the phrasal or nexal syntax with which they become incorporated into actual speech. Thus thierousalēm n-brre "the new Jerusalem" is less proper than thierousalēm by virtue of its phrasal syntax. In this sense, properness and commonness do not reside in the lexemes, but characterize them as the lexemes are incorporated one way or another into syntax at the will of the speaker.

Theory aside, more than half the book is devoted to extremely reliable specifics of noun syntax at various points along the spectrum of properness, primarily of course at the high properness end. Worthy of note are a very full treatment of naming and calling constructions, and a suggestive final section on the *Textgrammatik* of the noun.

Polotsky's last major article on Coptic concerns the adjectival meaning of nouns such as t-me "truth." me is grammatically feminine, but it can qualify a *masculine* pronominal subject in sentences like ou-me pe "he is true or truthful," and it can qualify a masculine article in phrases like p-me "the grammatically masculine one who is true." Polotsky derives p- in p-me as the transposition of an underlying sentence, either ou-me pe or f-o m-me, thus explaining the apparent discrepancy between the ways that ou- and p- govern the noun lexeme in light of Ernštedt's theory. He does not bring the attributive construction into the argument.

Simultaneously, I published an essay on the article and its noun governance, where my aim was to demonstrate a structural distinction, within the broad word class of noun, between two subclasses: one subclass having potentially stable gender, limited syntactic options as a modifier, the semantic potential to either denote or qualify, and membership in a very numerous set, for example, me 'truth, true' and rro 'king, royal'; and the other subclass having flexible gender, more syntactic options as a modifier, a semantic potential limited to qualification, and membership in a very small set, for example noc 'big'. The results are incomplete, since each of these subclasses would have to be subdivided much further.

In conclusion: I have spoken of a crisis in the investigation of the noun. This crisis, as I understand it, has two equally sharp focal points. The *first* is *the determinators*. We do not yet understand the full range of syntactic behavior of each determinator. We need a comprehensive description that analyzes not the determinator morphs as such, but rather their grammatical categories as they bundle together into distinct syndromes under specific conditions.

The *second* focal point lies in *the system of subclasses that make up the noun,* each subclass having *its* own syntactical relationships, which must be investigated in the same categorial way. Funk's *Nominal Sentence,* Shisha-Halevy's monographs, and my own recent article have begun the structural isolation of some of these subclasses and some of these category syndromes, but not in an overall systematic way. There is urgent need to conduct the investigation more rigorously and more completely.

A special difficulty is going to lie in not letting the description of either of these two, determinators and nominal subclasses, encroach detrimentally upon the domain of the other.

I am convinced that the time is ripe for a systematic monograph on the syntax of noun lexemes and determinators. Let us wait and see what the next four years of progress in Coptic linguistics will have to offer.

Recent Bibliography on Coptic Linguistics[2]

Alcock, Anthony. 1987. "Coptic Words for 'Priest'," *Zeitschrift für ägyptische Sprache* 114: 179.

Biedenkopf-Ziehner, Anne. 1987. "nefsōtm und nefsōtm pe: Funktionen von 1./2. Tempora und NE (wn-n3w)," *Göttinger Miszellen* 95: 21-34.

Browne, Gerald M. 1990. "Coptico-Nubiana: A Coptic Vorlage for an Old Nubian Text," *Journal of Coptic Studies* 1: 137-139.

Cannuyer, Christian. 1988. "Un mot copte absent des dictionnaires: hoseb (s), 'cordeau'," *Göttinger Miszellen* 104: 71-74.

Cartreau, Frederic. 1988. "Système 'codique' et système 'codé': Pertinence linguistique de la variante graphique en copte," *Langues orientales anciennes, Philologie et linguistique* 1: 33-47.

Coptic Encyclopedia, The. 1991. Vol. 8. Ed. Aziz S. Atiya. New York: Macmillan.

Dembska, Albertyna. 1987. "Remarks on the Origin of Coptic t Suffix-pronoun 1st pers. sing. c.," *Société d'Égyptologie de Genève, Bulletin* 11: 27-36.

Depuydt, Leo. 1987. "Specificity or Emphasis in Egyptian and Coptic Nominal Sentences?," *Chronique d'Égypte* 61: 358-367.
—1988. "New Horizons in Coptic and Egyptian Linguistics," *Chronique d'Égypte* 63: 391-406.
—1989. "The Contingent Tenses of Egyptian," *Orientalia* 58: 1-27.

Diebner, Bernd J. and Rodolphe Kasser (eds.). 1989. *Hamburger Papyrus Bil. 1.*

---

2.   Kindly supplied by Prof. Tito Orlandi. Note: *CoptEnc* 8 = *The Coptic Encyclopedia*. Vol. 8. Ed. Aziz S. Atiya. New York: Macmillan, 1991.

Die alttestamentlichen Texte des Papyrus Bilinguis 1 der Staats- und Universitätsbibliothek Hamburg. (Cahiers d'orientalisme, 18). Genève: Patrick Cramer.

Funk, Wolf-Peter. 1988. "Dialects Wanting Homes: A Numerical Approach to the Early Varieties of Coptic," in: Jacek Fisiak (ed.), *Historical Dialectology, Regional and Social.* (Trends in Linguistics, Studies and Monographs, 37). Berlin: Mouton de Gruyter. 149-192.
— 1991. "Dialects, Morphology of Coptic." *CoptEnc* 8: 101-108.
— 1991. "Formen und Funktionen des interlokutiven Nominalsatzes in den koptischen Dialekten [part 1]," *Langues orientales anciennes, Philologie et linguistique* 3: 1-75.

Gignac, Francis Thomas. 1991. "Phonology of the Greek of Egypt, Influence of Coptic on the." *CoptEnc* 8: 186-188.

Godron, Gérard. 1990. "A nouveau LIMEN (Compléments)," *Bulletin de la Société d'archéologie copte* 29: 43-48.

Green, Michael. 1987. *The Coptic šare Pattern and Its Ancient Egyptian Ancestors: A Reassessment of the Aorist Pattern in the Egyptian Language.* Warminster: Aris & Phillips.

Gregorius, Anba. 1991. "Greek Loan Words in Coptic: Greek Conjunctions in Coptic," *Bulletin de la Société d'archéologie copte* 30: 77-92.

Ishaq, Émile Maher. 1991. "Egyptian Arabic Vocabulary, Coptic Influence on." *CoptEnc* 8: 112-118.

Kasser, Rodolphe. 1987. "Subdialectes en Mesokémique?" in: *Miscellania papirologica Ramon Roca-Puig.* Barcelona: Fundacio S. Vives Casajuana. 159-170.
— 1988. "Aleph initial ou final en copte," *Orientalia* 57: 139-144.
— 1988. "Graphèmes coptes jumeaux (KXC ambivalents à double origine possible)," *Orientalia Lovaniensia Periodica* 19: 117-121.
— 1988. "Nommer les principaux graphèmes vieux-coptes?" *Société d'Égyptologie de Genève, Bulletin* 12: 53-57.
— 1989. "Le copte vraiment vivant, ses idiomes écrits (langues, dialectes, subdialectes) au cours de leur millénaire (IIIe-XIIe siècles environ)," *Bulletin de la Société d'archéologie copte* 28 [1986-89]: 11-50.
— 1989. "Le grand-groupe dialectal copte de Basse-Égypte et son extension véhiculaire panégyptienne," *Société d'Égyptologie de Genève, Bulletin* 13: 73-82.
— 1989. "Sigles des dialectes coptes: Propositions pour une convention permettant d'unifier les divers usages systématiques actuellement en vigueur," in: *Études coptes III. Troisième journée d'études...* (Cahiers de la Bibliothèque copte, 4). Louvain-Paris: Peeters. 1-10.

— 1990. "A propos des caractéristiques lexicales des dialectes coptes dans divers textes bibliques," in: W. Godlewski (ed.), *Coptic Studies: Acts of the Third International Congress of Coptic Studies, Warsaw, 20-25 August, 1984*. Warszawa: Państwowe Wydawnictwo Naukowe. 187-194.

— 1990. "Marius Chaine et la thèse d'une relation phonologique privilégiée entre les langues coptes saïdique et bohaïrique," *Journal of Coptic Studies* 1: 73-77.

— 1990. "A Standard System of Sigla for Referring to the Dialects of Coptic," *Journal of Coptic Studies* 1: 141-151.

— 1991. "Aleph." *CoptEnc* 8: 27-30.

— 1991. "Alphabet in Coptic, Greek." *CoptEnc* 8: 30-32.

— 1991. "Alphabets, Coptic." *CoptEnc* 8: 32-41.

— 1991. "Alphabets, Old Coptic." *CoptEnc* 8: 41-45.

— 1991. "'Ayin." *CoptEnc* 8: 45-47.

— 1991. "Bashmuric." *CoptEnc* 8: 47-48.

— 1991. "Bodmer Papyri." *CoptEnc* 8: 48-53.

— 1991. "Cryptophoneme." *CoptEnc* 8: 69-70.

— 1991. "Dialect H (or Hermopolitan or Ashmuninic)." *CoptEnc* 8: 76-79.

— 1991. "Dialect I (or Proto-Lycopolitan or Proto-Lyco-Diospolitan)." *CoptEnc* 8: 79-82.

— 1991. "Dialect P (or Proto-Theban)." *CoptEnc* 8: 82-87.

— 1991. "Dialect, Immigrant." *CoptEnc* 8: 70-73.

— 1991. "Dialects." *CoptEnc* 8: 87-97.

— 1991. "Dialects, Grouping and Major Groups of." *CoptEnc* 8: 97-101.

— 1991. "Djinkim." *CoptEnc* 8: 111-112.

— 1991. "Fayyumic." *CoptEnc* 8: 124-131.

— 1991. "Gemination, Vocalic." *CoptEnc* 8: 131-133.

— 1991. "Geography, Dialectal." *CoptEnc* 8: 133-141.

— 1991. "Greek Transcriptions." *CoptEnc* 8: 141-145.

— 1991. "Languages, Coptic." *CoptEnc* 8: 145-151.

— 1991. "Memphitic." *CoptEnc* 8: 159-161.

— 1991. "Mesodialect." *CoptEnc* 8: 161-162.

— 1991. "Metadialect." *CoptEnc* 8: 165-166.

— 1991. "Phonology." *CoptEnc* 8: 184-186.

— 1991. "Protodialect." *CoptEnc* 8: 191-194.

— 1991. "Syllabication." *CoptEnc* 8: 207-214.

— 1991. "Vocabulary of Egyptian Origin, Autochthonous Coptic." *CoptEnc* 8: 224-226.

— 1991. "Vocabulary, Copto-Greek." *CoptEnc* 8: 215-222. — and Ariel Shisha-Halevy. 1991. "Dialect B (or Bashmuric or Mansuric)." *CoptEnc* 8: 74-76.

Layton, Bentley. 1990. "The Coptic Determinator Syntagm and Its Constituents," *Journal of Coptic Studies* 1: 79-97.

Lucchesi, Enzo. 1988. "'Martyre' de Zacharie et Protévangile de Jacques," *Le Muséon* 101: 65-76. Especially Appendix III.

Mikhail, Louis B. 1989. "The Second Tenses in Practice: The Sahidic Dialect," *Zeitschrift für ägyptische Sprache* 116: 60-71.

Nagel, Peter. 1991. "Akhmimic." *CoptEnc* 8: 19-27.
—1991. "Lycopolitan (or Lyco-Diospolitan or Subakhmimic)." *CoptEnc* 8: 151-159.

Osing, Jurgen. 1987. "Einige koptische Etymologien," *Annales du Service des antiquités d'Égypte* 71: 205-212.

Polotsky, Hans Jacob. 1987. "Egyptology, Coptic Studies and the Egyptian Language," in: J. D. Ray (ed.), *Lingua Sapientissima*. Cambridge: Faculty of Oriental Studies. 5-21.
— 1989. "Zur Determination im Koptischen," *Orientalia* 58: 464-472.
— 1990. *Grundlagen des koptischen Satzbaus. Zweite Hälfte.* (American Studies in Papyrology, 29). Atlanta (Georgia, U.S.A.): Scholars Press. Comprises pages 169-272 of the whole work.
— 1991. "'Article' and 'Determinative Pronoun' in Coptic," *Lingua Aegyptiaca* 1: 241-42.

Quaegebeur, Jan. 1991. "Pre-Coptic." *CoptEnc* 8: 188-190.
— 1991. "Pre-Old Coptic." *CoptEnc* 8: 190-191.

Quecke, Hans. 1990. "Zur direkten und indirekten Rede im Koptischen," *Journal of Coptic Studies* 1: 129-135.

Roquet, Gerard. 1988. "L'esprit de géometrie: Le jeu et son empreinte culturelle dans l'Égypte dynastique et copte. De znt à SHNE. A propos de Luc 9:14," *Langues orientales anciennes, Philologie et linguistique* 1: 157-165.

Satzinger, Helmut. 1991. "Bohairic, Pronunciation of Late." *CoptEnc* 8: 60-65.
— 1991. "Old Coptic." *CoptEnc* 8: 169-175.

Schenkel, Wolfgang. 1990. *Einführung in die altägyptische Sprachwissenschaft.* (Orientalistische Einführungen). Darmstadt: Wissenschaftliche Buchgesellschaft.

Schenke, Hans-Martin. 1989. "Mittelägyptische 'Nachlese' I: Bemerkungen zum Adverb hitrour 'schnell' anlässlich der Edition von Restfragmenten der Mailander mittelägyptischen Handschrift der Paulusbriefe mit einem neuen Beleg," *Zeitschrift für ägyptische Sprache* 116: 160-174.
— 1990. "Ein Brief als Textzeuge für den mittelägyptischen Dialekt des koptischen (P.Mich. Inv. 525)," *Journal of Coptic Studies* 1: 59-72.
— 1991. *Apostelgeschichte 1,1--15,3 im mittelägyptischen Dialekt des Koptischen*

(Codex Glazier). (Texte und Untersuchungen, 137). Berlin: Akademie Verlag.
— 1991. "Mesokemic (or Middle Egyptian)." *CoptEnc* 8: 162-164.
— 1992. "Mittelägyptische 'Nachlese' II: Ein Privatbrief im mittelägyptischen Dialekt des Koptischen [P.BL OR 11173[2]])," *Zeitschrift für ägyptische Sprache* 119: 43-60.

Shisha-Halevy, Ariel. 1988. *Coptic Grammatical Chrestomathy: A Course for Academic and Private Study*. Orientalia Lovaniensia Analecta, 30). Leuven: Peeters.
— 1989. *The Proper Name: Structural Prolegomena to Its Syntax—A Case Study in Coptic*. (Beihefte zur WZKM, 15). Wien; VWGO.
— 1989. "Work-Notes on Demotic Syntax, I," *Orientalia* 58: 28-60. Syntactic predecessors of Coptic.
— 1990. "The 'Tautological Infinitive' in Coptic: A Structural Examination," *Journal of Coptic Studies* 1: 99-127.
— 1991. "Bohairic." *CoptEnc* 8: 53-60.
— 1991. "Sahidic." *CoptEnc* 8: 194-202.
— 1991. "Shenutean Idiom." *CoptEnc* 8: 202-204.

Sidarus, Adel. 1990. "Bibliographical Introduction to Medieval Coptic Linguistics," *Bulletin de la Société d'archéologie copte* 29: 83-85.

Sismanian, Dana. 1989. "Le point et la prosodie: Quelques notes au sujet des parépigraphiques coptes," in: *Études coptes III. Troisième journée d'études...* (Cahiers de la Bibliothèque copte, 4). Louvain: Peeters. 50-85

Van der Vliet, Jan. 1988. "Note on jōk ebol, 'To Die'," *Enchoria* 16: 89-94.
— 1991. "Varia magica coptica," *Aegyptus* 71: 217-242.

Vycichl, Werner. 1991. "Etymology." *CoptEnc* 8: 118-124.
— 1991. "Vocabulary of Semitic Origin, Autochthonous Coptic." *CoptEnc* 8: 226-227.
— 1991. "Vocabulary, African Contacts with Autochthonous Coptic." *CoptEnc* 8: 214-215.
— 1991. "Vocabulary, Copto-Arabic." *CoptEnc* 8: 215.
— 1991. "Vocabulary, Cuneiform Transcriptions of Prototypes of Authchthonous Coptic." *CoptEnc* 8: 222-224.

C. Detlef G. Müller

DIE ERFORSCHUNG DER GESCHICHTE DER KOPTEN IN DEN JAHREN 1988 BIS 1992

Die Erforschung Ägyptens in christlicher Zeit nahm in dem Berichtszeitraum einen lebhaften Verlauf. Zu fast allen Zeiten und Aspekten erschienen Arbeiten. Zu einem erheblichen Teil handelt es sich um Beiträge zu Einzelfragen. Eine große Gesamtdarstellung hat nicht das Licht der Welt erblickt. Überhaupt leben wir ja im Zeitalter der Enzyklopädien und Lexika. Ein erheblicher Teil der gelehrten Arbeitskraft ist derartigen Werken gewidmet. So ist es keineswegs verwunderlich, daß auch in Lexikonartikeln erste Forschungsergebnisse und neue Ansichten geäußert werden, die man früher eher in wissenschaftlichen Zeitschriften, versehen mit ausführlichem Anmerkungsapparat und in steter Auseinandersetzung mit anderen Forschern gesucht hätte.

An der ägyptischen Geschichte zwischen Alexander dem Großen und dem Arabereinmarsch haben sich seit jeher große Gelehrte, vornehmlich Papyrologen versucht: Wilhelm Schubart, Sir Idris Bell.[1] Eine moderne Darstellung, allerdings in Neuauflage, erschien 1990 (Bowman), reich bebildert. Eher konventionell werden Land, Obrigkeit, das Verhältnis der Untertanen zu ihr, die soziale Frage, Griechen und Ägypter, Religion und die Stadt Alexandrien abgehandelt. Die Darstellung ist griffig. Die Frage einer neuen Epocheneinteilung, Chalkedon (451) als Einschnitt gelangte nicht in das Gesichtsfeld des Autors.[2] Eine andere größere Darstellung (Griggs) behandelt

---

1.   Wilhelm Schubart: Ägypten von Alexander dem Großen bis auf Mohamed, Berlin 1922. - H. Idris Bell: Egypt from Alexander the Great to the Arab Conquest, Oxford 1948.

das alte Christentum Ägyptens und schließt bezeichnenderweise mit
dem Jahre 451. Sie sieht schon vor diesem Datum Chalkedon) in
Folge der politischen und religiösen Differenzen eine de facto Trennung der ägyptischen Kirche von der Reichskirche - eine Trennung,
die durch Chalkedon(451) eben nur formale Gestalt gewann. Das
Buch schildert zunächst den Charakter der ältesten Christenheit, um
dann zu den ersten ägyptischen Christen überzugehen. Unter Be-
nutzung zur Zeit zugänglicher Quellen sucht es ihr Bild farbiger zu
gestalten, bleibt jedoch bei der alten Erkenntnis, daß das ägyptische
Christentum alt sein muß, neben Alexandrien auch in anderen Teilen
Ägyptens früh existierte und stark gnostisch geprägt war. Weiter wird
das Aufkommen von Orthodoxie und Häresie geschildert. Ab Mitte
des 3. Jahrhunderts erst sieht der Verfasser, sich lehrmäßige Einheit
und kirchenleitende Autorität entwickeln. Jetzt tritt Alexandrien erst
wirklich in eine Führungsposition ein. Doch sieht Griggs hier schon
im 3. Jahrhundert alle Elemente für den großen Konflikt von 451 klar
am Tage, wenn er die innere Lage Ägyptens und insbesondere die
Christengruppen schildert. Er geht dann zum 4. Jahrhundert über und
beginnt mit dem melitianischen Schisma. Die arianische Kontroverse
sieht er als ägyptisches Problem an, da sie in Alexandrien geschah.
Die Sonderstellung Alexandriens neben Ägypten wird dabei ignoriert.
Den Streit in Alexandrien bezeichnet er als zunächst politisch und
dann erst als lehrmäßig bedeutend. Athanasios der Apostolische wird
in diesem Zusammenhang natürlich ausführlich dargestellt, wie auch
das Mönchswesen. Ein letztes Kapitel führt bis zur Trennung von 451,
wobei wohl der häufige Schwebezustand der Folgezeit nicht genügend
beachtet wird. Die Stärke des Buches liegt in der Heranziehung
zahlreicher und vor allem auch koptischer Originalquellen, während
die bisherige Forschung eher selektiv genutzt worden ist. Das Bild
wird so farbiger, wenn auch nicht unbedingt neuer.

   Neben diesen Gesamtdarstellungen aus dem vorislamischen
Ägypten stehen zahlreiche Arbeiten, die Teilaspekte behandeln oder

---

2.   Ein erster Versuch einer derartigen Epocheneinteilung findet sich bei C. Detlef
G. Müller: Grundzüge des christlich-islamischen Ägypten von der Ptolemäerzeit bis
zur Gegenwart, Darmstadt 1969 (Grundzüge, Band 11).

weitere Quellen zugänglich machen. Entscheidend für die historische Entwicklung sind die theologischen Streitigkeiten gewesen. Besonderes Interesse hat die Forschung zur Arianismusfrage gefunden (Ritter). Herausgestellt wurde die Bedeutung der Christologie für die Gedankenwelt dieses Mannes, was zu der Entwicklung der ägyptischen Kirche gut paßt. Allerdings liegt hier eine adoptianische Christologie vor. Der sittliche Gehorsam macht den Heiland zum Sohne. In sofern, wäre er nach Römer 8,29 der Erstgeborene unter vielen Brüdern. Gerade für die Asketen wäre diese Lehre attraktiv gewesen, indem sie dem sittlichen Vorbild des Erlösers nachstreben konnten, um im Eschaton zur gleichen Sohnschaft zu gelangen. So hätte Athanasios die Vita Antonii auch geschrieben, um den großen Mönchsvater für das nizänische Lager und dessen "essentialistisches" Erlösungskonzept zu vereinnahmen. Christos wird seinsmäßig und in Ewigkeit mit Gott verbunden. Die Position des Arios hingegen läßt sich am leichtesten aus seiner Verwurzelung im Transzendentalismus der Platoniker erklären. Dieser Einfluß ist weit stärker als in der Durchschnittstheologie seiner Zeit. Zwar hat Arios 327 dem Kaiser ein als zureichend angesehenes orthodoxes Bekenntnis unterbreitet - allerdings, unter Vermeidung der Begriffe ὁμοούσιος und οὐσία und sozusagen "Widerruf" geleistet. Athanasios hat ihn jedoch nicht wieder aufgenommen, auch wenn er die Bedingungen erfüllt hatte, die Kaiser Constantin für die Wiedergewährung der Kirchengemeinschaft gestellt hatte. In dem Sinne hat er bestimmte in Nikaia verurteilte Spitzensätze eben nicht wiederholt, aber auch nicht in klassischem Sinne widerrufen. So bleibt die Frage, ob Athanasios überhaupt noch dogmatische oder nicht eher ausschließlich kirchenpolitische Gründe für die Verweigerung der Kirchengemeinschaft hatte. Die Frage der Beziehungen zu den Melitianern, soweit sie Arios unterhielt, spielt hier auch mit hinein. Es geht für Athanasios sicher auch um die ganze Frage des Bischofsamtes, überhaupt der Kirchenorganisation und der in Ägypten damit zusammenhängenden Probleme. In diesem Zusammenhang ist zu bemerken, daß die These von Arios als Repräsentant einer spezifisch antiochenischen Theologie aufgegeben werden muß. Alles ist viel ägyptischer als man denkt. Betrachtet man nun die ein-

schlägigen Artikel in der neuen koptischen Enzyklopädie: Arius
(Roncaglia), Athanasius I (Atiya), Council of Nicaea (Torjesen), Meli-
tius (Timbie), so stellt man eine mehr traditionelle Abfassung fest.
Man findet die einschlägigen Tatsachen und ihre übliche Auslegung.
Die neuen Impulse in der Patristik und die einschlägigen Auseinandersetzungen haben hier kaum einen Niederschlag gefunden, was auch
die Literaturverzeichnisse beweisen. Das Problem der Marginal-
isierung Athanasiū und damit der ägyptischen Beitrages zur
christlichen Theologie ist nicht gesehen. Von koptologischer Seite
wünscht man sich für die Zukunft eine stärkere Durchforschung der
Situation im damaligen Ägypten und Klärung der ägyptischen Geis-
tesgeschichte. Hier sind allerdings ägyptologische Kenntnisse er-
forderlich. Das innerhalb der Ägyptologie neu aufgebrochene Interesse an Geistes- und Religionsgeschichte stimmt aber verheißungs-
voll.[3]

Hier weiterschreitend sei auf das Monumentalwerk von Alois
Grillmeier (und Theresia Hainthaler) "Jesus der Christus im Glauben
der Kirche" aufmerksam gemacht. Das mehrbändige, bisher noch
nicht abgeschlossene Werk wird die Diskussion in der Zukunft bestim-
men und christologisch maßgebend sein. Ein ähnlich monumentales
Werk wird so leicht nicht wieder erscheinen. Als den derzeitigen
Forschungsstand fixierend, wird das Werk seine Bedeutung für die
Dauer behalten. In Band 2/1 wird das Konzil von Chalkedon behandelt,sowie Rezeption und Widerspruch bis 518 dargestellt. Der neue
Band 2/4 behandelt die Kirche von Alexandrien mit Nubien und
Äthiopien bis 451. Hier ist erstmals in ein derartiges Werk die kopto-
logische Forschung voll eingegangen. Schenūte der Große von Atripe
wird als Begründer der koptischen Christologie gewürdigt, der Patriarch Damian ausführlich behandelt. Die Artikel der koptischen Enzyklopädie über Schenūte (Kuhn) und Damian (Hardy) nehmen davon
noch keinerlei Notiz.

---

3.   Dazu jetzt mit zahlreichen bibliographischen Hinweisen Elke Blumenthal: Vom
Wesen der altägyptischen Religion, in Theologische Literaturzeitung, Vol. 117
(1992), coll. 889-896.

Johannes V. der Almosengeber, der melkitische Patriarch (610-619) ist abschließend auch eingeordnet worden (Müller). Infolge seiner exzessiven Liebestätigkeit hat man ihn seit Michel Le Quien, der sich auf Ibn al-Kabar stützt, immer wieder auch als Heiligen der Koptischen Kirche einzuordnen gesucht. Er ist aber im Grunde acharnierter Chalkedonenser, der der ausgleichenden Kirchenpolitik des Kaisers Herakleios (610-641) nichts abzugewinnen vermochte. Doch für einen wirklichen Kampf gegen die Diplophysiten kam er zu spät. Man war des ewigen Streites um die beiden Naturen des Heilandes müde, da alle Argumente ausgetauscht waren und vermochte einer Erneuerung dieses Kampfes nichts mehr abzugewinnen.

Eine Fülle von kleineren Studien oder Beiträgen in Sammelwerken behandelt einzelne Probleme oder erwähnt die ägyptischen Christen. Genannt sei eine Analyse der koptischen Tradition über Kaiser Diokletian und ihre Prüfung auf den historischen Gehalt (Berg-Onstwedder). Es zeigt sich - vielleicht überraschend - daß die koptischen Quellen auch dazu beitragen. Zwar stimmen sie nur teilweise mit Lactantius und Euseb überein, zeigen aber doch den erschreckten Kaiser und den Beginn der Verfolgungen in der Armee. Das Feuer im Palast in Nikomedien, wie auch die Krankheit und Abdankung des Kaisers spiegeln die koptischen Quellen durchaus wider. Natürlich stimmen sie stark mit Johannes von Nikiū überein. Interessant ist, daß hieroglyphische und demotische Texte die gleichen langen Daten für die Regierungszeit des Kaisers haben. Christliche und heidnische ägyptische Daten stimmen also überein. Auch war die Herkunft des Kaisers lange unbekannt. So ist es keineswegs völlig verwunderlich, daß man Diokletian als Herrscher über Ägypten ansah und zum Ägypter machte. Auch andere Aussagen der Texte werden behandelt, dem Wissen der Kopten gegenübergestellt und ihre Auslegungen und Erklärungen analysiert. Das wichtigste Ergebnis ist die Feststellung, daß die literarischen koptischen Texte nicht nur über eine entsprechende literarische Qualität verfügen, sondern auch historische Tatsachen überliefern, die eines genauen Studiums wert sind, wie auch die in ihnen enthaltenen Nachrichten über die Lebensverhältnisse im damaligen Ägypten.[4]

Daß die Bedeutung Schenūte des Großen von Atripe für Oberägypten über seine Klosterfunktion und kirchliche Wirksamkeit hinausgeht, zeigt sich erneut anläßlich der Analyse seiner Rede "Über die Pflichten von Richtern" (Johannes Hahn). Flavianus, Praeses (ἡγεμών der Thebaïs war damals, nach 400, mit seinem Gefolge anwesend. Flavian dürfte Zivilgouverneur der nördlichen Thebaïs gewesen sein, während der gefährdete Süden wohl eher einem Dux unterstand, der Militär- und Zivilgewalt in einer Hand vereinigte. Die Bedeutung Schenūte's und seines Klosters erhellt daraus, daß der Praeses den weiten Weg zu diesem nicht besonders verkehrsgünstig gelegenen Ort nicht scheute und das Kloster persönlich besuchte. Schenūte's Macht und großer Einfluß sind bekannt. Er vermochte sich ohne weiteres Behörden und Gerichten gegenüber durchzusetzen. So wird Flavian durchaus nicht nur in das Weiße Kloster gereist sein, um sich eine Katechese über das Richteramt anzuhören, sondern auch um Angelegenheiten des öffentlichen Lebens und der Verwaltung in der nördlichen Thebaïs zu erörtern. Überhaupt sind Fragen der Verwaltungssituation auf Grund neuer oder erst jetzt erschlossener Quellen vielfach zur Sprache gekommen und haben uns in der Kenntnis der Lage in Ägypten weiter gebracht: Sei es die Höhe der Wohnungsmiete (Worp), sei es das Personal der Finanzverwaltung (Delmaire; 94 Namen), seien es schließlich zwei Dokumente von 531/32 und 533/34, die eine Art historische Zusammenstellung der jährlichen Naturalsteuern (= κανών) der Stadt Antaeopolis und eine Festlegung des geltenden κανών bieten (Gascou). Die besondere Situation des von der Pest des 6. Jahrhunderts wenig berührten Ägyptens zeigt schließlich Durliat.

Die neuesten Forschungen zur ägyptischen Patriarchengeschichte schilderte mein Vorgänger ausführlich in Louvain-la-Neuve. Das Werk von Johannes Den Heijer ist inzwischen erschienen. Es hat Zustimmung gefunden (Zanetti). Friedhelm Winkelmann hat in seiner sonst

---

4.   Dazu bereits C. Detlef G. Müller: Die alte koptische Predigt (Versuch eines Überblicks), Diss. Heidelberg 1953 (gedruckt 1954 in Darmstadt), p. 2.

mehr der klassischen Historiographie gewidmeten Arbeit auf den Den Heijer verwiesen und festgestellt, daß der arabischen Geschichte der alexandrinischen Patriarchen eine koptische Bearbeitung und Fortführung der Kirchengeschichte Euseb's zu Grunde liegt. In der koptischen Enzyklopädie (J. den Heijer) ist die Genesis der Patriarchengeschichte nochmals ausführlich dargelegt worden. Der Artikel über Sāwīrus ibn al-Muqaffaʿ (Atiya) hält allerdings an der Autorschaft dieses Mannes fest.

Das führt uns zu einer Würdigung der koptischen Enzyklopädie, die in zahlreichen Artikeln der Geschichte der ägyptischen Christen breiten Raum gewährt. Zunächst einmal dürfen wir froh sein, daß es ein derartiges Werk gibt, daß man in übersichtlicher Weise sich über zahlreiche Fragen, Personen und Probleme orientieren kann, die man sonst nicht in dieser Weise auf engem Raume zusammen hat. Das Gesamtwerk trägt das Siegel seines Herausgebers, der auch von ihm nicht verfaßte Artikel bearbeitet, ja sogar verändert hat. Auf diese Weise ist ein Werk aus einem Guß entstanden, mit allen Stärken, aber auch Schwächen eines solchen. So ist man in dem Artikel Dates and succession of Patriarchs (Atiya) bei den alten Regierungszeiten geblieben, hat etwa für das 5./6. Jahrhundert von den verbesserten Ansätzen Jülichers[5] keine Notiz genommen und so auch für Benjamin I. (Müller) eine heutzutage nicht mehr vertretbare Datierung vorgenommen; ja ist im Grunde auch hinter der von Marcus Simaika Pascha erarbeiteten Datierung[6] zurückgeblieben. Die einzelnen Artikel können hier nicht analysiert werden, denn jeder Patriarch hat einen eigenen Artikel. Bekannte Gestalten der alten Zeiten, wie auch des

5. Adolf Jülicher: Berichtigung von Daten im heraklianischen Jahrhundert, in Festgabe von Fachgenossen und Freunden A. von Harnack zum siebzigsten Geburtstag dargebracht, Tübingen 1921, pp. 121-133; und besonders: Die Liste der alexandrinischen Patriarchen im 6. und 7. Jahrhundert, in Festgabe für D. Dr. Karl Müller zum siebzigsten Geburtstag dargebracht von Fachgenossen und Freunden, Tübingen 1922, pp. 7-23.

6. Marcus Simaika Pasha, Yassa ʿAbd al-Masiḥ Effendi: Catalogue of the Coptic and Arabic Manuscripts in the Coptic Museum, the Patriarchate, the Principal Churches of Cairo and Alexandria and the Monasteries of Egypt, Vol. II/1 (Kairo 1942), pp. 491-508 (Arabisch und Englisch).

Mittelalters werden ausführlich gewürdigt. In anderen Fällen bleibt man ganz an dem Bericht der Patriarchengeschichte kleben. So wird im Falle des Patriarchen Anastasius (Atiya), unter dem es 616 zu der Versöhnung mit den Westsyrern kam, nur die Patriarchengeschichte wiedererzählt, ohne die syrischen Quellen zu konsultieren oder wenigstens die Forschungen Jean Maspero's heranzuziehen.[7] Das gezeichnete Bild entspricht daher nicht den historischen Tatsachen.

Zunehmend wird die Bedeutung der mittelalterlichen Periode für die Entwicklung der Kopten erkannt, die Verhältnisse in der nun islamischen Zeit differenziert gesehen. So hat selbst das Lexikon des Mittelalters für die Kopten (Müller) einen relativ großen Raum vorgesehen. Die Lebensverhältnisse, kirchliche Entwicklung und Beziehungen zu der islamischen Obrigkelt kommen ausführlich zur Sprache. Angeschnitten wird auch die Nubienfrage und hier insbesondere das Vorhild der koptischen Schrift aus griechischen Lettern und Kursivhieroglyphen für die nubische Schrift herausgestellt.

Dankenswert ist, daß in der koptischen Enzyklopädie nicht nur die Lage der Kopten unter den einzelnen islamischen Dynastien in jeweils separaten Artikeln zur Sprache kommt, sondern daß auch - wenigstens kurz - das Arsenal von Tunis (Chiarelli) behandelt wird. Es geht darum, daß zahlreiche Kopten und ihre Familien als Schiffbauer und Schiffsausrüster auf Veranlassung von 'Abd al-Malik dorthin gesandt wurden. Es wurden dann durch den Patriarchen auch Bischöfe zur Versorgung der dortigen nordafrikanischen Kopten abgesandt. Hier liegt ein Ansatz vor, die Bedeutung der christlichen Ägypter für die islamische Seefahrt zu würdigen. Grundsätzlich wäre allerdings auch die vorislamische Zeit mit heranzuziehen, um ein zuverlässiges Bild zu gewinnen. Doch bedingt das noch die Nutzung weiterer Quellen.

Nicht zufällig findet nach wie vor die Fāṭimīdenzeit und die Wirkungsmöglichkeiten für die Christen in ihr große Beachtung (Lev). Quellen und Forschung über sie fließen reichlich. Nach der teilweisen

---

7.   Jean Maspero (Ad. Fortescue/Gaston Wiet): Histoire des Patriarches d'Alexandrie depuis la mort de l'Empereur Anastase jusqu'à la reconciliation des Églises Jacobites (518-616), Paris 1923 (Bibliothèque de l'École des Hautes-Études 237), pp. 319-342, 385.

Islamisierung der Bevölkerung im Gefolge der Islamisierung Ägyptens im 9. Jahrhundert, erfolgte in der Fāṭimīdenzeit keine weitere Islamisierung. Die Kopten blieben ein starkes Bevölkerungselement und bildeten an einigen Plätzen sogar die Mehrheit; darunter in Städten, die wichtige Zentren der Textilmanufaktur darstellten. Auf dem Lande blieb die Kirche religiöse Autorität und war Landbesitzer, der Abgaben von Seiten der Bauern empfing. Zwischen dem Eintreffen der Araber in der Omayyadenzeit und der Unterdrückung der Steuerrebellion im 9. Jahrhundert einerseits, sowie der endgültigen Islamisierung unter den Mamlūken andererseits gab es trotz aller Unruhe eine Zeit der gedeihlichen Entwicklung für die Kopten. Grundsätzlich waren religiöse Gebäude geschützt. Mit al-Fusṭāṭ war eine Muslimsiedlung inmitten einer christlichen Umgebung errichtet worden. Allerdings siedelten dort von Anfang an auch christliche arabische Truppen aus Syrien im Stadtteil al-Ḥamrā. Koptische Siedler kamen ebenfalls. 735/36 A.D. (117 A.H.) hatte der Gouverneur den Bau einer koptischen Kirche in al-Ḥamrā genehmigt, wurde jedoch von fanatischen Muslimen angegriffen. So ist bis zu dem 9. Jahrhundert der Bau neuer Kirchen, aber auch die Zerstörung anderer bezeugt. Im 10. Jahrhundert änderte sich die Situation. 938 wird an dem Beispiel der Schenūte-Kirche die Frage akut, ob beschädigte oder verfallende Kirchen wieder aufgebaut werden dürfen. Einerseits war das lediglich eine Frage der Bestechungsgelder. Andererseits mußte die Regierung - auch gegen ihren Willen - auf antichristliche Gefühle der Muslimbevölkerung Rücksicht nehmen. A. D. 976/77 (A.H. 366) erlaubte al-ʿAzīz die völlige Wiederherstellung der Schenūte-Kirche. In dieser Zeit drangen lokale antichristliche Fanatiker nicht durch. Diese positive Entwicklung hält bis zu den Anfängen al-Ḥākim's an vor dem Beginn seiner religiösen Verfolgungen. Trotz gegenteiliger Entscheidung des Untersuchungsrichters al-Ḥusayn ibn al-Ǧawhar ließ er dann eine von den Christen aufgebaute Kirche in Rāšīda einreißen, eine Moschee auf dem Platze errichten und umliegende Kirchen auch zerstören wegen zu großer Nähe zu dieser Moschee. Weitere Zerstörungen belegen die Tatsache, daß auch in Kairo Kirchen existierten. Ohne Genehmigung oder stillschweigende Zustimmung der Regierung war ein Kirchenbau in Kairo nicht möglich. Grundsätzlich gab es unter den Fāṭimīden keine Probleme von Regierungsseite, wohl aber von der muslimischen Bevölkerung. Sie sah die zahlenmäßig umfangreicheren Christengemeinden als gefährlicher an als die kleinen Judengruppen. So beschwert sich ein Qāḍī, daß das Dorf Damrū , in dem der Patriarch residierte Constantinopel ähnele. Im Bürgerkrieg unter al-Mustansir wurden viele Kirchen zerstört und Mönche getötet, genauso in der Schlußphase der Fāṭimīdenherrschaft in Ägypten von den Truppen Nūr al-Dīn's . Im Gegensatz zu der Mamlūkenzeit führte unter den Fāṭimīden die Tätigkeit von Christen oder auch Juden kaum zu Spannungen. Man sah im allgemeinen keine Zurücksetzung der Muslime und eine Erniedrigung des Islams darin. Die Kopten hielten sich auf allen Stufen der Verwaltung. Man denke an die sehr komplizierte Verwaltung der Ländereien und alle damit zusammenhängende Probleme des Landmannes. Um hier zu reussieren, gehörten erhebliche Kenntnisse und Verwaltungsfähigkeiten dazu. In der Praxis blieben die Kenntnisse der Verwaltungsmaschinerie in der Familie, vererbten sich vom Vater auf den Sohn und erlaubten der betreffenden Familie ein gutes Auskommen und. vor allem die dauerhafte Besetzung des betreffenden Postens. Die große Zahl von Christen in der Verwaltung ist darüber hinaus Beweis für die erst teilweise Islamisierung Ägyptens, die jedenfalls unter den Fūṭimīden nicht weiter vorangetrieben wurde. Der Aufstieg in höchste Positionen war den Christen allerdings nur unter al-'Azīz und al-Hāfiz möglich, die beide tolerant und ohne Starrsinn waren. Ersterer hatte überdies eine melkitische Christin zur Frau. Nur einmal in der Fūṭimīdenzeit gab es wirklichen Protest und nur zweimal gab es umfängliche Entlassungen von Christen. Zumindest einmal sind es die zu aktiven Armenier, die die Situation verschuldet haben.

Zum Schluß sei noch die Teilnahme von Muslimen an christlichen Festen angesprochen - unter den Mamlūken wieder streng verpönt, von den Fāṭimīden ganz anders betrachtet. Teilnahme von Muslimen und Gegenwart von Herrschern beim Epiphaniasfest mit der Eintauchungszeremonie war gang und gäbe. Auch die Palmsonntagsprozession wurde begeistert gefeiert. Das mehr synkretistische Verhalten der Bevölkerung stand jedoch nicht isoliert da. Auch die Regierung machte mit. Muslimische sowohl wie christliche Feste wurden von ihr benutzt, um Kleider und Geld zu verteilen. Schließlich war auch die Bedeutung der christlichen Heiligen für die Muslime offensichtlich. Für Lev gehört zu den Gründen für die Haltung der Fāṭimīden auch die Tatsache, daß sie sich als von Gott geleitete, unfehlbare 'Imāme fühlten und sich nicht um die religiösen Autoritäten kümmerten und von ihnen ahhängig waren, wie die Sunnitenherrscher.

Über die folgenden Geschichtsperioden bis hin zur Gegenwart geben hauptsächlich die zahlreichen, einschlägigen Artikel der koptischen Enzyklopädie Auskunft. Der Gegenwart widmet man sich auch in Ägypten. So schreibt Ḥasanain Über die Zeit von 1952 bis 1981 auch in religiöser Hinsicht. Huwaidī widmet sich dem Problem der religiösen Auseinandersetzungen und damit der Lage der Christen in der Gegenwart, Ḥabīb dem Verhältnis der koptischen Kirchen und christlicher Intellektueller zum islamischen Staat in Ägypten, während Mūrū den Papst kritisiert. Man ersieht daraus, wie die historische Forschung bis in die Gegenwart voranschreitet, weite Gebiete umfaßt und auch in dieser Berichtsperiode seit 1988 an vielen Punkten uns bereichert und Klarheit geschaffen hat.

Bibliographie

Ahrweiler, Hélène, 1988: Géographie historique du Monde Méditerranéen, Paris 1988 (Publications de la Sorbonne: Byzantina Sorbonensia 7).

Altheim-Stiehl, Ruth, 1992: The Sasanians in Egypt - some evidence of historical interest, in Bulletin de la Société d'archéologie copte, Vol. 31(1992), pp. 87-96 = verkürzt in The Copt. Enc., 1938-1941 (Persians in Egypt).

Anawati, G. C., 1990: The Christian communities in Egypt in the Middle Ages, in M. Gervers & Ramzi Jibran Bikhazi: Conversion and Continuity: Indigenous Christian communities in Islamic lands, eighth to eighteenth centuries, Toronto 1990 (Papers in Mediaeval Studies 9), pp. 237-251.

Anawati, G. C., 1988: Le Frère Martin Edouard S. Sabanegh (1916-1985), in Institut Dominicain d'Études Orientales du Caire, Mélanges (MIDEO), Vol. 18 (1988), pp. 407-409 - Le Père Joseph Cuoq (1917-1986), in MIDEO, Vol. 18 (1988), pp.

406sq. - Louis Gardet (1904-1986), in MIDEO, Vol. 18(1988), pp. 406-407.

Anawati, G. C., & Platti, E., 1988: Textes arabes anciens édités en Égypte au cours des années 1985-1986, in MIDEO, Vol. 18 (1988), pp. 243-334.

Aubert, R., 1990: Héron, évêque de Thennesos en Égypte, in Dict. d'histoire et de géographie eccl., 24,1 (1990), 156 (Mitte des 5. Jh. Teilnehmer am Konzil von Chalkedon); - Héron, évêque de Diospolis en Thébaïde Seconde, in Dict. d'hist. et de géogr. eccl., 24,1 (1990), 156 (Mitte 4. Jh.); - Heraclius, in Dict. d'hist. et de géogr. eccl., fasc. 137 (1990), 1346.

Ayad, Boulos A., 1989: The continuation of the Ancient Egyptian Culture through the Coptic Immigrants, in Coptologia, Vol. 10 (1989), pp. 99-102.

Badawy, H., 1990: The Treaties of Egypt and of Alexandria, a Model for a Treaty or Final Treaties (640-646 A.D.), in Communications grecques présentées au VIe Congrés International des Études du Sud-Est Européen, Athen 1990, pp. 287-296 (Kentro Spoudōn Notioanatolikēs Eurōpēs).

Balard, M., 1988: Les croisades, les noms, les thèmes, les lieux, MA Éditions 1988.

Berg-Onstwedder, Gonnie van den, 1990: Diocletian in the Coptic tradition, in Bulletin de la Société d'archéologie copte, Vol. 29 (1990), pp. 87-122.

Bitonto Kasser, Anna di, 1989: Deir Apa Samuele: Localizzazione e storia di un monastero della regione tebana, in Aegyptus, Vol. 69 (1989),pp. 165-177.

Borkowski, Z., 1990: Local cults and resistance to Christianity, in The Journal of Juristic Papyrology, Vol. 20 (1990), pp. 25-30.

Bourguet, P. du, 1988 (1991²): Les Coptes, Paris 1988 (Que sais-je? 2398).

Bowman, Alan K., 1990: Egypt after the Pharaohs, Oxford 1990 (332 B.C. - A.D. 642).

Brennecke, H. Chr., 1988: Studien zur Geschichte der Homöer. Der Osten bis zum Ende der homöischen Reichskirche, Tübingen 1988 (Beiträge zur historischen Theologie 73).

Calament, Florence, 1989: Antinoë, in La Revue du Louvre, Vol. 39 (1989), pp. 336-342.

Caltabiano, M., 1985: L'assassinio di Giorgio di Cappadocia, in Quaderni Catanesi, Vol. 13 (1985), pp. 17-59.

Camelot, P.-Th., 1990: Héraclide d'Oxyrrhinque, in Dict. d'hist. et de Géogr. eccl., fasc. 137 (1990). 1341.

Carroll, Scott T., 1989: The Melitian schism, Coptic Christianity and the Egyptian Church (Diss. Oxford), Ohio 1989.

Chatzephotes, I. M., 1991: 'Αλεξάνδρεια, οἱ δύο αἰῶνες τοῦ Νεωτέρου 'Ελληνισμοῦ, 1903-20, Athen 1991.

Clarke, G. (B. Croke/Alanna Emmett Nobbs/R. Mortley), 1990: Reading the past in Late Antiquity, Rushcutters Bay/Elmsford N.Y., Kronberg etc., Australian National University Press 1990.

Coquin, René-Georges, 1991: Fragments d'une Chronique, relatifs à un Patriarche d'Alexandrie, sans doute Théodose (535-566 A.D.), in Bulletin de la Société d'archéologie copte, vol. 30 (1991), pp. 1-14.

Criscuolo, Lucia - Geraci, G. (a cura di), 1989: Egitto e storia antica dall'Ellenismo all'età araba. Bilancio di un confronto. Atti del colloquio internazionale, Bologna 1989 = 469-473.

Le origini della civiltà copta, 497-502 MacCoull.

Delmaire, R., 1988: Le personel de l'administration financière en Égypte sous le Bas Empire Romain (IVe-VIe siècles), in Cahiers de recherche de l'Inst. de Pap. et d'Égyptologie de Lille, Vol. 10 (1988), pp. 113-138.

Demandt, A., 1989: Die Spätantike: Römische Geschichte von Diocletian bis Justinian 284-565 n. Chr., München 1989 (Handbuch der Altertumswissenschaft III,3,6).

Doresse, Jean, 1989: Deir al-Gizaz, ou couvent de Samuel, un monastère thébain oublié... et même disparu, in Aegyptus, Vol. 69 (1989), pp. 153-163.

Durliat, Jean, 1989: La peste du VIe siècle, in Hommes et richesses dans l'Empire Byzantin, Tome I, IVe- VIIe siècles (réalités byzantines), Paris 1989 (edidit Pierre Zech), pp. 107-119.

Ebeid, Mona Makram, 1988: Le rôle de l'opposition officielle en Égypte, in Maghreb Machrek, Vol. 119 (1988), pp. 5-14.

Fahd, T., 1989: L'Arabe préislamique et son environment historique et culturel, Leiden 1989.

Fedalto, G., 1988: Hierarchia Ecclesiastica Orientalis: I. Patriarchatus Constantinopolitanus, II. Patriarchatus Alexandrinus, Antiochenus, Hierosolymitanus, Padova 1988 (2 Vols.).

Frend, W. H. C., 1988: Archaeology and History in the Study of Early Christianity, London 1988 (Collected Studies Series 282).

Gabra, Gawdat, 1990: Zur Vita des Bane (Abū Fāna), eines Heiligen des 4. Jahrhunderts, in Bulletin de la Société d'archéologie copte, Vol. 29 (1990), pp. 27-42.

1987: The Coptic Legacy, in G. Vitiello: Cairo, the site and the history, 1987 (Mobil Oil Egypt/S. A. E.).

1988: Hatre (Hīdra), in Mitteilungen des deutschen archäologischen Instituts, Abteilung Kairo, Vol. 44 (1988), pp. 91-94.

Garcín, J.-C., 1991: Kairo, in Lexikon des Mittelalters, Vol. V (1991), coll. 849-850.

Gascou, Jean, 1989: La table budgétaire d'Antaeopolis (p. Freer 0845c-d) = Hommes et richesses dans l'Empire byzantine, Tome I: IVe-VIIe siècles (réalités byzantines), Paris 1989 (ed. Pierre Zech), pp. 279-313, Tafeln VI - IX.

1990: Un nouveau calendrier de saints égyptiens (P. IAND. INV. 318), in Analecta Bollandiana, Vol. 83 (1990), p. 226.

Gayed, N., 1989: The Coptic Church in Australia, in Coptologia, Vol. 10 (1989), pp. 95-98.

Gervens, M. / R. J. Bikhazi, 1990: Conversion and Continuity; indigenous Christian

Communities in Islamic Lands Eighth to Eighteenth Centuries, Toronto 1990 (Papers in Medieval Studies 9): pp. 237-251 (G. C. Anawati: The Christian Communities in Egypt in the Middle Ages), 253-261 (Linda S. Northtup: Muslim-Christian Relattons during the reign of the Mamluk Sultan al-Manșūr Qalāwūn, A.D. 1278-1290), 263-288 (D. P. Little: Coptic Converts to Islam during the Baḥrī Mamlūk Period).

Girgis, Girgis Daoud, 1988: Abba Benjamin, the Coptic Patriarch in the 7th Century, in P. 0. Scholz/R. Stempel: Nubia et Oriens Christianus, Cöln/Rhein 1988, pp. 17-27.

Gregorius, Paulos Mar, 1989: Koptisch-Orthodoxe Kirche, in Evangelisches Kirchenlexikon, Vol. 2: (1989), pp. 1440-1442.

Griggs, C. Wilfred G., 1990: Early Egyptian Christianity from its origins to 451 C.E. (Coptic Studies 2), Leiden 1990.

Grillmeier, Alois, 1990/91: Jesus der Christus im Glauben der Kirche, Band 2/1 = Das Konzil von Chalcedon (451), Rezeption und Widerspruch (451-518), Zweite Auflage 1991; 2/4 Die Kirche von Alexandrien mit Nubien und Äthiopien nach 451, Freiburg/Breisgau-Basel-Wien 1990 (Großrezension zu dieser Frage L. Renwart: Jésus un et multiple, Chronique de christologie, in Nouv. rev. théol., Vol. 112 (1990, p. 718-730).

Grossmann, P., 1990: On the urbanistic arrangements in Abū Mīnā, in Acts of the first international colloquium of the ESGRS, Alexandria 22-24 Nov. 1986, Kairo 1990, pp. 40-61 mit 9 Abbildung.

Grottanelli, C., 1989: Appunti sulla fine dei sacrifici in Egitto, in Vic. Oriente, Vol. 12 (1989), pp. 175-192.

Ḥabīb, Rafīq, 1990: Al-Masīḥīya al-Siyāsīya fī Miṣr; Madḫal ila 'l-Taiyārāt al-Siyāsīya lada 'l-Aqbāt, 1990.

Hahn, J., 1991: Hoher Besuch im Weißen Kloster, Flavianus, Praeses Thebaïdis bei Schenute von Atripe, in Zeitschrift für Papyrologie und Epigraphik, Vol. 87 (1991), pp. 248-252.

Hanson, R. P. C., 1988: The search for the Christian Doctrine of God, the Arian Controversy 318-381 A.D., Edinburgh 1988.

Harīdī, Ṣalāḥ Aḥmad, 1987/88: Al-Gāliyāt al-Urubbīya fi 'l-Iskandarīya fi 'l-'aṣr al-'uṯmānī: «Dirāsa waṯā'iqīya min Siğillāt al-Maḥkama al-Šar'īya» (923-1213 A.H./1517-1798 A.D,), Alexandrien 1987/88.

Ḥasanain, Ḥasan Ḥanafī: Al-Dīn wa'l-Ṯaura fi Miṣr, 1952-1981, Kairo.

Heijer, Johannes Den, 1989: Mawhūb ibn Manṣūr ibn Mufarriğ et l'historiographie Copto-Arabe, Löwen 1989 (Corpus Scriptorum Christianorum Orientalium 513 " Subsidia 83).

Hellholm, D., 1989: Apocalypticism in the Mediterranean World and the Near East, Tübingen 1989.

Huwaidī, Fahmī: Ḥattā la Takūna fitna, Kairo 1989.

King, Karen L., 1988: Images of the feminine in gnostics, Philadelphia 1988 (Studies in Antiquity and Christianity).

Kolta, K. S.: Ärztenamen der kopto-arabischen Sprache, in R. Schulz/M. Görg: Lingua restituta orientalis, Wiesbaden 1990 (Studien zur Geschichte, Kultur und Religion Ägyptens und des Alten Testaments 20), pp. 190-194.

Kretschmer, G., 1988: Die Wahrheit der Kirche im Streit der Theologen, Überlegungen zum Verlauf des Arianischen Streites, in Vernunft des Glaubens, Göttingen 1988, pp. 289-321.

Leclant, J./Gisèle Clerc, 1990: Fouilles et travaux en Égypte et au Soudan, 1988-1989, in Orientalia, Vol. 19 (1990), pp. 335-439.

Lev, Yaacov, 1991: State and Society in Fatimid Egypt, Leiden 1991 (Arab History and Civilization I).

1988: Fāṭimids and Egypt 301-358/914-969, in Arabica, Vol. 35 (1988), pp. 186-196.

Liebeschuetz, J.H.G.W., 1990: From Diocletian to the Arabic conquest, Aldershot 1990 (Collected Studies, Series CS 310).

Lorenz, R., 1989: Zur Chronologie des Pachomius, in Zeitschrift für die neutestamentliche Wissenschaft und die Kunde der älteren Kirche, Vol. 80 (1989), pp. 280-283.

MacCoull, Leslie S. B., Patronage and the social order in Coptic Egypt = pp. 497-502 in Criscuolo.

1988: Coptic alchemy and craft technology in Islamic Egypt, the papyrological evidence, in M. J. Chiat & K. L. Reyerson: The Medieval Mediterranean crosscultural contacts, St. Cloud (U.S.A.) 1988 (Medieval Studies at Minnesota 3), pp, 101-104.

1989: A note on Rufus of Hypselis in the History of the Patriarchs, in Le Muséon, Vol. 102 (1989),pp.267-269.

1990: Verso una nuova comprensione dell'Egitto Copto, in Studi e ricerche sull'Oriente Crist.,Vol. 13 (1990), pp. 3-17.

1990: The paschal letter of Alexander II, Patriarch of Alexandria, a Greek defence of Coptic theology under Arab rule, in Dumbarton Oaks Papers, Vol. 14 (1990), pp. 27-40.

Martin, A., 1989: Le fil d'Arius: 325-335, in Rev. Hist. Eccl., Vol. 84 (1989), pp. 297-333.

Martin, M.P., 1990: Les coptes catholiques 1880-1920, in Proche-Orient Chrétien, Vol. 40 (1990), pp. 33-55.

Martin, M.P./Ch. van Nispen/F. Sidarouss, 1990: Les nouveaux courants dans la communauté copte orthodoxe, in Proche-Orient Chrétien, Vol. 40(1990), p. 247 sq..

Minnen, P. van/K. A. Worp, 1989: Proceedings of the council of Hermopolis A. D. 322, in Zeitschrift für Papyrologie und Epigraphik, Vol. 78 (1989), pp. 139-142.

Müller, C. Detlef G., 1990: Gabriel II. ibn Turaik, 70. Papst und Patriarch des Mis-
sionsbereiches des Heiligen Markos, in Oriens Christianus, Vol. 74 (1990),
pp.168-186.
1991: Kopten, in Lexikon des Mittelalters, Vol. 5 (1991), coll. 1438-41.
1992: Johannes V. der Almosengeher, in Biographisch-bibliographisches Kirchenlexikon, Vol. 3 (1992), coll. 251-253.
Mūrū, Muḥammad: Al-Bābā Sinūda, Hiwar ǧadīd, Kairo 1990.
Nagel, Peter, 1990: Carl Schmidt-Kolloquium an der Martin-Luther-Universität
1988 = M.-L.-Univ. Halle-Wittenberg, Wissenschaftliche Beiträge 1990/23 (K9),
Halle (Saale) 1990 (besonders pp. 25-35 F. Winkelmann: Carl Schmidt als
Kirchenhistoriker).
N. N., 1990: Hénotique,᾽Ενωτικόν, in Dictionnaire d'Histoire et de Géographie Ec-
cl., fasc. 136 (1990), 1044.
Nessim Youssef, Yuhanna, 1989: La genèse d'une légende copte sur l'enfance du roi
Dioclétien, in Bulletin de la Société d'archéologie copte, Vol. 28 (1986-89), pp.
107-109.
Orlandi, Tito, 1990: Koptische Kirche, in Theologische Realenzyklopädie, Vol. XIX
(1990), pp. 595-607.
Palme, B., 1989: Das Amt des ἀπαιτητής in Ägypten, Wien 1989 (Mitteilungen
aus der Papyrussammlung der Österreichischen Nationalbibliothek 20).
Pearson, B. A., 1990: Gnosticism, Judaism, and Egyptian Christianity, Minneapolis
1990.
Pereira Menaut, G., 1988: Actas del Ier Congreso Peninsular de Historia Antigua,
Santiago de Compostela 1988, Band III. pp. 177-186 = J. M. Blazquez: La His-
pania del Bajo Imperio, relaciones con Oriente.
Pryor, J. H., 1988: Geography, Technology, and War, studies in the Maritime History
of the Mediterranean 648-1571, Cambridge 1988 (Past and Present Publ.).
Ritter, A. M., 1990: Arius redivivus? Ein Jahrzwölft Arianismusforschung, in Theol-
ogische Rundschau, Vol. 55 (1990), pp. 153-187.
Simonetti, M., 1990: Il Concilio di Alessandria del 362 e l'origine della formula
trinitaria, in Augustinianum, Vol. 30 (1990), pp. 353-360.
Sirinian, Annna, 1990: Autori greci in lingue del Vicino e Medio Oriente (VIII), in
Studi e ricerche dull'Oriente crist., Vol. 12 (1989), pp. 117-119.
Skreslet, Stanley H., 1987: The Greeks in Medieval Islamic Egypt: A Melkite Dhim-
mi Community under the Patriarch of Alexandria (640-1095), Diss. Yale Univer-
sity 1987.
Solzbacher, R., 1989: Mönche, Pilger und Sarazenen, Studien zum Frühchristentum
auf der südlichen Sinaïhalbinsel von den Anfängen bis zum Beginn der islamis-
chen Herrschaft, Altenberge 1989 (Münsteraner Theol. Abhandlungen 3).
Stierlein, H.: Byzantinischer Orient, Stuttgart-Zürich 1988, pp.97-126.
Šukrī, Gālī: Al-Aqbāṭ fī Waṭan mutaġaiyir, 1990.

Syriany, Samuel al-/B. Habib, 1990: Guide to ancient Coptic Churches and Monasteries in Upper Egypt, Kairo 1990 (Institute of Coptic Studies).

Tedeschi, S.: Etiopi e Copti al Concilio di Firenze, in Annuar. Hist. Concilior., Vol. 21 (1989), pp. 380-407.

Thümmel, H. G., 1988: Die Kirche des Ostens im 3. und 4. Jahrhundert, Berlin 1988 (Kirchengeschichte in Einzeldarstellungen I/4).

Timm, S., 1988/1991: Das christlich-koptische Ägypten in arabischer Zeit, Teil 4 (Wiesbaden 1988 = Beihefte zum Tübinger Atlas des Vorderen Orients, B/41/4), Teil 5 (1991).

Walsh, Efthala Makris, 1989: The Ascetic Mother Mary of Egypt, in Greek Orth. Theol. Rev., Vol. 34 (1989), pp. 59-69.

Watterson, Barbara: Coptic Egypt, Edinburgh 1988.

Williams, J. A., 1988/89: Al-Ṭabarī: The early 'Abbāsīd Empire, Vol. 1/2, Cambridge 1988/89.

Winkelmann, Friedhelm, 1991: Historiographie, in Reallexikon für Antike und Christentum, Vol. IV (Stuttgart 1991), coll. 724-765 (hier col. 761).

Wipszycka, Ewa, 1988: La Christianisation de l'Égypte aux IVe-VIe siècles, aspects sociaux et ethniques, in Aegyptus, Vol. 68 (1988), pp. 117-165.

Worp, K. A., 1988: Bemerkungen zur Höhe der Wohnungsmiete in einigen Papyri aus dem byzantinischen Ägypten, in Tyche, Vol. 3 (1988), pp. 273-275.

Yoffee, N./G. L. Cowgill, 1988: The collapse of Ancient States and Civilisations, Tucson 1988.

Zanetti, U., 1990: L'Histoire des Patriarches d'Alexandrie n'est pas due à Sévère, in Analecta Bollandiana, Vol. 108 (1990), p. 292.

Tito Orlandi

THE STUDY OF BIBLICAL AND ECCLESIASTICAL LITERATURE, 1988-1992

This report is the third in a series that began with a paper read in 1976 at the Cairo congress[1] (it was a survey of the state of research at that time, though the title was «The Future of Studies...»), and continued in 1988 at the Louvain-la-Neuve congress.[2] Therefore I shall not repeat the general observations that I made on those occasions, but I shall proceed directly to report on the studies that have appeared in the last four years. This report cannot be exhaustive, because of lack of time, and possibly of information on the most recent publications; but I have tried to mention all the important contributions. More full and detailed bibliographical information may be found in our Coptic Bibliography.[3]

1. Collections of manuscripts

Alla I. Elanskaya has published a catalogue of the literary manuscripts in Moscow's Pushkin Museum,[4] thus filling a gap in our knowledge of the Russian collections. Though information on such

---

1. Tito ORLANDI, The Future of Studies in Coptic Biblical and Ecclesiastical Literature, in: R. McL. WILSON (ed.), The Future of Coptic Studies, p. 1-22, Leiden, Brill, 1978.
2. The Study of Coptic Literature, 1976-1988, in: M. RASSART-DEBERGH – J. RIES, Actes du IVe congrès Copte, Louvain-la-Neuve, 1992: vol. II, p. 211-223.
3. Corpus dei Manoscritti Copti Letterary, Coptic Bibliography, XI ed., Roma, 1993.
4. Alla I. ELANSKAYA, Coptic Literary Texts of the Pushkin State Fine Arts Museum in Moscow, Budapest, Univ. Loránd Eötvös, s.d. (1991). 306 p., 72 pl. = Studia Aegyptiaca, 13

collections is still far from satisfactory, we expect that the recent opening of Russia to the West may change also this situation for the better.
Elanskaya had already produced a catalogue of the St. Petersburg
(then Leningrad) Saltykov-Schedrin Public Library collection,[5] and
her latest catalogue is conceived more or less along the same guide-
lines, providing not only a list of the material and paleographic information, but also transcriptions of the unpublished fragments. Due—I
think—to an inability to travel abroad and also to access all the relevant bibliography, some of the information given about the fragments
(especially as they relate to the complementary material in other collections) appears to be incomplete and sometimes erroneous. But on
the whole the catalogue remains a very useful tool, also because it is
accompanied by extensive reproductions of the fragments; and it is
only to be regretted that the distribution is—at least for the time being—almost clandestine.

   The Coptic collection of the Beinecke Library of Yale University is
a somewhat minor one; but the accurate catalogue of the biblical fragments by Stephen Emmel is no less welcome.[6] Also we mention the
work of Stephen Emmel on the recostruction of Shenutean codices
from the fragments of all known collections, which is not published
yet (it will be first presented as a doctoral dissertation at Yale), but by
our personal knowledge it is in a very advanced stage and will give an
enormous amount of new information on this fundamental part of
Coptic studies.

   We wish to mention at this point that the catalogue of the Coptic
manuscripts of the Pierpont Morgan Library in New York by Leo
Depuydt is announced as imminent; and that the archaeological discovery of the remains of the library of the old monastery of Neklone

---

5.   Alla I. ELANSKAYA, Koptskaya Rukopisi... = Palestinski Sbornik 20 (83),
Leningrad, 1969.
6.   Stephen EMMEL, Antiquity in Fragments: A Hundred Years of Collecting
Papyri at Yale, The Yale University Library Gazette 64 (1989) 38-58; cp. also
Stephen EMMEL, Marginalia, The Yale University Library Gazette 64 (1990)
174-175; Stephen EMMEL, Coptic Biblical Texts in the BeineckeLibrary, Journal of
Coptic Studies 1 (1990) 13-28.

(in the Fayum), which are still to be catalogued and investigated, seems to be important also for the literary material.[7]

Finally, the «Corpus dei Manoscritti Copti Letterari,» under our direction in Rome, has produced an electronic data base for Coptic manuscripts and the works of Coptic literature, which can be consulted directly from the computer in the Facoltà di Lettere, University of Rome (also by telephone network), or is distributed on a personal basis.[8] Contacts in order to establish permanent collaboration are being negotiated with the Louvre Museum, the Patristic Bibliography project in Toronto, and the Swiss Apocrypha project.

2. Biblical Texts

Two articles on the general problems relating to the biblical versions have been published in *The Coptic Encyclopedia*: one by Peter Nagel for the Old Testament, and one by Bruce M. Metzger for the New Testament.[9] Both are unfortunately rather brief and necessarily vague, and in this respect not very different from the articles that can be found in other non-specialized encyclopedias; but they are commendable for the soundness of the opinions which the authors bring forth, though briefly and without discussion, and should be taken more seriously than their length suggests.

Both authors rightly affirm that we are still very far from a good assessment of the «Coptic» versions in the frame of biblical philology. Two points are essential: the relationship of the different versions among themselves, which requires linguistic as well as philological research; and the relationship between the «groups» of manuscripts emerging from that research with the families of Greek manuscripts. It

---

7.   Wlodzimierz GODLEWSKI - Thomasz HERBICH - Ewa WIPSZYCKA, Deir el Naqlun (Nekloni) 1986-87. First Preliminary Report with Appendix from 1988 by Jaroslaw Dobrowolski, Nubica 1-2 (1990) 171-208.

8.   Cf. T. ORLANDI, The Corpus dei Manoscritti Copti Letterari, Computers and the Humanities 24 (1990) 397-405.

9.   Aziz S. ATIYA, The Coptic Encyclopedia, New York etc., Macmillan, 1991. 8 vols. P. NAGEL, Old Testament, Coptic Translation of: VI 1836-1840; B. M. METZGER, New Testament, Coptic Version of the, VI 1787-1789.

is important to mention that Peter Nagel states that, for the Sahidic version of the Old Testament, the evidence presently available suggests a twofold tradition, represented by the White Monastery codices on the one hand, and the Hamuli codices on the other. On another point, however, we would disagree with both authors. For the date of the versions, they tend to assume as valid the information in Athanasius' Life of Antony: first, that Antony did not understand Greek; and second, that he heard a Bible reading in a church around the year 270. Though the latter statement may be a historical fact, the former is far from sure, especially after Samuel Rubenson's reassessment of Antony's letters (Letters, pp. 141ff.).[10] For this reason, we cannot affirm that Antony in 270 heard the Bible read *in Coptic*, and in any case that he was not able to understand it *in Greek*.

Two important projects continued during the past four years: for the Old Testament, Peter Nagel is carrying on the work for the complete edition, and has continued to publish fruits of the preliminary research. In 1983 and 1984 he had published an accurate and detailed list of the White Monastery codices which can be reconstructed from a sufficient number of presently dispersed folios, preceded by an exhaustive report on the state of studies in this area, but without paleographic or codicological description. In 1987 he published the diplomatic edition (also without paleographical remarks, but with full photographic reproduction) of some fragments not published before, from those in the 1983-84 list.[11] This part of the work is necessary, because the apparatus of the future edition will refer to material which is supposed to be already available to the scholars.

All this is impressive, but also leads to some reflections on the feasibility of a «complete» edition in the traditional sense. The use that scholars make of the variant readings of fragmentary manuscripts is very different from that of variant readings coming from well preserved manuscripts. Moreover, the difference between versions and different testimonies of the «same» text is difficult to appreciate, but

---

10.   Samuel RUBENSON, The Letters of St. Antony: Origenist Theology, Monastic Tradition and the Making of a Saint, Lund, Lund University Press, 1990.

essential. Problems like these and the many others which could be mentioned, seem to recommend a «diversified» edition, taking advantage also of the new technologies.[12] A kind of database, containing the full texts of the manuscripts easily consulted by means of detailed reference points, accompanying a printed edition of the most important complete (or semi-complete) manuscripts, could be one solution. The use of CD-ROM for the reproduction of the manuscripts might also be envisaged.

For the New Testament, Franz-Jürgen Schmitz and Gerd Mink, working in the «Institut für neutestamentliche Textforschung», are carrying on a similar preparatory task, on a larger and more complete scale. In 1986, they had published the first volume of their *Liste der koptischen Handschriften des neuen Testaments, part 1, Die sahidischen Handschriften der Evangelien*, and the remaining two volumes have appeared in 1989 and 1991.[13] The general project has been described in full by Kurt Aland,[14] and I think that here also the observations made above on the edition of the Old Testament are relevant. The two last volumes testify to the progress in the use of computer technology, but—as it seems—only for printing. The idea of a philological and codicological database is not taken into consideration.

---

11. Peter NAGEL, Sahidische Pentateuchfragmente, ZAS 114 (1987) 134-166. Cp. the preceding Peter NAGEL, Studien zur Textüberlieferung des sahidischen Alten Testaments, Teil I, ZAS 110 (1983) 51-74; Peter NAGEL, Griechisch-koptische Bilinguen des Alten Testaments, in: P. NAGEL (ed.) Graeco-Coptica, p. 231-257, Halle, Martin-Luther-Univers., 1984; Peter NAGEL, Aufgaben und Probleme einer kritischen Edition der Sahidischen Version der Septuaginta, in: T. ORLANDI, F. WISSE (eds.), Acts of the Second Int. Congress of Coptic Studies, Roma, CIM, 1985; Peter NAGEL, The Present State of Work in the Edition of the Sahidic Version of the Old Testament, in: W. GODLEWSKI (ed.), Coptic Studies. Acts of the Third Int. Congr. of Coptic Studies, Warsaw, 20-25 Aug. 1984, p. 281-284, Warszawa, PWN - Panstwowe Wydawnictwo Naukowe, 1990.

12. For such problems and for information on what is going on in this field, one can refer to the very interesting "Electronic Discussion Group" AIBI (Association Intern. Bible et Informatique), on Bitnet (and Internet), address AIBI-L@uottawa.bitnet.

14. Kurt ALAND, The Coptic New Testament, R. H. FISCHER (ed.), A Tribute to Arthur Voobus, p. 3-12, Chicago, 1977.

The list includes sixteen complete or particularly old codices (nos. 1-16), and 255 items (nos. 101-355) of reconstructed fragmentary codices of very different extents. Also the lectionaries are taken into consideration, and every item is provided with an extensive codicological and paleographical description, which is derived from observation of photos, or dependent on publications (vol. 1.1, p. xviii). The authors rightly mention the uncertainty of some statements (p. xxii), which of course cannot be considered a fault in this kind of work. On the contrary, the reader would like very much to have access to the enourmous amount of information in a way much more flexible than the indexes provide. But here again, only electronic processing of the data could provide what is wanted.

Such lists are fatally never complete. Apart from manuscripts simply overlooked by the authors (for which an example is the appendix in the 3rd volume), Coptic manuscripts of the gospels are being discovered every day, but also some collections known for a long time are still difficult to manage. For what I have verified, the authors do not have complete information of the material preserved in the Louvre Museum, in the Michigan University Library, in the Vienna Papyrussammlung, in the groups of fragments 661B, 664A-B, 665 of the Morgan Library, in the Cologne Papyrussammlung, and in one so-called Oslo collection, which according to our investigation is now nowhere to be found.[15] A final note should be made on the identification number of the fragments, which sometimes does not coincide with the last reorganization made in the collections.

---

13. F.-J. SCHMITZ, G. MINK (Bearb.), Die sahidischen Handschriften der Evangelien. 1. Teil, Liste der koptischen Handschriften des Neuen Testaments, ANT 8, Berlin New York, De Gruyter, 1986. Franz-Jurgen SCHMITZ und Gerd MINK (Bearb.), Die Sahidischen Handschriften der Evangelien. 2. Teil, 1. Halbband, , Liste der Koptischen Handschriften des Neuen Testaments, I, Berlin - New York, De Gruyter, 1989, Arbeiten zur Neutestamentlichen Textforschung, 13; Franz-Jurgen SCHMITZ und Gerd MINK (Bearb.), Die Sahidischen Handschriften der Evangelien. 2. Teil, 2. Halbband, , Liste der Koptischen Handschriften des Neuen Testaments, I, Berlin - New York, De Gruyter, 1991, Arbeiten zur Neutestamentlichen Textforschung, 15.

As for the publication of individual codices, we register first the long awaited edition of the biblical part of the important bilingual papyrus 1 from Hamburg.[16] The long and complicated story of the successive phases of the work on this codex are reported in detail in the preface. Initially (ca. 1930) Carl Schmidt, who was publishing the Greek Acta Pauli (pp. 1-11 of the manuscript),[17] had entrusted the late A. Kropp with the edition of the rest. After the war, other scholars in one way or another worked on it, beside Kropp: Christian Voigt, Bernd Jörg Diebner, and Rodolphe Kasser.[18] In the end, the edition took the present magnificent shape, with the collaboration of Enzo Lucchesi, and thanks also to the munificence of the publisher, Patrick Cramer. The book of 532 pages and 53 plates (the biblical part of the manuscript is completely reproduced) is impressive. The very fragmentary Coptic text has been tentatively reconstructed for the benefit of the «general» reader, and on the whole it is a wise choice, because it gives at least an idea of what the original texts might have been. Also a German translation is provided, accompanied by the parallel versions in Sahidic and Bohairic, and by the Greek text. The Greek text of Ecclesiastes is reproduced in diplomatic transcription, with a critical apparatus. The so-called «Index of Coptic Words» is really a detailed lexicological study, which shows also the rendering of the Greek words by the Coptic translator. Also to be mentioned are the 90 pages devoted to the Coptic dialect, which is rather a monograph on

---

15. In the famous «armoir Lefort», now in the Catholic University of Louvain-la-Neuve, Institut Orientaliste, one of the boxes contains the photos from «Oslo, Université». But they are not (or no more) in the University Library of Oslo, nor—as it seems—anywhere else in Oslo.

16. Bernd Jörg DIEBNER et Rodolphe KASSER (Hrsgg.), Hamburger Papyrus Bil. 1. Die alttestamentlichen Texte des Papyrus Bilinguis 1 der Staats- und Universitätsbibliothek Hamburg, Genève, Cramer, 1989. 532 p., 53 pl. = Cahiers d'Orientalisme 18

17. Carl SCHMIDT, Acta Pauli, Leipzig, 1904 (II ed. 1905; rist. Hildesheim, 1965).

18. Cp. Bernd Jörg DIEBNER, Die biblischen Texte des Hamburger Papyrus Bilinguis 1 in: T. ORLANDI, F. WISSE (eds.), Acts of the Second Int. Congress of Coptic Studies, Roma, CIM, 1985.

the Coptic dialects. In a word, the quality of this edition perfectly matches the importance of the manuscript.

The only preserved semi-complete Sahidic Evangeliarium is the Morgan Library codex M569, which was fully reproduced in the famous photographic edition, but never published in a critical edition. Gonzalo Aranda had published in 1984 the the Gospel of St. Matthew from this manuscript,[19] and in 1988 he has continued the work with the Gospel of St. Mark[20] (in the meantime the variant readings of Luke and John could be found in Hans Quecke's edition of the Barcelona gospel manuscript).[21] Gonzalo Aranda is particularly keen on the textual problems;[22] his general views were expressed in the first volume, and are not repeated in the second. The text is not presented in diplomatic transcription, but in continuous lines. There are two critical apparatuses, one for the non-significant or less significant variant readings, the other for the significant ones.

The so-called Crosby-Schöyen Codex, formerly in the University of Mississippi and then in the private collection of the Norwegian bibliophile Martin Schöyen, has been known for a long time for its antiquity and importance. Besides the text of Melito of Sardis *On the Pascha*, and another homily not identified, three biblical texts are

---

19. Gonzalo ARANDA, El Evangelio de San Mateo en copto sahidico, = Textos y estudios "Cardinal Cisneros" 35, Madrid, Inst. Arias Montano, 1984.
20. Gonzalo ARANDA PEREZ, El Evangelio de san Marcos en copto sahidico (Texto de M 569 y aparato critico), Madrid, Instituto de Filologia, CSIC, 1988 = Textos y estudios "Cardenal Cisneros", 45.
21. Hans QUECKE, Das Lukasevangelium Saidisch, = Studia et Textus 6, Barcelona, Papyrologica Castroctaviana, 1977. Hans QUECKE, Das Johannesevangelium saidisch. Text der Handschrift PPalau Rib. Inv.-nr. 183 mit den Varianten der Handschriften 813 und 814 der Chester Beatty Library und der Handschrift M 569, = Papyrologica Castroctaviana, Studia et Textus 11, Roma Barcelona, Papyrologica Castroct., 1984.
22. Gonzalo ARANDA PEREZ, Autour de la version sahidique du Nouveau Testament: s'agit-il d'une tradition textuelle unique? Étude des manuscrits M 569 et Bodmer XIX, , W. GODLEWSKI (ed.), Coptic Studies. Acts of the Third Int. Congr. of Coptic Studies, Warsaw, 20-25 Aug. 1984, p.21-26, Warszawa, PWN - Panstwowe Wydawnictwo Naukowe, 1990. 506 p.,

copied: *2 Macchabees* (in part), *1 Peter*, and *Jonah*. It has now been finally published, by a team of scholars under the general editorship of James Goehring.[23]

Another codex has been published recently, after much delay, due to the decease of the late Paulinus Bellet, to whom the edition had been entrusted. In the meantime, the codex (known as the Glazier codex, after the name of the previous owner) has been deposited in the Morgan Library, and Hans-Martin Schenke has provided the edition, with complete information on codicology, language and textual comparisons.[24]

Due to circumstances, we cannot make a sufficiently detailed report of the meticulous work done by Goehring and Schenke on these codices, but the readers will appreciate the high level of their achievement.

We wish to mention also two important codices which have been recently discovered, or at least made known: one, of the fourth or fifth century, is in the Vatican Library and contains the text of the Minor Prophets in Bohairic, a dialect rarely attested from so early a period; the other codex is in Cairo, a testimony to the Middle Egyptian version of the Psalms.[25] The publication of both codices is announced as imminent, by Hans Quecke and Rodolphe Kasser for the Minor Prophets, and by Gawdat Gabra for the Psalms. Finally we announce that most of the available Coptic text of the Bible has been encoded in machine-readable form under the direction of Robert Kraft at the University of Pennsylvania and is available to interested scholars.

In sum, the work on biblical texts has been very successful on the side of the editions; it is to be hoped that detailed philological studies will be encouraged in the future for the whole of the Coptic versions.

---

23. James E. GOEHRING, The Crosby-Schöyen Codex Ms 193 in the Schöyen Collection, Leuven, Peeters, 1990.

24. Hans-Martin SCHENKE, Apostelgeschichte 1, 1 - 15, 3 im mittelägyptischen Dialekt des Koptischen (Codex Glazier), Akademie-Verlag, Berlin 1991.

25. Cf. e.g. Newsletter-Bulletin d'Information, IACS, 18 (April 1986), p. 10.

3. Apocrypha

Apocrypha have always been a special part of Coptic literature. When Coptic texts first began to be known in good numbers, scholars noticed the great quantity of narratives pertaining to Sacred History, but not exactly coinciding with the biblical text. A common opinion was formed that Coptic literature was mainly composed of *apocrypha*. Later, with a better appreciation especially of the fragments, it was understood that such texts generally belong to homilies, which draw inspiration from the Bible, but are aimed at satisfying the listeners' taste for the fabulous and the extraordinary. The texts which could be classified as proper apocrypha after all were relatively few.

Those few presented intricate philological problems, so their study was neglected for a while. It was the constitution of the group around François Bovon, investigating the New Testament apocrypha in all late-antique and medieval languages, which gave new impulse to this work.

Bovon's enterprise, now an official institution with the patronage of the Union Académique Internationale, has initiated a new series of editions and a journal. In the Series Apocryphorum of the Corpus Christianorum, where Junod and Kaestli had published the versions of the *Acta Iohannis*,[26] Jean-Marc Prieur has published, together with the Greek and Latin texts, the fragments of the Coptic version of the *Acta Andreae*, with translation and commentary (1989).[27] The new journal, named: *Apocrypha: Le champs des Apocryphes*, will certainly publish (inter alia) articles on the Coptic tradition of the apocrypha.

It is to be hoped that the sparse publication of the individual *Acta* does not prevent the continuation of the general study, begun by Françoise Morard,[28] of the process by which the Coptic tradition

---

26. E. JUNOD, J. D. KAESTLI, Acta Iohannis (Corpus Christianorum, Series Apocryphorum 1-2), Turnhout, Brepols, 1983, 2 Vols., XXI 949 p.
27. Jean-Marc PRIEUR, Acta Andreae. (I) Praefatio, Commentarius. (II) Textus, Turnhout, Brepols, 1989. XXVI 848 p. (= Corpus Christianorum 5-6).
28. Le recueil copte d'Actes Apocryphes des Apôtres. Un exemple: le codex R, Augustinianum 23 (1983) 73-82.

brought the individual *Acta* together into some kind of collection, to be found partly in some White Monastery codices, and then in at least one Bohairic codex, as also in Arabic.

In the same field of studies is to be mentioned the new edition, much improved, of the classic work edited by Wilhelm Schneemelcher, *Neutestamentliche Apokryphen in deutscher Übersetzung* (Tübingen: Mohr, 1987; 5. Auflage der von Edgar Hennecke begründeten Sammlung); the English translation by James Charlesworth of the *Old Testament Pseudepigrapha*;[29] and the volume of the Pleiade collection of the *Écrits Intertestamentaires*.[30]

4. Ecclesiastical Literature

Given the well known scarcity of studies pertaining to Coptic literature in its entirety, I must begin by mentioning some contributions of my own, which synthesize (following the ideas that I had already set forth in my 1988 report) my view of its development, and should go together with the documentary work done in the frame of the Corpus dei Manoscritti Copti Letterari. In *The Coptic Encyclopedia*,[31] the articles on *Literature; Hagiography, Cycles,* and the articles on individual Coptic authors (real or attributed), form a compendium of Coptic Literature. A contribution for Quacquarelli's *Complementi interdisciplinari di Patrologia* deals with Patristic texts;[32] one for Nagel's *Schmidt Colloquium* treats the beginnings of Coptic literature;[33] one for a book edited by Paolo Siniscalco (in the press) deals with the relationship of Coptic literature and Egyptian Church history.

29. J. H. Charlesworth, *The Old Testament Pseudepigrapha*, 2 vols., Garden City NY, Doubleday, 1983-85.
30. AA VV, La Bible: écrits intertestamentaires. Éditions publiées sous la direction d'André Dupont-Sommer, Paris, Gallimard, 1987 (Bibliothèque de la Pléiade).
31. Aziz S. ATIYA, The Coptic Encyclopedia, New York etc., Macmillan, 1991. 8 vols.
32. Tito ORLANDI, La patrologia copta, in: A. QUACQUARELLI (ed.), Complementi interdisciplinari di Patrologia, p. 457-502, Roma, Città Nuova, 1989.
33. Egyptian Monascticism and the Beginnings of the Coptic Literature, in: P. NAGEL (ed.), Carl-Schmidt Kolloquium..., Halle, 1990, p. 129-142.

I wish to summerize what seem to me the most original interpretations in these works: (1) the Coptic literary language is a cultural acquisition, not necessarily dependent on the pastoral needs of the church; (2) Pachomian and Shenutean literary attitudes should be kept separate, just as should be done with their monastic organizations and their relations with the ecclesiastical and civil authorities; (3) the Origenistic-anthropomorphite controversy represents a turning point also for Coptic literature; (4) the golden age of Coptic literature is the time of Damianus; (5) the clandestine activity of the «cyclical» schools around the eighth century is emphasized; and (6) the synaxarian arrangement of the individual works in the codices of the ninth century is recognized.

Regarding the publication of texts, I shall mention first Iain Gardner's edition of further literary papyri (theological in a broad sense) from the Vienna Papyrussammlung,[34] continuing the work done by me some years ago.[35] Gardner has identified some of the fragments which I could not identify (I take the occasion to note that no. 20 has been identified by Xavier Martinez as part of Ps.-Methodius' *Apocalypse*),[36] and by joining other little fragments has reconstructed what remains of a codex, or possibly two codexes (the explanations at pp. 12-13 are very confusing), which contained a translation of Epiphanius' *Ancoratus* in the first (?) part (foll. 1-13), and other unidentified works in the following parts, including a title of an otherwise unknown epistle of Gregory to Basil (foll. 14-67; no translation is provided for these fragments, mostly very little). Gardner has also reconstructed one folio and part of another, with an exegetical homily, otherwise not identified. The miscellaneous book closes unexpectedly

---

34. Iain GARDNER, Coptic Theological Papyri II. Edition, Commentary, Translation, with an appendix: The Docetic Jesus, Wien, Hollinek, 1988. 2 vols. = Mitteilungen aus der Papyrussamml. der Österr. Nationalbibliothek N.S. 21
35. Tito ORLANDI, Papiri copti di contenuto teologico, Wien, Osterr. Nationalbibl., 1974.
36. Francisco Xavier MARTINEZ, Eastern Christian Apocalyptic in the Early Muslim Period: Pseudo-Methodius and Pseudo-Athanasius, Dissertation Washington Cathol. Univ. 1985, Roma, CIM, 1985, Microfiche.

with some notes on the Manichaean fragments of Vienna, and a contribution on *The Docetic Jesus*.

In 1988 I published what remains of the ascetic writings of Paul of Tamma, one of the monks unknown to the Greco-Latin tradition, but frequently mentioned in Coptic sources.[37] There is also a *Life* of him, in more than one version, unfortunately of little historical use. The most important feature of these works is that probably they were written originally in Coptic, in the fourth century. On the other hand, they fit well in the ascetic literature together with, e.g., the letters of Antony, those of Ammonas, perhaps those of Pachomius, the so-called *Teachings of Silvanus*, the *Liber* of Horsiesi, and later the writings of Isaiah of Scetis and perhaps Barsanuphius and Iohannes.

Evagrius Ponticus' work seemed only indirectly attested in the Coptic literary tradition,[38] and consequently its influence on Coptic theology had been underestimated. Sometime ago I had pointed to some possible relations between Evagrius (or his school) and Pachomian monasticism, with implications also for the research on the milieu of the Nag Hammadi texts.[39] Now two rather large fragments, whose existence has been known for a long time, have been published. They demonstrate the existence of complete Coptic translations, probably fallen under the damnatio of the Origenistic school. An ostracon from the Berlin Museum with three sentences from the *De octo virtutibus*... has been published and commented on in detail by Hans-Martin Schenke,[40] and some folios from a little codex (probably some sort of personal monastic vademecum) in Toronto with ample extracts

---

37. Tito ORLANDI, Paolo di Tamma, Opere, Roma, CIM, 1988.
38. Joseph MUYLDERMANS, Evagriana Coptica, Le Muséon 76 (1963) 271-276; cp. the citation in Walter Ewing CRUM, Der Papyruscodex Saec. VI-VII der Phillipps-Bibliothek in Cheltenham. Koptische theologische Schriften, Strassburg, Trubner, 1915, p. 38,29-35.
39. Tito ORLANDI, A Catechesis against Apocryphal Texts by Shenute and the Gnostic Texts of Nag Hammadi, HTR 75 (1982) 85-95.
40. Hans-Martin SCHENKE, Ein koptischer Evagrius, in: P. NAGEL (ed.) Graeco-Coptica, p. 231-257, Halle, Martin-Luther-Univers., 1984 = Wiss. Beitrage 48; Hans-Martin SCHENKE, Das Berliner Evagrius-Ostrakon (P.Berol. 14700), ZAS 116 (1989) 90-107.

from the Speculum monachorum have been published and annotated by Hans Quecke.[41]

Coming now to studies of Coptic literature, some very good news from the past four years is the beginning of extensive critical work (and consequently of discussions) on some texts published, something that had happened very rarely before. I myself was worried by the fact that, although the number of texts published and made known was not very large (cf. our 1988 paper), the capacity of the «Coptological community» to include them in a living discussion on their value and their historical and cultural position was almost nonexistent.

Fortunately it seems that we are at a turning point, due especially to several monographs, in which Coptic texts play a large part. First, in a new volume of the monumental work of Aloys Grillmeier on *Christ in the Christian Tradition*, in which post-Chalcedonian Egyptian theology is studied in great detail, for the first time the Coptic sources are much in evidence.[42] The most important of these sources is a work by Shenute, preserved with some lacunae, written (as it seems) at the request of the Patriarch Dioscorus, who had been alerted of the fact that there were in Upper Egypt (Achmim) some Origenistic enclaves. I had published this work in 1985 under the title *Shenute contra Origenistas*.[43] The attribution to Shenute has been challenged by Lucchesi,[44] but so far with no evidence.[45]

Grillmeier, who is not a specialist of Coptology, has recognized the importance of this work, not only for our knowledge of the personality of Shenute—who appears much more learned and theologically informed than he was supposed to be—but also for our knowledge of

---

41. Hans QUECKE, Eine koptische alphabetische Akrostichis, Orientalia 61 (1992) 1-9.
42. Alois GRILLMEIER, Jesus der Christus im Glauben der Kirche. 2/4: Die Kirche von Alexandrien mit Nubien und Äthiopien nach 451, Freiburg etc., Herder, 1990, cf. p. 167-264.
43. Tito ORLANDI, Shenute contra Origenistas, Roma, CIM, 1985.
44. 318 ou 319 Pères de Nicée?, Analecta Bollandiana 102 (1984) 394-396, note 9.
45. On the contrary, the paper read by S. Emmel, in the vol. 2 of the Acts of this same Congress (in the press), definitely states that the text was attributed to Shenute in the White Monastery tradition.

the theological situation of Upper Egypt in the fifth century. The work is directed especially against Nestorians and Origenists. But it is clear from the arguments and quotations that under this second category, Shenute had in mind people who read not only works of Origen, but also works very near in contents to those known to us from the Nag Hammadi codices. This from one side establishes a relationship between Origenism and the Nag Hammadi texts; from the other it puts the Nag Hammadi texts in a very delimited environment, for the first time. It is true that this happens about one century after the codices known to us were written; but this is interesting in order to trace the upward road of the texts (rather than the downward one, as is usually done, if at all). At the end of this road we find together people who held «true» Origenistic opinions (e.g., the interpretation of the Seraphim in Isa 6:2; cf. pp. 185-86; or the question of prayer, pp. 188-91), with late Arian opposers of the *homoousios* (p. 187), readers of apocrypha of the Nag Hammadi kind, possibly sharers of some Manichaean ideas.

The Shenutean position may instead be matched by older Coptic texts like the Life of Aphou and the «revised» Agathonicus. We find the late convergence of many different schools in two main streams, originating in the Origenistic (anthropomorphite) controversy of the beginning of the fifth century. Here is the key to understanding the cultural setting of the Coptic world, and especially the monastic part of it, with a strong Origenistic current in the north (led by Evagrius, and his successors), a strong anthropomorphite current in the south (from which the Atripe-Shenutean orthodoxy seems to derive), with the Pachomians in a less defined position, but probably until about 410 more Origenistically oriented than not. Set in this environment, also the problem of the Pachomian origin of the Nag Hammadi «library» receives new light, and the results of the papyrological, philological, and theological studies so far obtained may be placed on a better basis than is provided by the evidence of the Lives of Pachomius, which are an a posteriori hagiographic arrangement.

As we are dealing with the literary activity of Shenute, this may be the place to mention a strange polemic concerning the original language of his works. Enzo Lucchesi has identified the contents of a few fragments from a very ancient bilingual Greco-Coptic codex as being parallel to the text of a papyrus codex in the Turin collection.[46] Some evidence points to Shenute as the author of the Turin text, and therefore Lucchesi not only attributes also the bilingual fragments to Shenute (adding a note against Shenutean attributions too easily done!), but concludes that Greek was the original language of this, and possibly also of other, works of Shenute, protesting that nobody had recognized Shenute's Greek culture.

This is not the place to enter into details, but some general points may be usefully clarified. The study of Coptic literature is rather peculiar, because of the very particular characteristics of its manuscript tradition. So we have very few certainties, but many realistic possibilities, whose value cannot depend so much from data established above any reasonable doubt, but rather from the coherence with the general picture of Coptic literature and culture in which each particular question is inserted. This is why, from one side, the whole literary situation should be always kept in mind, and from the other, we may expect that some or much of that general situation may change because of the addition of new data, or new appreciation of old data. For what concerns us here, the good theological and literary (and therefore Greek) culture of Shenute had already been recognized before the article of Lucchesi.[47] But that Shenute is to be considered first of all a Coptic author cannot be put in doubt even after it. And there is more: the bulk of the works that we now attribute to Shenute certainly belong to him, even though this or that fragment may be recognized in the future as belonging to other authors. We have a fairly good idea of Shenute as a Coptic author. The fact that there existed Greek versions of some of

---

46. Enzo LUCCHESI, Chenoute a-t-il écrit en grec?, in: AA VV, Melanges Antoine Guillaumont, p. 201-210, Genève, Cramer, 1988 = Cahiers d'Orientalisme, 20. Cp. now the reaction of J. HELDERMANN in Bibliotheca Orientalis, ***; and it should be stressed that Crum had already recognized the parallelism of the texts, without so much fuss: cp. Coptic Dictionary, s.v. ειαβε, 76B.

47. Tito ORLANDI, Shenoute d'Atripe, Dictionnaire de Spiritualité, t. XIV, coll. 797-804, Paris, Beauchesne, 1989.

his works (so far only one is in question) certainly does not prove that he habitually wrote in Greek; and strictly it does not even prove that this one work was written in Greek and translated into Coptic, rather than vice versa.[48] As a matter of fact, we personally are in favour of the Shenutean attribution of this work, and of the view that the original was in Greek. But this does not alter very much the general judgment on the work of Shenute as a whole, as it has been recently assessed against the old opinions of Leipoldt.

Another significant improvement in the study of an important part of Coptic literature, historiography, is a splendid monograph dedicated by Johannes den Heijer to the the Arabic History of the Patriarchs of Alexandria.[49] Den Heijer had previously published some articles which were centered on the problem of the «first» author of this work: not Severus of Ashmunein, as is currently believed, but a much less known Mauhoub al-Mansur. The question is surely important, but given that the attribution to Severus had been no basis for any historical assessment of the work itself, we may leave it to the specialists of Christian Arabic literature. More significant for us is that we have in this monograph a first complete exposition of the philological problems concerning this work, which is still unsatisfactorily published and has not been studied enough in its genesis and use of the sources, which—as it seems—were both Coptic and Greek. The first part of the book treats the (Arabic) manuscripts, which are accurately listed and annotated, as also the differences between the two versions resulting from their comparison. It is now to be hoped that den Heijer himself will publish a complete critical edition and translation at least of the Lives 1-74. The second part of the monograph deals with the problem of the author. Finally the third part, which particularly concerns us here, studies the use of the Coptic sources, and especially the Coptic History of the Church. Here all previous contributions are taken into due account, and properly evaluated, and the synthesis which emerges

---

48. Leo DEPUYDT, In Sinuthium graecum, Orientalia 59 (1990) 67-71.
49. Johannes Den HEIJER, Mawhub Ibn Mansur et l'historiographie copto-arabe. Étude sur la composition de l'Histoire des Patriarches d'Alexandrie, Louvain, Peeters, 1989. = CSCO 513 = Subsidia 83

will serve for a long time as the reference point for interested scholars. We cannot enter into detail, of course, but we may say that, as the Arabic text is fundamental in turn to the reconstruction of the fragmentary Coptic history, the synthesis of den Heijer remains a great help for the Coptic scholar who works on a new critical edition of and commentary on the Coptic History of the Church (as I myself am doing).

In another important monograph, Alberto Camplani has studied once again the question of the festal letters of Athanasius,[50] one of the few cases in which—thanks to the work of Lefort—Coptic texts have assumed relevance in a broader context of ecclesiastical history. But Camplani's work began from the lack of a reliable edition and translation of the Syriac text. The Coptic text also requires a new edition, though that done by Lefort is still very good. But some new fragments have been found, and the improvements in the Syriac text have consequences also for the Coptic. On the other hand, Camplani has reviewed *de novo* the problem of the chronology of the letters, and many other historical problems. From the point of view of Coptology, the main results are: (1) a new basis on which to prepare the new edition of the Coptic text, which in fact Camplani is preparing; and (2) a series of historical assessments relating to Athanasius himself, the Melitians in the time of Athanasius and later on, and the liturgical developments of the Paschal festivities. All this is helpful in many ways also for the study of Coptic literature.

Another book, which though valuable *per se* is also a preparation for a critical edition, is that of Samuel Rubenson on the letters of Antony.[51] It represents a kind of revolution in the appreciation of this long neglected corpus and its author. The attribution of the seven letters to Antony is vindicated against the many doubts which had prevailed so far, and then the Antony who had been regarded as perfectly representative of the uneducated, popular kind of Egyptian monasticism, with no knowledge of Greek, theologically agnostic, and only

---

50. Alberto CAMPLANI, Le Lettere Festali di Atanasio di Alessandria. Studio storico-critico, Roma, CIM, 1989, (Corpus dei Manoscritti Copti Letterari).
51. Samuel RUBENSON, The Letters of St. Antony: Origenist Theology, Monastic Tradition and the Making of a Saint, Lund, Lund University Press, 1990.

following the teaching of the church and the patriarch, appears from Rubenson's study as an intelligent Origenist (though not an extremist) perfectly conscious of the spiritual debate of his time. And also the Coptic culture of his time is described as much more active and valid than is generally assumed. It must be said that, though we agree in general with these opinions, we are far less enthusiastic than others are about the correct use of the literary evidence. In a Coptological context, we cannot leave unmentioned that the letters are not preserved in «two folios of a papyrus codex dating presumably from the seventh century»; rather they belong to a parchment codex from the White Monastery, dating at least from the ninth century. But what seems especially unconvincing, in Rubenson's method of demonstrating authorship, is the weight given to the contents, in particular the theological contents, of the letters, and the weight given to the lack of contradictory documents. In demonstrating authorship, admittedly a difficult task, one wants above all to have stylistic arguments, with clear divergences from the other possible authors. On the other hand, the content of these texts, interesting as it may be, is not so peculiar that it could not have been written by any educated monk of Lower Egypt in the fourth and fifth centuries.

The book dedicated to Peter of Alexandria by Tim Vivian[52] may be seen as somewhat preparatory for an edition of the Coptic texts attributed to Peter, as well as being an effort to give a new appreciation of the personality of the Alexandrian bishop, using the Coptic sources alongside the «classical» ones. Here also the use of the evidence does not appear entirely correct, and some conclusions frankly are unconvincing. We may also point out the new conclusions reached by Pearson in the introduction to the edition of the texts (prepared by Vivian, Pearson, and Donald Spanel).[53]

Now in the press (but already available in its original form as a doctoral dissertation) is Mark Sheridan's complete edition of what re-

---

52. Tim VIVIAN, St. Peter of Alexandria Bishop and Martyr, Philadelphia, Fortress Press, 1988 = Studies in Antiquity and Christianity.
53. Birger PEARSON and Tim VIVIAN, with the assistance of D. B. Spanel, Two Coptic Homilies Attributed to Saint Peter of Alexandria, Roma, CIM, 1993.

mains of the works of Rufus, bishop of Shotep in the time of the Patriarch Damianus,[54] and one of the group of literati who wrote the best
original Coptic works after Shenute. After Garitte called attention to
Rufus in 1956, listing the known fragments, no one took on the job of
publishing them. Also providing a historical and theological study and
full commentary, Sheridan's book will be an important contribution to
our knowledge of late Egyptian biblical exegesis and its relationship
to the Alexandrian school.

Just out of the press is a welcome volume in which Leo Depuydt
and some collaborators publish a number of homilies from the codices
in the Pierpont Morgan Library.[55] Although the publication of texts is
always to be considered with favor, I must say that this book just goes
against the recommendation which I presented to the 1998 Louvain
congress: «What really matters is the honesty and the clarity of an edition. The editor should make clear which problems he has tried to
solve, and which he has devoted less attention to, and the edition
should be used according to such declarations".[56] So, from a literary
point of view, there is an introduction by Rowan A. Greer, which simply ignores all the recent studies on Coptic literature and their achiev-
ments; and ther is no commentary on the texts; while also linguistic
notes and accurate paleographic description are absent.

In conclusion, we observe that the study of Coptic literature has
progressed in the last four years at least as much as in the previous
years. Many important codices have been published, and new texts are
now known, even if we are still far from possessing an edition of most
Coptic manuscripts. All the main collections of texts (CSCO, Cahiers
d'Orientalisme, CMCL...) have published new books, a new journal

---

54. Mark J. SHERIDAN, The Homilies of Rufus of Shotep on the Gospels of
Matthew and Luke, Ann Arbor, University Microfilm International, 1990. 5
microfiche
55. Leo DEPUYDT (General Editor), Homiletica from the Pierpont Morgan
Library. Seven Coptic Homelies Attributed to Basil the Great, John Chrysostom, and
Evodius of Rome, Louvain, Peeters, 1991.
56. The Study of Coptic Literature, cit., p. 219.

sponsored by our Association is being published, and the existing enterprises have been continued.

But above all we think that the most satisfactory feature of recent years is the new interest that scholars have shown in the study of Coptic works as a necessary complement to the other Christian sources for a good knowledge of the history of Christianity and of Christian thought. This is the best proof that the efforts to make Coptic literary works known is appreciated by colleagues in related fields. And of course we hope that such a trend may continue and expand in the future.

BIRGER A. PEARSON

GNOSTICISM 1988-1992

In this report of scholarship on Gnosticism in the past four years, I shall discuss, first and rather summarily, the most important general treatments of Gnosticism that have appeared, and then, as is appropriate to this congress, give a more extensive report on the Coptic texts from Nag Hammadi and related Coptic sources. I reach back to the year 1987 in a few instances for particularly important items not discussed by Hans-Martin Schenke in his report at Louvain-la-Neuve.[1] Needless to say, this report is not at all complete. My intention is to treat, selectively, those books and articles that I deem the most important to appear on our topic in the past four years. Of course, as should be expected, my task has been made easier by the bibliographical work of David Scholer, whose articles supplementing his *Nag Hammadi Bibliography*[2] continue to appear regularly in *Novum Testamentum*.[3]

1. Gnosticism

As is well known "Gnosticism" and "Gnosis" conjure up very different images in the minds of people, scholars and laypersons alike, ranging from the disapproval of traditionalist theologians to the various approving appropriations of cultists of various sorts, from the sen-

---

1. "Gnosis-Forschung 84-88," in *Actes du IVe Congrès Copte*, 2:321-33.
2. D. M. Scholer, *Nag Hammadi Bibliography 1948-1969* (NHS 1; Leiden: Brill, 1971).
3. See D. M. Scholer, "Bibliographia Gnostica: Supplementum XVII," *NovT* 30 (1988) 339-72; and Supplementa XVIII-XX, *NovT* 31 (1989) 344-78, 32 (1990) 349-73, 34 (1992) 48-89.

sationalist accounts of journalists to the more sober treatments of historians of religions and other scholarly professionals.

With a tip of the hat to the ancient heresiologists of the Church, I cite first an example of the disapproving view: P. J. Lee, *Against the Protestant Gnostics*.[4] Lee briefly discusses Gnosticism as a "type of religion" ("Judaism gone berserk," p. 6) and "heresy," but then turns to his main preoccupation: the ascendance of "Gnosticism" in North American Protestantism. He laments such trends as emphasis on private illumination, "escapism," "syncretism," and "narcissism." Lee ends by pointing to the steps that Protestants need to take to "degnosticize" itself.

The polar opposite to Lee is a real-live "Gnostic": Stefan Hoeller, Bishop of the Ecclesia Gnostica in Hollywood, California. His book, *Jung and the Lost Gospels*, was inspired by a remark made by Prof. James M. Robinson, visiting a Good Friday service of the Gnostic church: "We scholars have completed our work, it is time now for a Gnostic to write about the Gnostic scriptures." (Preface, p. xvii.) Hoeller's book tells the story of the "two heresies," the Essenes of Qumran and the Gnostics; analyzes some of the basic Gnostic myths, especially with reference to the psychological theories of C. G. Jung;[5] and then discusses three of the "other gospels": *Thomas, Philip,* and *Egyptians.* He concludes that the only hope in the face of the coming cosmic catastrophe, which he says was prophesied by C. G. Jung (232ff.), is the recovery of the human self.

It should here be noted that Hoeller's attempt to relate Gnosticism to Jungian thought has rightly been challenged by Robert Segal (in *The Gnostic Jung*), who argues that Jung's thought is much more compatable with that of the ancient alchemists than with Gnosticism. The monistic worldview of alchemy must be contrasted with the dualistic worldview of Gnosticism.

As an example of journalistic enthusiasm for Gnosticism I cite To-

---

4.   For bibliographical data on this and other items discussed here see the appended select bibliography.

5.   Cf. his other book, *The Gnostic Jung and the Seven Sermons to the Dead* (Wheaton IL: Theosophical Publishing House, 1982).

bias Churton's *The Gnostics*. This book was prepared as a companion work to a British television series on the Gnostics produced by Churton, a program initially inspired by Elaine Pagel's best-seller, *The Gnostic Gospels*. In the book Churton ranges from the burial and discovery of the Nag Hammadi Codices, Hermetism, and the medieval Cathars, to the revival of Hermetism in the Renaissance. It concludes with an interview with Joseph Ritman, a Dutch businessman and avowed "Gnostic," founder of the Hermetic Philosophy Library in Amsterdam.

By way of transition to a discussion of scholarly publications on Gnosticism, I cite Andrew Welburn's *The Beginnings of Christianity*. This is not a book on Gnosticism per se, but it does devote considerable attention to Gnosticism and Gnostic literature. An exceedingly erudite work, it is dominated, from beginning to end, by an interpretive approach that is based on the "spiritual investigations" of Rudolf Steiner, the founder of Anthroposophy. Ranging from ancient Iran, Mesopotamia, and Egypt, to Essenism, Gnosticism, and early Christianity, this book concludes that Christianity, i.e. in its primitive pre-Imperial forms, is "uniquely valuable among the world religions" because its essential message is that the history of man's consciousness has spiritual meaning (p. 296).

A more traditional comparative approach is taken by Andrea Diem in *The Gnostic Mystery*,[6] where she compares the mysticism found in ancient Gnosticism with that of the Sant tradition of 14th- and 15th-century India. Her approach is phenomenological; she wisely refrains from attempting to draw lines of historical continuity between the two traditions.

A recent book by Graziano Benelli, *La gnosi*, treats Gnosticism as an intellectual current in Western history from ancient to modern times, with special focus on the various attempts that have been made to explain the origin of evil. Ioan Couliano's posthumously published book, *The Tree of Gnosis*,[7] is a study of western dualism that rejects

---

6.   The original version of this book was presented as a M.A. thesis at the University of California, Santa Barbara.

the traditional methods of the history of religions in favor of what Couliano (a.k.a. Culianu) calls "morphodynamics," a structuralist approach that also pays attention to diachrony. This approach reduces western dualism, and religion in general, to "mind games" consisting of mental systems made up of binary switches. What emerges in the book is an account of Gnostic dualism and its variants in western culture, including a chapter on "Modern Nihilism" (ch. 11). In his preliminary acknowledgments Couliano refers to his exile from his native Romania in 1972 as contributing to his personal interest in Gnosticism. He writes that the trauma of exile was cured in December of 1989 when he saw on television "the bodies of the executed Archon of that world and his equally evil consort." Unfortunately, as we now know, the agents of that dead Archon were able to seek him out and murder him in his place of refuge.

Meanwhile, Couliano's scholarly targets, historians of religions, are alive and well. The most notable for the study of Gnosticism is, of course, Kurt Rudolph, whose *Die Gnosis* is out in a third edition.[8] His Italian counterpart, Giovanni Filoramo, now has his fine work out in an English version, *A History of Gnosticism,*[9] which will now probably attract the attention it deserves, even if its use of American and northern European scholarship is somewhat spotty. The classic of Gnostic scholarship, Hans Jonas' *Gnosis und spätantiker Geist* (vol. 1: mythological gnosis) is out in a fourth edition.[10] Simone Pétrement's massive, idiosyncratic defense of the traditional understanding of the origins of Gnosticism, i.e. as a Christian heresy, is also now available in an English version, unfortunately not up-dated.[11] Maddalena Scopello has recently published an introduction to Gnosticism, *Les*

7.　This is a revised translation of *Les gnoses dualistes d'Occident* (Paris: Editions Plon, 1990).

8.　It was first published in 1977 (Leipzig: Koehler & Amelang). ET: *Gnosis: The Nature and History of Gnosticism* (Edinburgh: T. & T. Clark / San Francisco: Harper & Row, 1983).

9.　See *L'attesa della fine: Storia della gnosi* (Roma/Bari: G. Laterza & Figli, 1983).

10.　It was first published in 1934.

gnostiques, that deals with the sources, historical influences, and the message of Gnosticism, as well as its symbolism and ways of thinking.

Several books of discrete essays on Gnosticism have appeared in the period under review. Alexander Böhlig's two volumes, *Gnosis und Synkretismus*, contain 27 articles of his on Gnosticism, Manichaeism, and the Nag Hammadi texts published in the period from 1966 to 1988. (The three latest essays, published in 1988, deal with Manichaeism.) The second volume contains a combined index of the two volumes plus his earlier collection, *Mysterion und Wahrheit*.[12] Ithamar Gruenwald's collection of studies on apocalypticism, merkabah mysticism, and Gnosticism contains several articles on Gnosticism previously published, as well as a new one on the *Second Apocalypse of James* (see below). A selection of essays on Gnosticism and the New Testament by the late George MacRae has been published by two of his former colleagues. Seven of the essays, published from 1970 to 1983, deal specifically with Gnosticism and the Nag Hammadi Codices, including his now-classic study, "The Jewish Background of the Gnostic Sophia Myth" (ch. 12).[13] The book also contains a complete bibliography of MacRae's publications.

Miroslav Marcovich's collected essays, *Studies in Graeco-Roman Religions and Gnosticism*, includes revised versions of four items related to our topic published between 1969 and 1981, as well as three entirely new essays, one on Justin's *Baruch* (ch. 10), one on new Gnostic texts isolated from Hippolytus' *Refutatio* (ch. 11),[14] and one on the system of Monoimus the Arab (ch. 12). Essays by Eric Segel-

---

11. The English version is an unrevised translation of the original French: *Le Dieu séparé: les origines du gnosticisme* (Paris: Cerf, 1984). See my review, "Early Christianity and Gnosticism: A Review Essay," *Religious Studies Review* 13 (1987) 1-8, esp. 4-6.

12. *Mysterion und Wahrheit: Gesammelte Beiträge zur spätantiker Religionsgeschichte* (Leiden: Brill, 1968).

13. *NovT* 12 (1970) 86-101.

14. See his magisterial edition of Hippolytus: *Hippolytus, Refutatio omnium haeresium* (PTS 25; New York / Berlin: De Gruyter, 1986).

berg on Gnosticism and Mandaeism, published between 1960 and 1983, are included in a volume of his own essays gathered together and published by Uppsala colleagues and presented to him as a Festschrift. The book also contains a previously unpublished essay by Segelberg: "Mandaean - Jewish - Christian. How does the Mandaean tradition relate to the Jewish and Christian traditions?," an analysis of ritual features in Mandaeism that, he argues, show both early ("late") Jewish and early Christian influences. My own volume, *Gnosticism, Judaism, and Egyptian Christianity*, contains revised versions of 10 items published between 1972 and 1986, as well as three new essays, one on the traditions related to the "Cainites" (ch. 6), one on the figure of Melchizedek (ch. 7),[15] and one on Gnosticism in the history of early Egyptian Christianity (ch. 13).

Other collections of essays include those presented at a conference at Claremont and Anaheim in 1985, organized by Karen King, on the theme "Images of the Feminine in Gnosticism." The volume with the same title edited by King contains essays and responses by 31 different scholars, and has already opened the way to new areas of research on the role of gender in Gnosticism and in the history of religions generally.

Papers from another conference, on "Neoplatonism and Gnosticism," organized by the late Richard T. Wallis and held at the University of Oklahoma in 1984, have finally (in 1992) been published in a volume with the same title. The conference brought together specialists in Gnosticism and in Platonic philosophy in a very fruitful exchange. Of the 21 chapters in the book, six are by scholars of Gnosticism: Francisco Garcia Bazan ("The 'Second God' in Gnosticism and Plotinus's Anti-Gnostic Polemic"), Birger A. Pearson ("Theurgic Tendencies in Gnosticism and Iamblichus's Conception of Theurgy"), Pheme Perkins ("Beauty, Number, and Loss of Order in the Gnostic Cosmos"), Gedalyahu G. Stroumsa ("Titus of Bostra and Alexander of Lycopolis: A Christian and a Platonic Refutation of Manichaean Dualism"), John D. Turner ("Gnosticism and Platonism: The Pla-

---

15.   This essay was presented at the IACS Congress in Louvain-la-Neuve, 1988.

tonizing Sethian Texts from Nag Hammadi in their Relation to Later Platonic Literature"), and Michael A. Williams ("Higher Providence, Lower Providences and Fate in Gnosticism and Middle Platonism"). The most notable of the other papers are those of A. H. Armstrong ("Dualism: Platonic, Gnostic, and Christian"), Jean Pépin ("Theories of Procession in Plotinus and the Gnostics"), and Richard T. Wallis ("Soul and Nous in Plotinus, Numenius and Gnosticism").

Gilles Quispel has edited a volume in Dutch on Gnosis as "the third component of the European cultural heritage," with papers presented at a symposium on that theme held in Amsterdam in 1986. It contains articles by Rouel van den Broek on "the Unknown God in Gnosis," by Jarl Fossum on "Helena," by Quispel on "the woman in Gnosis," by Esther A. de Boer on "Mary Magdalene and her gospel," by Th. G. Sinnige on "Plotinus and Gnosis," as well as articles by Jan Helderman and Maria de Groot on the Nag Hammadi tractates *Gospel of Truth* and *Thunder* respectively (see below). It also contains several other articles on such related topics as "Androgyny in Jacob Boehme" (B. Koole) and "the universal Gnosis" (J. R. Ritman, the aforementioned gnostic businessman).

The Festschrift for Helmut Koester, edited by me, contains five articles related to our topic (R. Cameron, "The *Gospel of Thomas* and Christian Origins" ([ch. 30]; H.W. Attridge, "'Masculine Fellowship' in the *Acts of Thomas*" [ch. 32]; P. Perkins, "New Testament Christologies in Gnostic Transformation" [ch. 35]; E. H. Pagels, "The 'Mystery of Marriage' in the *Gospel of Philip* Revisited" [ch. 36]; and B. A. Pearson, "Pre-Valentinian Gnosticism in Alexandria" [ch. 37].

Several new encyclopedias containing general articles on Gnosticism have appeared in the past four or five years. I single out for mention here the three most important for our purposes (in order of their appearance): *The Encyclopedia of Religion, The Coptic Encyclopedia,* and *The Anchor Bible Dictionary.* In *ER* the main entry is divided into three parts, with Gilles Quispel dealing with "Gnosticism from Its Origins to the Middle Ages" (but he ignores the imposed limit and brings the discussion of "this perennial philosophy" into the modern period), Ioan Culianu (a.k.a. Couliano) dealing with "Gnosticism from the Middle Ages to the Present," and Pheme Perkins discussing "Gnosticism as a Christian Heresy." Quispel traces the origins of Gnosticisim to an Alexandrian milieu, both here and in his shorter article in *CE*. A more traditional history-of-religions approach is taken by Kurt Rudolph in his article in *ABD*. His article is a succinct summary of his book, *Gnosis*. He traces the origins of Gnosticism to a Syro-Palestinian milieu. Rudolph has also published a new Forschungsbericht in *Theologische Rundschau* which deals with publications on Gnosticism and the Nag Hammadi corpus published from about 1981 to 1988.[16] Six journal articles on Gnosticism are singled out for mention here: Gilles Quispel (in *VC* 46), with special attention to a saying on self-knowledge in a Hermetic gnomology preserved in Armenian, explores the role of Alexandrian Hermetism in the origins of Gnosticism. M. J. Edwards (in *JTS* 40) argues that the term "gnostic" was never used by the Valentinians, at least in its main phase, because Valentinus avoided the name both as a Platonist and as a Christian. In another article the same author (in *JTS* 41) refers to Plotinus' treatise *Against the Gnostics* (*Enn*. II.9) and other Neoplatonic sources as "neglected texts" that shed important light on ancient Gnosticism. Walter Beltz (in *ZRGG* 40) analyzes the historical component in gnostic thinking, and defines the gnostic approach to history as "anti-history." Howard Jackson (in *VC* 43) argues for the origin in magical traditions of such Sethian Gnostic names as Ialdabaoth and Barbelo. The same author (in *NovT* 32) refers to the Gnostic apocalypses mentioned by Porphyry (*Vit. Plot.* 16) and relates some of the Nag Hammadi texts to them. He then goes on to explore the various sources available on one figure mentioned by Porphyry, the seer Nikotheos.

In an article in the Klijn Festschrift Gerard Luttikhuizen examines the Gnostic myths relating to Sophia and the anthropogony, and concludes that these two components of Gnostic mythology cannot have originated in a Jewish milieu. By the same logic one could argue that early Christian traditions, because of their distinctive features, could not have developed in a Jewish milieu. This article betrays an unfortu-

---

16. His last report appeared in *ThR* 50 (1985) 1-40.

nate lack of understanding as to the historical factors at work in the development of new religious complexes out of older ones. George MacRae, whose classic article on Sophia Luttikhuizen attempts to refute, had a much better grasp on the issues.

Finally, I mention here an article of mine in a collection of essays on *Mikra* (the Hebrew Bible) in the series "Compendia Rerum Iudaicarum ad Novum Testamentum," on the various ways in which the Old Testament is interpreted in Gnostic sources.

2. The Coptic Gnostic Library

Turning now to the Nag Hammadi corpus and related texts, I treat: 1) new translations and editions, 2) studies on the Nag Hammadi corpus in general (books and articles), and 3) studies (books and articles) on individual tractates of the Coptic Gnostic Library, in the order of their occurrence in the manuscripts (NH and BG) as presented in *The Nag Hammadi Library in English*. (NB: In the appended bibliography books and articles are listed separately, and in alphabetical order.) Again, I have had to be selective, especially with respect to articles on the *Gospel of Thomas*. (E.g. I omit articles that treat only a single saying.)

I mention first the widely used anthology published under the general editorship of James M. Robinson, *The Nag Hammadi Library in English*, now out in a third, revised edition.[17] In some cases the revised translations represent improvements in the translations of the critical edition published by Brill (since 1975) as a subseries ("The Coptic Gnostic Library") of "Nag Hammadi Studies."[18] Of course, this anthology suffers somewhat from the inconsistencies that are inevitable in a group project.[19] The other anthology of translations cited

---

17. The first edition was published in 1977, with Marvin Meyer serving as Managing Editor (Leiden: Brill / San Francisco: Harper & Row).
18. The first volume to be published in this series was Alexander Böhlig and Frederik Wisse's edition of the *Gospel of the Egyptians: Nag Hammadi Codices III,2 and IV,2: The Gospel of the Egyptians (The Holy Book of the Great Invisible Spirit)* (NHS 4: Leiden: Brill, 1975).

here is the recently revised edition of volume 1 of the famous Hennecke-Schneemelcher collection of New Testament apocrypha, now out both in German and in English. Included in this volume of "Gospels and Related Writings" are translations of seven tractates of the Nag Hammadi corpus: *The Gospel of Philip* (NHC II,*3*), introduced and translated by Hans-Martin Schenke; *The Book of Thomas* (NHC II,*7*), introduced by Schenke and translated by Einar Thomassen; *The Apocryphon of James* (NHC I,*2*), introduced by Dankwart Kirchner and translated by Thomassen; *The Dialogue of the Savior* (NHC III,*5*), introduced by Beate Blatz and translated by Thomassen; *The First Apocalypse of James* (NHC V,*3*), introduced and translated by Wolf-Peter Funk; *The Second Apocalypse of James* (NHC V,*4*), introduced and translated by Funk; and *The Letter of Peter to Philip* (NHC VIII,*2*), introduced and translated by Hans-Gebhard Bethge.

Several critical editions have appeared since 1988. The "Coptic Gnostic Library" series has been augmented by four new editions. Bentley Layton's edition of NH Codex II, tractates 2-7, comprises two volumes and represents the work of several contributors. It includes the fragment of II,*5* (*Orig. World*) found in NH Codex XIII, and the British Library fragments (in Subakhmimic Coptic) of the same tractate, as well as the Oxyrhynchus fragments (in Greek) of the *Gospel of Thomas*. Douglas Parrott's one-man edition of *Eugnostos* and *The Sophia of Jesus Christ* (NHC III,*3* and V,*1*; NHC III,*4* and BG,*3*) is set up in four parallel columns, Coptic and English, so that one gets a synoptic presentation of the two tractates, showing their relationships and the variations in the two versions of each. His edition also includes the Greek fragments of *Soph. Jes. Chr.* from Oxyrhynchus. John Sieber's edition of Codex VIII contains the *editio princeps* of *Zostrianos* (text edited by B. Layton, translation and notes by Sieber), and a new edition of *The Letter of Peter to Philip* (by F. Wisse and M. Meyer). Charles Hedrick's edition of Codices XI, XII, and XIII, with several contributors, contains *editiones principes* of XI,*1* (*Interp.*

---

19.   39 members of the Coptic Gnostic Library Project of the Institute for Antiquity and Christianity in Claremont CA are listed as contributors to the anthology.

Know.), XI,*3* (*Allogenes*), XI,*4* (*Hypsophrone*, a few fragments, all by
J. D. Turner), and the unidentified fragments of Codex XII (by F.
Wisse), as well as full critical editions of the other tractates. It also
contains a dialectical analysis by Rodolphe Kasser of the Lycopolitan
(Subakhmimic) texts in the Nag Hammadi corpus.

Two new critical editions have appeared in Germany in the series
"Texte und Untersuchungen." Dankwart Kirchner's edition of the
Apocryphon of James (NHC I,*2*) originated as a dissertation submitted
to the Humboldt-Universität Berlin (1977) as part of the work of the
Berliner Arbeitskreis für koptisch-gnostische Schriften directed by
Hans-Martin Schenke. Schenke himself has published a fine new edition of *The Book of Thomas* (NHC II,*7*), in which he also presents a
translation of what he has isolated as the Vorlage of the tractate, a hypothetical apocryphal epistle of the Old Testament patriarch Jacob,
"the Contender" *par excellence.*

The French Canadian project based at Laval University in Québec,
"Bibliothèque copte de Nag Hammadi," is represented by a beautiful
edition, with commentary, of *The Tripartite Tractate* (NHC I,*5*), based
on a dissertation prepared by Einer Thomassen at St. Andrews University in 1982.[20] There is now also a computer-generated concordance
of Codex VII that inaugurates a new component of the Bibliothèque
copte de Nag Hammadi series ("Concordances"), edited by Régine
Charron. It includes a full transcription of Codex VII, making this the
first "edition" (except for the Facsimile Edition) of Codex VII in its
entirety. Finally, a massive edition of *The Teachings of Silvanus* (NHC
VII,*4*) by Jan Zandee has been posthumously published, having been
completed shortly before the author's death in January, 1991. It features a very extensive commentary, with six excursuses.

Before discussing the various studies of the Coptic Gnostic texts

---

20. Until recently BCNH consisted of two subseries, one of "Textes," the other of
"Études." See Jacques-É Ménard, "La Bibliothèque copte de Nag Hammadi," in R.
M. Wilson, ed., *Nag Hammadi and Gnosis* (NHS 14; Leiden: Brill, 1973) 108-12.
The first critical edition published in the "Textes" section was Ménard's *La lettre de
Pierre à Philippe* (Québec: Laval Université, 1977). Charron's work is the first, and
as yet the only, volume in the new "Concordances" subseries.

produced by professional scholars, I want to mention here a fine example of journalistic writing, John Dart's *Jesus of Heresy and History*. Dart is a religion writer for the Los Angeles *Times*, and got interested in the Nag Hammadi discovery in the early '70's. He obtained a leave from the *Times* to consult with scholars (myself included), and read the various translations and studies that had appeared. As a result of these efforts he published in 1976 a book entitled *The Laughing Savior*[21] (deriving the title from the crucifixion scene in the *Apocalypse of Peter* [NHC VII,*3*: 81,4-83,15]), giving an account of the discovery of the Nag Hammadi library and its contents. The current book is a revised and expanded version of the earlier one, and contains material on the *Gospel of Thomas* and the historical Jesus that reflects Dart's more recent interests. Dart's work represents responsible religious journalism at its best.

I also want to mention here the second volume of essays in honor of James M. Robinson, *Gnosticism & the Early Christian World*, which contains essays on Nag Hammadi tractates that will be referred to here in due course (K. L. King, "Ridicule and Rape, Rule and Rebellion: The Hypostasis of the Archons"; L. H. Martin, "Genealogy and Sociology in the Apocalypse of Adam"; G. Robinson, "The Trimorphic Protennoia and the Prologue of the Fourth Gospel"; and B. A. Pearson, "The Apocalypse of Peter and Canonical 2 Peter"). Helmut Koester's *Ancient Christian Gospels* contains extensive discussion of three Nag Hammadi tractates (*Gos. Thom.*, *Dial. Sav.*, *Ap. Jas*; see below).

A very fine book on the Nag Hammadi Codices has been published in Russian by Alexander Khosroyev of the Institute of Oriental Studies in the St. Petersburg branch of the Russian Academy of Sciences. In this book the author discusses the Nag Hammadi texts in the context of a general discussion of early Christianity, especially in Alexandria. He devotes separate chapters to four of the tractates, all of which are situated in Alexandria: *The Teachings of Silvanus* (VII,*4*), *The Ex-*

---

21. *The Laughing Savior: The Discovery and Significance of the Nag Hammadi Gnostic Library* (San Francisco: Harper & Row, 1976).

egesis on the Soul (II,6), *Authoritative Teaching* (VI,3), and *The Testimony of Truth* (IX,3). The book includes at the end a Russian translation of each of the four tractates, a catalog of the Coptic Gnostic Library, bibliography, indices, and (fortunately!) an English summary. Khosroyev regards the four texts he treats as products of a "vulgarization of thought and literature of higher standards," circulating among people "whose intellectual demands were rather modest" (275).

The most important encyclopedia articles published in the last four years on the Nag Hammadi Codices are those of Stephen Emmel in the *Coptic Encyclopedia* and myself in the *Anchor Bible Dictionary*. The former describes the manuscripts, and the latter includes not only codicological data but also an account of the publication history of the manuscripts and an assessment of their contents.

Three other articles cited here deal with aspects of the Nag Hammadi codices and their relative importance for the study of Gnosticism. M. J. Edwards (in *OrChrP* 55) takes a cautionary stand, warning that scholars have been prone to exaggerate the importance of the Nag Hammadi Codices vis-a-vis the heresiological sources. Wincenty Myszor is more appreciative of the Coptic sources in his comparative study (in *JAC* 32) of the letters of St. Anthony and some of the Nag Hammadi texts, esp. *The Teachings of Silvanus* (VII,4) and *Authoritative Teaching* (VI,3), texts whose connection to classic Gnosticism is minimal. Myszor traces the thought world and asceticism of St. Anthony and the comparable texts from Nag Hammadi to a Christianized Platonism. J. van der Vliet studies the concept of *parrhesia* ("frank speech") in *The Apocryphon of James* (I,2) and other Gnostic texts against the background of its use in Alexandrian Jewish thought, and interprets the concept to imply a manifestation of the divine in the sense-perceptible world of ordinary speech.

We turn now to a discussion of recent scholarship on individual tractates of the Coptic Gnostic Library, both books and articles.

Nag Hammadi Codex (Cairensis Gnosticus) I. From the famous "Jung Codex" two tractates have elicited studies included here for discussion: *The Apocryphon of James* (I,2) and *The Gospel of Truth* (I,3 + XII,2).

B. Dehandschutter (in *ANRW* II.25.6) presents a summary of the content of *Ap. Jas.* and research done on it (up to about 1982). He then discusses its genre and its use of New Testament traditions, concluding that it can appropriately be called a New Testament apocryphon. J. van der Vliet (in *VC* 44) discusses the tractate's rejection of prophecy, which demands outward signs, in favor of being "filled with the Spirit," a spiritual state given exemplary expression in martyrdom. Helmut Koester's treatment (in *Ancient Christian Gospels*, 187-200) discusses the text with special reference to its genre, its relationship to other gospel writings, and its use of an early tradition of Jesus sayings.

A full-scale study by Jacqueline Williams, *Biblical Interpretation in the Gnostic Gospel of Truth from Nag Hammadi* (originating as a Yale dissertation completed in 1983 under Bentley Layton) is an evaluation of the use of scripture, mostly what would become the New Testament, in *Gos. Truth*. With Layton and others she attributes the tractate to Valentinus himself and situates it in Rome. Valentinus' use of NT texts is allusive; he never quotes directly or cites a scriptural text. So Williams first establishes levels of probability in 73 cases where scripture passages are possibly reflected, and then analyzes Valentinus' "midrashic" method of interpretation. This is a very fine study, but I do take issue with her view that a fully developed Gnostic system is not presupposed in *Gos. Truth*. Indeed, the use of a basic Gnostic myth in that tractate can be detected using somewhat the same methods as Williams has done with scripture allusions, for Valentinus (if he is the author) utilizes the myth in his expository homily in the same way as he does scripture, i.e. allusively.

Jan Helderman (in *ANRW* II.25.5) has produced a lengthy study of research on *Gos. Truth*, and joins the developing "*communis opinio*" that Valentinus was its author, suggesting that Valentinus may have composed it for delivery as a sermon to a gnostically oriented house church in Rome. The same author (in *Gnosis: De derde component*, 57-70) discusses the theme of "the child" (e.g. the Logos as "child") in *Gos. Truth*. I cite one other study here, also by a Dutchman, Tijtze Baarda, on "the sabbath" in *Gos. Truth* 32,18-34 (in *NedTT* 41). Contrary to most interpreters, Baarda sees a negative interpretation of *sabbaton* in the text, as a symbol for the demiurgic cosmos.

Codex II. This is clearly one of the most important single Coptic codices ever discovered. I mention here recent studies on five of its tractates: *The Apocryphon of John* (II,*1* + III,*1*; IV,*1*; BG,*2*), *The Gospel of Thomas* (II,*2*), *The Gospel of Philip* (II,*3*), *The Hypostasis of the Archons* (II,*4*), and *On the Origin of the World* (II,*5* + XIII,*2*).

A very important full-scale study of *Ap. John* has appeared, published by a Japanese scholar, Takashi Onuki: *Gnosis und Stoa*. Onuki refers to the one-sided prominence accorded to Platonism, esp. Middle Platonism, in scholarly discussion of the intellectual milieu of Gnostic authors, and proposes to expand the horizon with reference to the Stoicism of the Empire. Onuki joins a number of other scholars in the view that *Ap. John*, as we now have it, is a Christianized text; the core composition, produced in Greek, was a non-Christian Gnostic work. Onuki analyzes first the large insertion in the long recension of Codex II (15,29-19,12), points to the Stoic elements that are found in it (part of a "Book of Zoroaster"), and shows how the Gnostic author reworked in polemical fashion the Stoic teachings. Onuki goes on to argue that *Ap. John* as a whole, both in its pre-Christian original, and in the later Christianized version, can be viewed as consistently anti-Stoic, reflecting a polemical stance that can be contrasted with the more favorable attitude toward Stoicism exemplified by the catholic church fathers.

An interesting article by Richard Valantasis (in *SecCent* 7) compares *Ap. John*'s presentation of the formation of Adam's body with comparable traditions in Origen's *Dialogue with Heraclides*. The common intellectual traditions of anthropological speculation, rooted in personal asceticism, is part of an esoteric system in *Ap. John*; Origen makes them exoteric.

The scholarship on *Gos. Thom.* shows no signs of abating. I single out for mention here six articles, plus Helmut Koester's important discussion in *Ancient Christian Gospels* (75-128). An extensive joint article by Francis T. Fallon and Ron Cameron (in *ANRW* II.25.6) presents a Forschungsbericht (into the early '80's) and highlights the sharply divided views among scholars on the text and its place in early Christian history, esp. on such issues as its relationship to the canonical New Testament and its relationship to Gnosticism. Ron Cameron presents his own views on such issues in a separate article (in the Koester Festschrift, 381-92) where he develops some ideas put forward over a number of years by Helmut Koester, and points to *Gos. Thom.* as evidence for a very early and enduring strand of Jesus tradition that is non-apocalyptic. *Gos. Thom.* thus forces us to reassess the origins of Christianity. Koester's own work on *Gos. Thom.*, extending over many years, is summarized admirably in *Ancient Christian Gospels*. He continues to hold that *Gos. Thom.* is early and independent of the canonical gospels, containing a core of sayings that is contemporary and overlapping with the first edition of the sayings source Q. It also contains material that shows relationship to the gospel of John, reflecting the independent use on the part of both gospels of an early tradition of dominical sayings. Some sayings in *Gos. Thom.* of an esoteric character (e.g. Log. 50) bring that gospel into close association with Gnosticism.

On the other hand, some scholars still view *Gos. Thom.* as late and secondary. Christopher Tuckett (in *NovT* 30) points to what he considers to be that gospel's use of redactional material from the canonical gospels, thus arguing against the view that *Gos. Thom.* is independent of the Synoptic gospels. Klyne R. Snodgrass (in *SecCent.* 7) is even more definite in his arguments that *Gos. Thom.* is late and secondary. Kenneth V. Neller (in *SecCent* 7) looks at the diversity reflected in *Gos. Thom.* as evidence for multiple sources and redactions, and thus an extended literary history. He argues that each saying has to be studied individually as to its relationship to canonical parallels, a view that in my opinion has much to commend it. The importance of studying each saying individually is also underscored by Charles Hedrick (in *SecCent* 7).

Thus, the divided state of scholarship on Thomas remains as sharp as ever, with no sign of any consensus emerging.

A number of studies on *Gos. Phil.* have appeared. Giulia Sfameni Gasparro (in *ANRW* II.25.5) presents a Forschungsbericht (to the early

80's), reporting on the various editions and translations, and commenting on the text's contents, structure, and doctrinal affinities. Jorunn Jacobsen Buckley (also in *ANRW* II.25.5) argues against the common view that *Gos. Phil.* is a collection of unrelated logia, in favor of an assumed coherence of the whole. She discusses its sacramental features and its polemical stance vis-a-vis the orthodox church. Jeffrey Siker (in *NovT* 31) discusses the social and theological tensions among Jews and Christians reflected in the text, and situates *Gos. Phil.* in second century Antioch. Elaine Pagels (in the Koester Festschrift, 442-54) discusses the various interpretations of the "bridal chamber" ceremony featured in the text and the issue whether the Valentinian "mystery of marriage" did or did not include actual marriage. She decides that the author of *Gos. Phil.* is deliberately ambiguous on the matter, regarding sexuality as a matter of indifference. Thus, she concludes, the same range of practice in matters of sexuality and asceticism existed among Valentinian Christians as among other second-century Christians.

Karen King (in the Robinson Festschrift, 3-24) analyzes *Hyp. Arch.* in terms of its gendered imagery, and the prominent symbolic role played by Norea in the text. Brian Glazer (in *NovT.* 33) proposes an Egyptian religious background for the fire-breathing figure of Zoe in *Hyp. Arch.*, in her battle against the chaotic forces of darkness. He brings in for comparison certain Egyptian myths featuring fire-breathing goddesses battling against the forces of death.

Louis Painchaud (in *VC* 44) argues that the anthropogony in *Orig. World* (117,27-118,2) is a reinterpretation of Paul's teaching in 1 Corinthians 15:45-47. He also situates the tractate as a whole in a Valentinian Christian milieu. In a more recent article (in *SecCent* 8) Painchaud assigns the aforementioned material to a first redaction of a more primitive text. He posits a second redaction as well, thus seeing in the text as we have it three levels of composition.

Codex III. Two tractates in Codex III have called forth studies that I want to mention here: *Eugnostos the Blessed* (III,3 + V,1) and *The Dialogue of the Savior* (III,5).

In a full scale study of the theology of *Eugnostos* (*The Transcen-*

dent God of Eugnostos) Demetrios Trakatellis situates the doctrinal and mythological teachings of that tractate in the context of second-century Middle Platonism and Gnosticism. Though he sees no obvious Christian elements in the text, Trakatellis is willing to admit of some indirect Christian influences here and there. His book includes a Koine Greek retroversion of the Coptic text of *Eugnostos*.

Douglas Parrott has a very different view of *Eugnostos* (in the Böhlig Festschrift), dating the tractate to the first century B.C.E. One reason for the early dating, according to Parrott, is that the author of *Eugnostos* does not include Platonists in his critique of "all the philosophers" [70,15], aiming his polemics instead at Stoics, Epicureans, and astrologers. But if (as Trakatellis et al. have argued) the main philosophical influence on *Eugnostos* is Middle Platonism, the absence of anti-Platonic polemic in that text is no criterion for an early date. Parrott goes on to argue that the author's view of the transcendent world is indebted in large measure to the influence of Egyptian religion, modified by Jewish elements.

Rouel van den Broek (in *Knowledge of God in the Graeco-Roman World*) argues that *Eugnostos* was written by a Jew in Alexandria. He also argues that the tractate shares a common source with the Christian apologist Aristides in their respective treatments of the transcendent God. Jerry Sumney (in *NovT* 31) also posits a Jewish background for Eugnostos, and views it as a bridge between Hellenistic Jewish speculation in Alexandria and later, more radically dualist, Gnostic systems. *Eugnostos* gives us a glimpse of Gnosticism as it was first emerging. Anne Pasquier, in a more specific study (in *Muséon* 103), relates the tractate's doctrine of the "name" to that preserved in a fragment of Valentinus (Clem. *Strom.* 4.89.6-90.1 = Frg. 5 [Völker]).

Dial. Sav. is treated extensively by Helmut Koester (in *Ancient Christian Gospels*, 173-87). Koester posits a first-century dialogue source for the tractate, made up of discrete sayings of Jesus, some of which are close to sayings in *Gos. Thom.* The text as we now have it, i.e. its Greek original, is dated to the early second century.

Codex V.[22] Three of the apocalypses in this codex have elicited studies mentioned here: *The (First) Apocalypse of James* (V,3), *The (Second) Apocalypse of James* (V,4), and *The Apocalypse of Adam* (V,5).

William Schoedel (in *NovT* 33) discusses the role of James the Just as an anti-catholic protagonist in *1 Apoc. Jas.* and that text's interpretation of James' martyrdom and the ensuing fall of Jerusalem. Ithamar Gruenwald ("Halakhic Material in Codex Gnosticus V,4: *The Second Apocalypse of James*?" in *From Apocalypticism to Gnosticism*, 279-94) examines the use of halakhic material in the account of James' martyrdom in *2 Apoc. Jas.*, and concludes that the Gnostic version is earlier than the martyrdom story in a fragment of Hegesippus' *Hypomnemata* (preserved in Eusebius' *Ecclesiastical History*), and comes closer to Jewish halakhah pertaining to execution.

Considerable scholarly attention has been paid to *Apoc. Adam*. One of the more original studies to appear on this text is the recent Lund dissertation of Per-Arne Linder, *The Apocalypse of Adam . . . Considered from its Egyptian Background*. Linder first presents a new transcription and translation, with comments on the structure of the text. He then analyzes the hymnic section dealing with the coming of the Illuminator (76,8-77,26), especially in terms of its meter as Coptic poetry. He concludes that this hymn was an integral part of *Apoc. Adam*, and was sung in a cultic context. He then analyzes the conclusion of *Apoc. Adam* (85,19-32), arguing that this passage, too, was meant to be sung. He finally concludes that the entire tractate reflects the influence of Egyptian cult and drama. He argues that the original Greek version was already written in an Egyptian context and under Egyptian influence, but that this Egyptian character was made all the stronger when it was rendered into Coptic. While the mythology of *Apoc. Adam* is essentially Gnostic, as well as its ritual, i.e. Gnostic baptism, its structure is similar to that of ancient Egyptian dramatic texts.

---

22. The severely damaged Codex IV contains only two tractates, *Ap. John* and *Eugnostos*, both of which are better preserved in other copies (discussed above).

An Egyptian background for the hymnic section of *Apoc. Adam* dealing with the Illuminator and the 13 kingdoms has also been argued by Douglas Parrott (in *NovT* 32). Parrott maintains that the repeated formula "and thus he came upon the water" reflects an Egyptian formula (a point also made by Linder), and therefore what is said of the 13 kingdoms preceding the "generation without a king" is also Egyptian. Parrott relates the thirteen kingdoms to a tradition found in Apuleius' *Metamorphoses* 11, according to which Egypt is the 13th of human domains over which Isis holds sway under her various names, reigning over Egypt in her true identity as "Isis." The Sethian author of *Apoc. Adam* has modified this tradition by presenting the Sethian Illuminator as the ultimate revealer who supersedes the previous revealers.

A different tack is taken by Andrew Welburn (in *ANRW* II.25.6). Welburn argues that *Apoc. Adam* is a very early text, traceable to the 1st century B.C.E. Analyzing in detail the passage dealing with the 13 kingdoms, Welburn argues that the passage as a whole can be elucidated with reference to Iranian, i.e. Zoroastrian, mythic traditions concerning the cyclical appearance of Zarathustra. The details of each strophe of the hymn are related not only to Iranian mythology but also to other mythologies, biblical, Greek, Babylonian, and Egyptian. Jewish messianism also plays a role in the text, but the Sethian Gnostic viewpoint of the author is reflected in the material that follows upon the discussion of the 13 kingdoms, i.e. that pertaining to the "generation without a king." Welburn's arguments for an early dating for *Apoc. Adam* can be contrasted with the view of Scott Carroll (in *VC* 44). On the basis of the place of the Solomonic lore in *Apoc. Adam* (78,27-79,12) in the chronological trajectory of the Solomonic legend in late antiquity, Carroll argues that *Apoc. Adam* is relatively late (late 2nd to 4th cent.).

In a very different kind of study, one which I find quite fascinating, Luther Martin (in the Robinson Festschrift, 25-36) utilizes insights derived from social anthropology and comparative jurisprudence to study the social role of kinship and fictive genealogy in *Apoc. Adam*'s delineation of the Sethian Gnostics over against the rest of humanity.

Martin chooses *Apoc. Adam* for his case study of Sethian Gnosticism because of its presumed early date and especially because it constitutes a "charter myth" in which privilege is established through a special genealogy. In *Apoc. Adam* Gnostics are treated as fictive descendents of Seth, claiming patrilineal descent from the heavenly Seth on the basis of an alliance secured by "adoption" (= "conversion" in religious terms). The Sethian Gnostics reject marriage alliances, which mark the children of Cain (i.e. the rest of humanity), and constitute a "kingless race" that also eschews political alliances.

Codex VI. Two tractates in this codex are treated in articles cited here: *The Acts of Peter and the Twelve Apostles* (VI,*1*) and *The Thunder, Perfect Mind* (VI,*2*). Stephen Patterson (in *VC* 45) proposes a solution to the compositional problems in *Acts Pet. 12 Apost.* with a three-source hypothesis, and an explanation of the purposes of the redactor of the text as we now have it. Far from being a Gnostic text this tractate has as its purpose to show that the true apostolic commission is this-worldly: to serve the poor and the sick and to promote social justice. Maria de Groot (in *Gnosis: De derde component*, 23-36) discusses *Thund.* in terms of its historical context (accepting Gilles Quispel's published views)[23] and its "I am" style and mode of expression. She goes on to provide a feminist interpretation of the text.

Codex VII. Two tractates in this codex have elicited studies cited here: *Apocalypse of Peter* (VII,*3*) and *The Teachings of Silvanus* (VII,*4*). *Apoc. Peter* is treated in an article by me (in the Robinson Festschrift, 67-74). I assess the relationship between the tractate and the canonical 2 Peter, and show how the New Testament text and the figure of the apostle Peter have been interpreted to serve the interests of an embattled anti-catholic Gnostic sect. Rouel van den Broek (in *NedTT* 42) shows that a combination of two sayings from the *Sentences of Sextus* (352 and 22) are combined in *Teach. Silv.* 102,16-22, a combination also attributed to Origen by Epiphanius (*Pan.* 64.7.3). *Teach. Silv.* and Origen thus reflect a later stage of the Sextine gnomo-

---

23.   She cites Quispel's article in *Les Textes de Nag Hammadi* ["Jewish Gnosis and Mandaean Gnosticism: Some Reflections on the Writing *Brontè*"], ed. J.-É Ménard (NHS 7: Leiden: Brill, 1975) 82-122.

logical tradition. Jan Zandee (in *LavThP* 46) discusses 53 excerpts from *Teach. Silv.*, followed by parallels from the writings of Origen, and concludes that *Teach. Silv.* is an important witness for the history of Christian doctrine. A complete presentation of Zandee's interpretation of *Teach. Silv.* is found in the aforementioned edition.

Codex IX.[24] The first tractate in this codex, *Melchizedek*, is treated in an article by Jacques-É. Ménard (in *RevSR* 64), where he analyzes the role of Melchizedek in the text, its Jewish background, and its anti-docetic christology. He argues that the typically Gnostic elements in the tractate are secondary. The third tractate, *The Testimony of Truth*, is the subject of a thorough study, with an Italian translation, by Claudio Gianotto. His fine work inaugurates a new series devoted to Egyptian Gnostic and Christian literature.

Codex XI.[25] The second tractate in this codex, *A Valentinian Exposition*, is analyzed by Einar Thomassen (in *Muséon* 102). Contrary to the suggestion of other scholars (e.g. E. H. Pagels and J. D. Turner) that *Val. Exp.* belongs to the Western branch of Valentinianism, Thomassen situates the tractate in the Oriental branch, largely on the basis of its lack of a rigid distinction between "spiritual" and "psychic."

Codex XIII.[26] The one extant tractate preserved (relatively intact) in this partial manuscript[27] is *Trimorphic Protennoia* (XIII,*1*). Gesine Robinson (formerly Gesine Schenke) argues (in the Robinson

---

24. No studies of the two tractates in Codex VIII are cited here, but cf. my comments (above) on Sieber's edition of Codex VIII, and the new translation of *Ep. Pet. Phil.* in the revised edition of Hennecke-Schneemelcher, *New Testament Apocrypha*, vol. 1.

25. The one tractate in the severely damaged Codex X, *Marsanes*, has not attracted much attention (understandably enough!).

26. The only material in the severely damaged Codex XII that is not elsewhere attested consists of the unidentified fragments (XII,*3*) edited by Frederik Wisse. See my discussion (above) of Charles Hedrick's edition of *Nag Hammadi Codices XI, XII, XIII*.

27. This material consists of eight leaves torn out of a codex and tucked into the leather covers of Codex VI in antiquity, before burial at the site of discovery near Nag Hammadi.

Festschrift, 37-50) that *Trim. Prot.* reflects a pre-Christian tradition of the descent of Wisdom that also informs the Prologue of the Gospel of John.

I conclude this discussion[28] with the observation that scholarship continues to go on apace, both on Gnosticism in its many facets and on the Coptic Gnostic texts. With respect to the individual tractates discussed here we note in some cases (e.g. *Gos. Truth*) that scholarly opinion is tending to converge, whereas in other cases (e.g. *Gos. Thomas*, *Eugnostos*, and *Apoc. Adam*) a considerable divergence of opinion is to be noted. Of course (fortunately, for some of us), the last word has not yet been pronounced on any of this. The next four years will produce a lot of grist for the mill of the one who will discuss this area at the next congress four years hence.

Select Bibliography

I. Gnosticism (general studies)

Books:

Benelli, G. C. *La gnosi: Il volto oscuro della storia.* (Uomine e religioni 58.) Milano: Mondadori. 1991.

Böhlig, A. *Gnosis und Synkretismus: Gesammelte Aufsätze zur spätantiken Religionsgeschichte.* 2 vols. (WUNT 47-48.) Tübingen: Mohr-Siebeck, 1989.

Churton, T. *The Gnostics.* London: Weidenfeld & Nicolson, 1990.

Couliano, I. *The Tree of Gnosis: Gnostic Mythology from Early Christianity to Modern Nihilism.* San Francisco: HarperCollins, 1992.

Diem, A. *The Gnostic Mystery: A Connection Between Ancient and Modern Mysticism.* Walnut CA: Mt. San Antonio College Press, 1992.

Filoramo, G. *A History of Gnosticism.* Trans. A. Alcock. Oxford: Blackwell, 1990.

Gruenwald, I. *From Apocalypticism to Gnosticism: Studies in Apocalypticism, Merkavah Mysticism and Gnosticism.* (BEATAJ 14.) Frankfurt: Peter Lang, 1988.

---

28. To my knowledge no major studies have appeared on the two singular tractates in the Berlin Gnostic Codex, or those in the Bruce and Askew Codices. But see the individual entries on these tractates, and on Nag Hammadi tractates not mentioned here, in the new *Anchor Bible Dictionary* (referred to above).

Hoeller, S. A. *Jung and the Lost Gospels: Insights into the Dead Sea Scrolls and the Nag Hammadi Library*. Wheaton IL: Theosophical Publishing House, 1989.

Jonas, H. *Gnosis und spätantiker Geist*. I: *Die mythologische Gnosis*. 4th ed. (FRLANT 33.) Göttingen: Vandenhoeck & Ruprecht, 1988.

King, K. *Images of the Feminine in Gnosticism*. (SAC 4.) Philadelphia: Fortress Press, 1988.

Lee, P. J. *Against the Protestant Gnostics*. Oxford: Oxford University Press, 1987.

MacRae, G. W. *Studies in the New Testament and Gnosticism*. (GNS 26.) Ed. D. J. Harrington and S. B. Marrow. Wilmington: Michael Glazier, 1987.

Marcovich, M. *Studies in Graeco-Roman Religions and Gnosticism*. (SGRR 4.) Leiden: Brill, 1988.

Pearson, B. A. *Gnosticism, Judaism, and Egyptian Christianity*. (SAC 5.) Minneapolis: Fortress Press, 1990.

Pearson, B. A. (ed.). *The Future of Early Christianity: Essays in Honor of Helmut Koester*. Minneapolis: Fortress Press, 1991. (articles by R. Cameron, H. Attridge, P. Perkins, E. H. Pagels, and B. A. Pearson.)

Pétrement, S. *A Separate God: The Christian Origins of Gnosticism*. Trans. C. Harrison. San Francisco: HarperSanFrancisco, 1990.

Quispel, G. (ed.). *Gnosis: De derde component van de Europese cultuurtraditie*. Utrecht: H. & S., 1988. (articles by R. v. d. Broek, J. Fossum, G. Quispel, E. v.d. Boer, Th. G. Sinnige, J. Helderman, M. de Groot, et al.)

Rudolph, K. *Die Gnosis: Wesen und Geschichte einer spätantiken Religion*. 3. Aufl., Göttingen: Vandenhoeck & Ruprecht, 1990.

Scopello, M. *Les gnostiques*. (BREF 37.) Paris: Cerf / Montreal: Fides, 1991.

Segal, R. *The Gnostic Jung*. Princeton: Princeton University Press, 1992.

Segelberg, E. *Gnostica - Mandaica - Liturgica* (ed. J. Bergman, J. Hjärpe, P. Ström). (AAU: Historia Religionum 11.) Uppsala: Almqvist & Wiksell, 1990.

Wallis, R. T. and J. Bregman (eds.) *Neoplatonism and Gnosticism*. (Studies in Neoplatonism: Ancient and Modern 6.) Albany NY: State University of New York Press, 1992.

Welburn, A. *The Beginnings of Christianity: Essene Mystery, Gnostic Revelation and the Christian Vision*. Edinburgh: Floris Books, 1991.

Articles:

Beltz, W. "Zum Geschichtsbild der Gnosis." *ZRGG* 40 (1988) 362-66.

Edwards, M. J. "Gnostics and Valentinians in the Church Fathers." *JTS* 40 (1989) 26-47.

Edwards, M. J. "Neglected Texts in the Study of Gnosticism." *JTS* 41 (1990) 26-50.

Jackson, H. M. "The Origin in Ancient Incantatory *Voces Magicae* of Some of the Names in the Sethian Gnostic System." *VC* 43 (1989) 69-79.

Jackson, H. M. "The Seer Nikotheos and His Lost Apocalypse in the Light of Sethian Apocalypses from Nag Hammadi and the Apocalypse of Elchesai." *NovT* 32 (1990) 250-77.

Luttikhuizen, G. P. "The Jewish Factor in the Development of the Gnostic Myth of Origins: Some Observations." *Text and Testimony: Essays on New Testament and Apocryphal Literature in Honour of A. F. J. Klijn* (ed. T. Baarda, A. Hilhorst, G. P. Luttikhuizen, A. S. van der Woude; Kampen: J. H. Kok, 1988) 152-61.

Pearson, B. A. "Use, Authority and Exegesis of Mikra in Gnostic Literature." Ch. 17 in *Mikra: Text, Translation, Reading and Interpretation of the Hebrew Bible in Ancient Judaism and Early Christianity* (ed. M. J. Mulder; CRINT II:1; Assen/Maastricht: Van Gorcum / Philadelphia: Fortress, 1988) 635-52.

Quispel, G. "Gnosticism." *The Coptic Encyclopedia* (New York: Macmillan, 1991) 4:1148-51.

Quispel, G. "Hermes Trismegistus and the Origins of Gnosticism." *VC* 46 (1992) 1-19.

Quispel, G.; Culianu, I. P.; Perkins, P. "Gnosticism." *The Encyclopedia of Religion* (New York: Macmillan, 1987) 5:566-80.

Rudolph, K. "Die Gnosis: Texte und Übersetzungen." *ThR* 55 (1990) 113-52.

Rudolph, K. "Gnosticism." *The Anchor Bible Dictionary* (New York: Doubleday, 1992) 2.1033-40.

II. The Coptic Gnostic Library

Books (translations, editions, etc.):

The Nag Hammadi Library in English. 3rd revised edition, ed. James M. Robinson and Richard Smith. San Francisco: Harper & Row, 1988.

Neutestamentliche Apokryphen in deutscher Übersetzung. I: *Evangelien.* 5. Aufl., hrsg. W. Schneemelcher und E. Hennecke. Tübingen: Mohr-Siebeck, 1987.

New Testament Apocrypha. I: *Gospels and Related Writings.* Rev. ed. W. Schneemelcher, ET ed. R. McL. Wilson. Cambridge: James Clarke & Co. / Louisville KY: Westminster/John Knox Press, 1991.

Charron, R. *Concordance des textes de Nag Hammadi: Le Codex VII.* (BCNH "Concordances" 1.) Québec: Université Laval, 1992.

Hedrick, C. .W. (ed.). *Nag Hammadi Codices XI, XII, XIII.* (NHS 28.) Leiden: Brill, 1990.

Kirchner, D. *Epistula Jacobi apocrypha: Die zweite Schrift aus Nag-Hammadi-Codex I.* (TU 136.) Berlin: Akademie-Verlag, 1989.

Layton, B. *Nag Hammadi Codex II,2-7 together with XIII,2*, Brit. Lib. Or. 4926 (1), and P. Oxy. 1, 654, 655.* 2 vols. (NHS 20-21.) Leiden: Brill, 1989.

Parrott, D. *Nag Hammadi Codices III,3-4 and V,1 with Papyrus Berolinensis 8501,3 and Oxyrhynchus Papyrus 1081: Eugnostos and The Sophia of Jesus Christ.* (NHS 27.) Leiden: Brill, 1991.

Schenke, H.-M. *Das Thomas-Buch (Nag-Hammadi-Codex II,7): Neu heraus-gegeben, übersetzt und erklärt.* (TU 138.) Berlin: Akademie-Verlag, 1989.
Sieber, J. *Nag Hammadi Codex VIII.* (NHS 31.) Leiden: Brill, 1991.
Thomassen, E. et Painchaud, L. *Le traité tripartite (NH I,5).* Texte établi, introduit et commenté par E. Thomassen; traduit par L. Painchaud et E. Thomassen. (BCNH "Textes" 19.) Québec: Université Laval, 1989.
Zandee, J. *The Teachings of Sylvanus (Nag Hammadi Codex VII,4): Text, Transla-tion, Commentary.* Leiden: Nederlands Instituut voor het Nabije Oosten, 1991.

Books (studies):

Dart, J. *The Jesus of Heresy and History: The Discovery and Meaning of the Nag Hammadi Gnostic Library.* San Francisco: Harper & Row, 1988.
Gianotto, C. *La testimonianza veritiera.* (Testi del Vicino Oriente antico: Letteratura egiziana gnostica e cristiana 1.) Brescia: Paideia, 1990.
Goehring, J. E.; Hedrick; C. W., Sanders; J. T.; with H. D. Betz (eds.). *Gnosticism & the Early Christian World: In Honor of James M. Robinson.* (FF 2.) Sonoma: Pole-bridge, 1990. (articles by K. L. King, L. H. Martin, G. Robinson, and B. A. Pear-son.)
Khosroyev, A. L. *Aleksandriyskoye Khristianstvo: Po Dannim Tekstov iz Nag Kham-madi* [with English summary]. Moskva: Nauka. Glavnaya redaktsiya vostochnoy lit-eraturi, 1991.
Koester, H. *Ancient Christian Gospels: Their History and Development.* London: SCM / Philadelphia: Trinity Press International, 1990.
Linder, P.-A. *The Apocalypse of Adam: Nag Hammadi Codex V,5 Considered from its Egyptian Background.* (LSAAR 7.) Ödeshög, 1991. (Lund diss.)
Onuki, T. *Gnosis und Stoa: Eine Untersuchung zum Apokryphon des Johannes.* (NTOA 9.) Freiburg: Universitätsverlag / Göttingen: Vandenhoeck & Ruprecht, 1989.
Trakatellis, D. *The Transcendent God of Eugnostos.* Brookline MA: Holy Cross Or-thodox Press, 1991.
Williams, J. *Biblical Interpretation in the Gnostic Gospel of Truth from Nag Ham-madi.* (SBLDS 79.) Atlanta: Scholars Press, 1988.

Articles (general):

Emmel, S. "Nag Hammadi Library." *The Coptic Encyclopedia* (New York: Macmil-lan, 1991) 6:1771-73.
Edwards, M. J. "New Discoveries and Gnosticism: Some Precautions." *OrChrP* 55 (1989) 257-72.
Myszor, W. "Antonius-Briefe und Nag-Hammadi-Texte." *JAC* 32 (1989) 72-88.
Pearson, B. A. "Nag Hammadi Codices." *The Anchor Bible Dictionary* (New York:

Doubleday, 1992) 4.984-93.
van der Vliet, J. "La *Parrhésie* anticosmique dans la Bibliothèque copte de Nag Hammadi." *Muséon* 105 (1992) 27-43.

Articles (specific tractates):

Baarda, T. "The Sabbath in the Parable of the Shepherd (Evangelium Veritatis 32 18-34)." *NedTT* 41 (1987) 17-28.
Buckley, J. J. "Conceptual Models and Polemical Issues in the Gospel of Philip." *Aufstieg und Niedergang der römischen Welt* II.25: *Religion (Vorkonstantinisches Christentum: Leben und Umwelt Jesu; Neues Testament [Kanonische Schriften und Apokryphen])* 5 (ed. W. Haase; Berlin: De Gruyter, 1988) 4167-94.
Carrol, S. T. "The *Apocalypse of Adam* and Pre-Christian Gnosticism." *VC* 44 (1990) 263-79.
Dehandschutter, B. "L'Epistula Jacobi apocrypha de Nag Hammadi (CG I,2) comme apocryphe néotestamentaire." *ANRW* II.25.6: 4529-50.
Fallon, F. T. and Cameron, R. "The Gospel of Thomas: A Forschungsbericht and Analysis." *ANRW* II.25.6: 4195-4251.
Glazer, B. "The Goddess with a Fiery Breath: The Egyptian Derivation of a Gnostic Mythologoumenon." *NovT* 33 (1991) 92-94.
Hedrick, C. W. "Thomas and the Synoptics: Aiming at a Consensus." *Second Century* 7 (1989/90) 389-56.
Helderman, J. "Das Evangelium Veritatis in der neueren Forschung." *ANRW* II.25.5: 4054-4106.
Ménard, J.-É. "Le traité de Melchisédek de Nag Hammadi." *RevSR* 64 (1990), 235-43.
Neller, K. V. "Diversity in the Gospel of Thomas: Clues for a New Direction?" *Second Century* 7 (1989/90) 1-18.
Painchaud, L. "The Redactions of the Writing Without Title (CG II,5)." *Second Century* 8 (1991) 217-34.
Painchaud, L. "Le sommaire anthropogonique de l'Écrit sans titre (NH II, 117:27-118:2) à la lumière de *1 Co* 15:45-47." *VC* 44 (1990) 382-93.
Parrott, D. M. "Eugnostos and 'All the Philosophers.'" *Religion im Erbe Ägyptens: Beiträge zur spätantiken Religionsgeschichte zu Ehren von Alexander Böhlig* (ed. M. Görg; ÄAT 14; Wiesbaden: O. Harrassowitz, 1988) 153-67.
Parrott, D. M. "The 13 Kingdoms of the Apocalypse of Adam: Origin, Meaning and Significance." *NovT* 31 (1989) 67-87.
Pasquier, A. "Étude de la théologie du nom dans le traité gnostique d'Eugnoste à partir d'un fragment de Valentin." *Muséon* 103 (1990) 205-14.
Patterson, S. J. "Sources, Redaction and *Tendenz* in the *Acts of Peter and the Twelve Apostles* (NH VI,1)." *VC* 45 (1991) 1-17.
Schoedel, W. "A Gnostic Interpretation of the Fall of Jerusalem: The First Apoca-

lypse of James." *NovT* 33 (1991) 153-78.

Sfameni Gasparro, G. "Il 'Vangelo secondo Filippo': rassegna degli studi e proposte di interpretazione." *ANRW* II.25.5: 4107-66.

Siker, J. S. "Gnostic Views on Jews and Christians in the Gospel of Philip." *NovT* 31 (1989) 275-88.

Snodgrass, K. R. "The Gospel of Thomas: A Secondary Gospel." *Second Century* 7 (1989/90) 19-38.

Sumney, J. L. "The Letter of Eugnostos and the Origins of Gnosticism." *NovT* 31 (1989) 172-81.

Thomassen, E. "The Valentinianism of the *Valentinian Exposition* (NHC XI,2)." *Muséon* 102 (1989) 225-36.

Tuckett, C. "Thomas and the Synoptics." *NovT* 30 (1988) 132-57.

Valantasis, R. "Adam's Body: Uncovering Esoteric Traditions in the *Apocryphon of John* and Origen's *Dialogue with Heraclides*." *Second Century* 7 (1989/90) 150-62.

van den Broek, R. "Eugnostos and Aristides on the Ineffable God." *Knowledge of God in the Graeco-Roman World* (ed. R.

van den Broek, T. Baarda and J. Mansfeld; EPRO 112; Leiden: Brill, 1988) 202-18.

van den Broek, R. "Silvanus en de Griekse gnomische traditie." *NedTT* 42 (1988) 126-33.

van der Vliet, J. "Spirit and Prophecy in the *Epistula Iacobi Apocrypha* (NHC I,2)." *VC* 44 (1990) 25-53.

Welburn, A. J. "Iranian Prophetology and the Birth of the Messiah: The Apocalypse of Adam." *ANRW* II.25.6: 4752-94.

Zandee, J. "Origène et *les enseignements de Silvain* (Nag Hammadi Codex VII,4)." *Laval Théologique et Philosophique* 46 (1990) 369-82.

Marguerite Rassart-Debergh

L'ART CHRÉTIEN DU NIL 1988-1992

Je souhaite, avant tout, annoncer la parution des actes du dernier congrès de l'I.A.C.S, édités par le professeur Ries et moi-même (1). Le premier volume est dédié à la mémoire du professeur Atiya, père de l'Encyclopédie Copte [*The Coptic Encyclopedia*], et regroupe les communications des deux sections "Art" et "Archéologie"; il est sorti en juin 1992, juste avant le Ve Congrès de l'IACS. Dans le second, *De la linguistique au gnosticisme*, sont publiés les textes des autres sections et un index de l'ensemble.

J'y avais conçu le rapport *L'art chrétien du Nil 1984-1988* (pp. 3-26) comme une bibliographie aussi exhaustive que faire se pouvait, avec mention des congrès et, sous forme d'appendice, celle des expositions. Le présent rapport diffère quelque peu dans sa présentation, bien que sa conception ait été identique à l'origine : les limites dans le temps et l'espace, la liste des revues dépouillées depuis 1988 et les abréviations y renvoyant restent les mêmes que celles données dans les actes du IVe congrès (pp. 7-9). Mais les quatre années qui se sont écoulées ont connu un très grand nombre de manifestations relatives à l'art copte et la somme des livres et articles atteignait plus de 500 titres; une telle masse de documents ne restait accessible que dans la mesure où elle s'accompagnait de commentaires et de nombreux *indices*; ce rapport devenait, – chose impossible, – un volume en soi. On trouvera donc ici les travaux qui m'ont paru illustrer au mieux les principales tendances de la recherche dans le domaine de l'art copte; je réserve à une autre occasion la publication de l'ensemble des références collationnées. Pour la peinture murale, on trouvera déjà des informations dans la revue *Apelles* (5).

Pour ne pas alourdir inutilement le présent texte, j'ai assigné à chaque titre un numéro auquel je renverrai dans le commentaire. Comme dans le rapport de 1988, la liste des principales publications sera suivie de celle, chronologique, des catalogues d'expositions et des congrès. J'y ajouterai une brève mention des travaux réalisés en Égypte : consolidations et restaurations, découvertes fortuites et fouilles aussi, mais abordées rapidement et uniquement si les objets découverts offrent de l'intérêt pour l'histoire de l'art copte en général.

1. PUBLICATIONS

Plusieurs projets, en cours lors de notre dernier congrès, ont maintenant abouti.

Il s'agit d'abord de la publication d'actes de congrès. Ceux de la rencontre de 1987 sur le thème *Egitto e storia antica* (27) ont paru en 1989.

En 1990, sortaient ceux du IIIe Congrès de l'IACS, - les *Coptic Studies* - publiés sous la direction de Wodek Godlewski (24), ceux du colloque de 1983 sur *Artistes, artisans* (7).

On saluera ensuite la parution d'un travail de longue haleine, les huit volumes de la *Coptic Encyclopedia* (23), que commenta Madame Atyia lors du Ve Congrès de l'IACS. Rappelons que ce projet, né en 1942 d'un "rêve utopique" d'Aziz S. Atiya, fut rendu public lors du premier Congrès de notre association au Caire et qu'il fut officiellement conçu lors du second, à Rome, en 1981. Dix ans plus tard, on peut en voir l'aboutissement.

Enfin, lancé en 1984, le recensement des objets coptes hors d'Égypte est maintenant contenu dans une brochure éditée par les soins de Stephen Emmel. Ouvrage utile s'il en est, cet *International Directory* (46) pourra être complété; dans son compte rendu (*BSAC*, XXXI, 1992, p. 136), R.-G. Coquin suggère d'ailleurs qu'on dresse aussi la liste des collections publiques et privées d'Égypte; l'idée est excellente, mais paraît difficilement réalisable pour les collections privées : dans quelque pays que ce soit, la plupart des collectionneurs tiennent à l'anonymat. Un premier pas pourrait être fait par le dépouillement et le relevé de tous les objets passant dans les ventes publiques; un tel travail implique l'aide active des grandes maisons de vente.

A. *Ouvrages généraux*

En 1990, l'Institut Hollandais du Caire a consacré un ouvrage au titre significatif, *Coptic Art and Culture* (22), à divers aspects de la civilisation copte. Présenté par l'éditeur H. Hondelinck et préfacé par G. Gabra, le livre réunit une série d'articles : P. Grossmann y donne un aperçu de l'architecture chrétienne, P. Van Moorsel s'interroge sur la signification des "saints" de l'Ancien Testament dans la liturgie et l'art copte médiéval, quelques-uns de ses étudiants s'intéressent aux problèmes d'iconographie (G. Van Loon, N. Van Dorn et J. Van der Vliet), aux tissus coptes (Ph. Van 't Hooft), aux icônes enfin (L. Langen, Z. Skalova et J. den Heijer). Ce dernier domaine fait l'objet d'articles dus aux mêmes auteurs dans les volumes 17 et 18 du *Monde Copte*, consacrés à *L'icône copte* (42, 43).

Nos collègues scandinaves disposent maintenant d'une histoire de l'art copte, due à Rostislav Holthoer; bien qu'il s'agisse d'un article (38), il m'a semblé utile de le mentionner tout comme le petit ouvrage dans lequel J. Frösén (34) évoque quelques aspects de l'art chrétien (pp. 8-10 et 20-22). R. Holthoer a en cours d'autres travaux dans ce domaine, notamment une présentation nouvelle des peintures du Deir Abou Hennis.

L'art tardif et chrétien de la vallée du Nil dans les collections russes se trouve mis à l'honneur dans les catalogues sur les arts égyptien ou byzantin, ainsi que par les articles et communications de chercheurs comme St. Y. Bersina, E. Kormycheva, N. Pomerantseva et A. Kakovkine (cf. *infra*).

Enfin, parmi les ouvrages traitant des Coptes, de leur culture ou des moines, on retiendra ceux de Chr. Cannuyer (17) et de L. Regnault (72), qui accordent une place certaine à l'art, montrant ainsi l'intérêt grandissant de l'ensemble du monde savant pour cette culture.

Malgré son titre, le livre de N. Samain (78) ne quitte guère le niveau de la simple compilation, sans note; en outre, il est pourvu d'un apparat critique bibliographique indigent et conçu en dépit de toute règle!

B. *Revues*

Lors de la réunion finale du congrès de Louvain-la-Neuve, fut annoncée la création d'une nouvelle revue, *The Journal of Coptic Studies*; le volume I a vu le jour déjà; dédié à A.I. Elanskaja, il ne comporte aucun article d'art (48); le deuxième, à la mémoire du Père du Bourguet, est sous presse; particulièrement intéressant pour notre domaine de recherches, il est attendu avec impatience.

C'est avec grand plaisir que l'on notera que le *Bulletin de la Société d'Archéologie Copte* a retrouvé un rythme régulier, que sa présentation comme la qualité des planches se sont améliorés; on trouvera la liste des articles traitant d'art copte dans la bibliographie exhaustive.

Le *Bulletin Archéologique d'Alexandrie* a recommencé à paraître; la moitié du n° 44 présente les fouilles de Kom el Dikka (matériel tardif et chrétien), un article sur les stèles de Kom Abou Billou et un aperçu des découvertes récentes à Abou Ménas.

A côté des *Newsletters*, bibliographie de Tito Orlandi pour le domaine copte, à laquelle correspondent les *Nubian Letters* pour la Nubie (avec parfois quelques notices sur l'Égypte chrétienne) et les *Fouilles et travaux* de Gisèle Clerc et Jean Leclant pour l'égyptologie en général (19), ont pris place deux nouvelles revues : le *Bulletin d'Information Archéologique* (14), patronné par l'IFAO et la *Polish Archaeology in the Mediterranean* (68-70), éditée par le "Polish Centre of Mediterranean Archaeology" de l'université de Varsovie. Traitant des recherches en Égypte, le *BIA* qui, comme l'a souligné Nicolas Grimal, ne souhaite en rien concurrencer les *Fouilles et travaux*, mentionne les travaux archéologiques, en réservant une place importante aux restaurations, signale les colloques, conférences, leçons .. qui se sont tenus en Égypte; et publie la traduction ou le texte des nouvelles parues dans les principaux journaux d'Égypte.

La revue polonaise donne des nouvelles de chacun des chantiers et missions à travers le bassin méditerranéen; l'Égypte y a bien entendu sa place; c'est aussi l'occasion d'annoncer des découvertes dès avant la publications des rapports préliminaires.

C. *Monographies*

Nous annoncions, en 1988, la création par l'IFAO d'une série nouvelle, les *Cahiers de la Céramique Égyptienne*; le deuxième volume, d'une qualité scientifique égale à celle du premier, est publié (15), le troisième, sous presse, constituera les actes d'une table ronde organisée à l'IFAO, sous la responsabilité de P. Ballet, en novembre 1990 (cf. *infra*).

Aucun volume n'est encore venu accroître le précieux *Corpus de la peinture murale copte au Moyen Age* de l'abbé Leroy, mais celui de P. Van Moorsel, P. Grossmann et K. Innemée sur Saint-Antoine est sous presse; on se reportera en attendant sa parution aux informations données par les auteurs dans les *Actes* du IVe congrès copte (1).

On soulignait, à ce même congrès, la générosité de la fille de Jean Clédat, Madame Mallet, qui avait offert au Louvre les archives de l'illustre savant : ce geste et ces documents ont suscité un colloque et une exposition à Périgueux à l'automne 1991 (cf. *infra*).

Enfin, comme l'ont bien montré, au cours du dernier congrès de l'IACS, les communications de Fatma Mahmoud et de Gaudat Gabra, les différents volumes du *Catalogue général du Musée Copte* sont en bonne voie. J'espère terminer celui des peintures des Kellia fin 1993; une centaine de peintures sont maintenant restaurées, une bonne partie se trouve déjà dans les réserves du musée; une dernière campagne, durant l'été 1993, devrait y conduire le reste.

Pour terminer, signalons l'ouvrage de Hilde Zaloscer consacré à l'art copte, qui rassemble utilement divers articles de l'auteur (93).

Passons aux nouveautés; on y retrouve les deux tendances qui se dessinaient en 1988 (*Actes*, I, p. 6) : un intérêt de plus en plus grand pour les objets dits "mineurs", par le biais de catalogues, et une double approche de l'art, où l'étude de la technique côtoie celle de l'histoire et de l'esthétique proprement dites.

On constate, en outre, l'attrait qu'exerce une Égypte qui n'est pas celle "des Pharaons", en dehors du domaine purement scientifique. En 1990, A. et E. Chevillat ont consacré un ouvrage aux moines égyptiens et à leur spiritualité (18); deux ans plus tard, Nicole Levallois publiait un livre "d'art" (55) sur les déserts d'Égypte; l'époque chrétienne y trouve sa place avec la nécropole de Khargeh et avec les couvents des Kellia. Aussi, *infra* "Guides généraux".

Des revues de bonne vulgarisation se sont, elles aussi, intéressées à l'Égypte chrétienne : en décembre 1988 *Archéologia* avec *Saint-Antoine et les moines du désert* (79) (préparant l'exposition de Genève) et en mars1990, *Le Monde de la Bible* avec *L'Égypte au début de l'ère chrétienne* (30).

La région alexandrine a été fort à l'honneur; j'ai déjà parlé de la reprise du *B(S)AA*; nos collègues polonais ont également enrichi leur série «Alexandrie» de deux volumes (51, 52). Enfin, sous l'impulsion de Jean Yves Empereur et avec l'appui de l'IFAO, plusieurs chercheurs ont entrepris la publication du matériel tardif et chrétien du si riche musée gréco-romain d'Alexandrie; dans ce but, on envisage la création d'une collection de petits guides (P. Roscam et M.-Fr. Boussac pour les intailles, D. Kassab pour les tanagra). De leur côté, les collègues italiens, à l'initiative de N. Bonacasa, de l'université de Palerme, s'attellent à la continuation du fameux *Repertorio* lancé par Achille Adriani (*infra, p.* ***).

En 1990, le Père Samuel a donné une version anglaise de son guide (en arabe) des églises et monastères depuis Assouan jusqu'au Caire, améliorée encore par l'ajout de références bibliographiques et de plans (84).

La même année, en attendant les publications (sous presse tant du côté français que suisse) des Kellia, une mise au point des connaissances, qui se présente en même temps comme un guide, a été publiée à l'occasion de l'exposition de Genève (*infra*, pp. 00-00); elle avait été préparée par le dossier que dirigea R.-G. Coquin pour *Archéologia* (79).

À côté de nombreux articles sur les collections du Louvre, Dominique Bénazeth a consacré deux volumes aux objets en métal; le premier concerne ceux conservés au Louvre (11), le second (10) ceux trouvés à Tôd entre 1933 et 1986, avec, en *addendum*, la campagne de 1989; on y découvre statuette humaine, animaux, bijoux, vaisselle, lampes d'époque copte (pp. 16-19, 22-23, 26- 28, 32, 36-39).

Plusieurs ouvrages, centrés surtout sur les textiles coptes, ont vu le jour ou sont en cours d'impression. Certains ont pour centre d'intérêt un thème précis, d'autres une collection.

Claudia Nauerth a redonné sous la forme d'un fascicule indépendant, le texte d'un article sur l'iconographie d'Héracles (64) et a publié les tissus conservés à Trèves (65).

Dans ses *Tissus coptes*, Marie-Hélène Rutschowscaya retrace une histoire des textiles d'Égypte (77). Partant de la riche collection du Louvre, dont elle rappelle l'origine, mais puisant ses comparaisons dans maints autres musées, elle évoque à l'aide de dessins très clairs les différentes techniques, mentionne les matériaux, énumère les thèmes inspirés de l'antiquité tardive ou du christianisme; ce superbe livre est abondamment illustré en couleurs.

La publication d'Annemarie Stauffer repose sur son travail de fin d'études universitaires; le catalogue de 99 tissus de la Fondation Abegg est accompagné de grands chapitres analoguement conçus : historique des fouilles, techniques, matériaux, thèmes, avec dans son chef un intérêt particulier pour l'apport du Proche-Orient (82).

Virpi Huhtala a, dans le même but, présenté les textiles du Musée National de Finlande (40) et Alexandra Lorquin a fait connaître ceux conservés au Musée de Cluny, à Paris; ce dernier volume (56) consacre une étude détaillée à plus de 150 tissus coptes et à une vingtaine d'islamiques, jusqu'alors inédits; les aspects techniques, les diverses utilisations font l'objet d'une particulière attention de la part de l'auteur; j'ai aussi beaucoup apprécié les nombreux dessins qui les illustrent et les tableaux montrant les variantes thématiques; c'est, à mon sens, un des ouvrages les plus novateurs dans le domaine.

En Allemagne, la publication de travaux de fin d'études universitaires a donné le jour à une nouvelle collection, les *ASKÄ*, éditée par Martin Krause (6) ; deux volumes sont déjà sortis de presse. Caecilia Wietheger traite, – essentiellement au départ des inscriptions mais sans oublier les peintures, – de l'histoire et de la vie du couvent de Saint-Jérémie à Saqqara (91) De son côté, Kristina Urbania-Walczak donne une bonne image du culte marial en Égypte, et réinterprête une peinture de la "chapelle de la Paix" à El-Bagawat (89).

La dissertation de Thelma Thomas sur les niches sculptées d'Oxyrhynchus et d'Héracléopolis Magna, déposée en décembre 1989 à l'Institute of Fine Arts de l'Université de New York, fera l'objet d'une publication revue et corrigée dans les prochaines années (86).

En 1988, Marie-Hélène Rutschowscaya annonçait (*Actes,* pp. 56-62, sp. 56) la prochaine publication des peintures conservées au Musée du Louvre; ce catalogue vient de paraître illustré de photos et de dessins; il présente peintures pariétales, sur bois et sur toile de lin (76).

Le volume qu'Ulrike Horak vient de consacrer aux papyri (39) permet d'établir d'étonnants rapprochements entre les sujets qui les décorent et l'iconographie des tissus et des peintures coptes.

Quel que soit le sujet de ces publications, l'aspect technique des productions a été longuement envisagé (voyez aussi *infra*, pp. 00-00).

Enfin, la revue *Le Monde Copte* a consacré son volume 17 au *Caire Copte* (16), les numéros 18 et 19 à *L'icône copte* (des origines à l'époque contemporaine) (42, 43) et le volume double 20-21 au *Monachisme*.

Nous mentionnerons pour terminer des ouvrages en cours de publication; deux volumes de Laszlo Török, *Coptic Antiquities*, sont à l'impression à Rome (88); Loretta della Francia attend la sortie de son catalogue des tissus coptes conservés au Musée égyptologique de Florence et Marianne Erikson prépare *Textiles in Egypt 200-1500 A.D.* Sont également attendus, dans le cadre du *Repertorio d'Arte dell'Egitto Greco-Romano*, serie B *Pittura, Ritratti di mummie* IV par K. Parlasca; serie C *Architettura*, III par P. Pensabene; plusieurs nouveaux volumes sont prévus sur les portraits romains (par N. Bonacasa), les lampes à huile décorées (par E. Joly), les ivoires et les os (par R.M. Carra Bonacasa).

D. *Catalogues et guides généraux*

Signe d'un intérêt grandissant pour les époques tardive et chrétienne, les grands musées leur accordent de plus en plus de place dans leurs catalogues généraux, quand ils ne leur consacrent pas un volume entier comme l'a fait le Musée du Louvre pour les bois, les tissus, les peintures, les métaux coptes (77, 76, 11). Il n'est guère possible de citer tous ces catalogues ici; mentionnons simplement qu'en Allemagne, Arne Effenberger et H.G. Severin donnent une large part au copte dans leur ouvrage sur l'art chrétien des "Staatliche Museen" de Berlin (Berlin-Dahlem et Bodenmuseum) (27); qu'en Belgique, à Morlanwelz, plus d'un dixième du "choix d'oeuvres" du Musée Royal de Mariemont sont des objets coptes (31); qu'en Italie, dans chacun des trois volumes sur le musée égyptologique de Turin qu'a patronnés A.-M. Donadoni, l'Égypte chrétienne est présente (60-62); qu'aux Pays-Bas, dans son récent catalogue de l'Allard Pierson à Amsterdam, R. Scheurleer consacre un chapitre aux Coptes (80).

Un phénomène analogue se remarque au sein des guides de voyage. Pour ne donner que deux exemples, E. Ambros décrit, dans son *Égypte* (3), les couvents du Ouadi Natroun (pp. 40-43), le Vieux Caire (pp. 68-69) et le Musée Copte (pp. 83-85), les couvents de Sohag (p. 133), de Saint-Siméon (pp. 194-195) et de Sainte-Catherine (pp. 213-214); le choix est partiellement différent dans *Le grand guide de l'Égypte* (36) publié chez Gallimard : généralités sur l'Égypte chrétienne (pp. 41-54), Le Caire copte (pp. 144-145), Alexandrie (p. 217), Saint-Ménas (pp. 227-228), couvents du Ouadi Natroun (p. 233), de Sainte-Catherine (pp. 244-245), de Saint-Paul et de Saint-Antoine (pp. 255), nécropole d'El Bagawat (p. 265).

De même, on constate que plusieurs byzantinistes s'attardent de manière plus précise et complète à l'Égypte chrétienne : ainsi dans son livre sur les icônes (12) H. Belting (aux pages 103-116 et *passim*), ou A. et H. Stierlin dans leur *Orient byzantin* (83).

Ce ne sont là que quelques exemples choisis mais significatifs.

Liste alphabétique (avec abréviations)

1. *Actes du IVe Congrès Copte. Louvain-la-Neuve, 5-10 septembre 1988*, édités par M. RASSART-DEBERGH et J. RIES, I. *Art et Archéologie*, Louvain-la-Neuve, 1992 (dorénavant cité : *Actes*).
2. *Ägyptisches Museum. Staatliche Museen zu Berlin, Stiftung Preussischer Kulturbesitz*, Berlin, 1991, *passim*.
3. E. AMBROS, *Égypte*, s.l., 1992, *passim* (*Nelles Guides*).
4. J. ANQUETIL, *Routes de la soie. Vingt-deux siècles d'Histoire. Des déserts de l'Asie aux rives du monde occidental*, s.l., 1992, pp. 83-88 (tisserands coptes) et 90-96
5. *Apelles. Bulletin de l'Association internationale pour la peinture murale antique*, I, *Bibliographie 1985-1990 et compléments d'années antérieures*, Avenches, 1992, sp. pp. 26. 33 et 64-65.
6. *Arbeiten zum spätantiken und koptischen Ägypten*, édités par M. KRAUSE, Altenberge.
7. *Artistes, artisans et production artistique au Moyen Age. Colloque international. CNRS . Université de Rennes II - Haute- Bretagne, 2-6 mai 1983*, organisé et édité par X. BARRAL I ALTET, III, Paris, 1990, pp. 211-221.
8. S. AUFRERE, J.-Cl. GOLVIN, J.-G. GOYON, *L'Égypte restituée. Sites et temples de Haute Égypte (1650 av. J.-C. - 300 ap. J.-C.)*, Paris, 1991, *passim*.
9. D. BÉNAZETH, C. METZGER, J. DURANT, *Éclosion de l'art chrétien*, Paris, 1989, *passim* (*Louvre, promenades*, 1)
10. D. BÉNAZETH, *Tod. Les objets de métal*, San Antonio, 1991, *passim*.
11. D. BÉNAZETH, *Musée du Louvre. Département des Antiquités Égyptiennes. L'art du métal au début de l'ère chrétienne*, Paris, 1992, *passim*.
12. H. BELTING, *Bild und Kult. Eine Geschichte des Bildes von dem Zeitalter der Kunst*, Munich, 1990, sp. pp. 103-116.
13. A. K. BOWMAN, *Egypt after the Pharaohs, 332 BC-AD 642, from Alexander to the Arab Conquest*, Oxford, 1990, *passim* .
14. *Bulletin d'Information Archéologique*, sous la direction de N. GRIMAL, Le Caire, 4 fascicules, 1990-1992 (dorénavant cité : *BIA*).
15. *CCE*, 2, Le Caire, 1991.
16. *Le Caire copte*, Limoges, 1990 (*MC*, 17).
17. Chr. CANNUYER, *Les Coptes*, Turnhout, 1990, *passim* (*Fils d'Abraham*).
18. A. et E. CHEVILLAT, introduction de M.M. DAVY, *Moines du désert d'Égypte*, Lyon, 1990.
19. G. CLERC et J. LECLANT, *Fouilles et travaux en Égypte et au Soudan* dans *Orientalia*, Rome, *passim* .
20. *Coptic and Nubian Pottery. International Workshop, Nieborów, August 29-31, 1988, Part I*, édité par W. GODLEWSKI, Varsovie, 1990 (*National Museum in*

Warsaw, Occasional Paper, N° 1)

21. *Coptic and Nubian Pottery. International Workshop, Nieborów, August 29-31, 1988, Part II*, édité par W. GODLEWSKI, Varsovie, 1991 (*National Museum in Warsaw, Occasional Paper*, N° 2).

22. *Coptic Art and Culture*, édité par H. HONDELINCK, Le Caire, 1990 (dorénavant cité : *Coptic Art*).

23. *The Coptic Encyclopedia*, édité par A.S. ATIYA, 8 voll., New York-Toronto-Oxford, 1991, *passim*.

24. *Coptic Studies. Acts of the Third International Congress of Coptic Studies, Warsaw, 20-25 August 1984*, édité par W. GODLEWSKI, Varsovie, 1990 (dorénavant cité : *Coptic Studies*).

25. Fr. DUNAND, J.-L. HEIM, N. HENEIN, R. LICHTENBERG, *et alii, Douch I. La nécropole. Exploration archéologique; monographie des tombes 1 à 72. Structures sociales, économiques, religieuses de l'époque romaine*, Le Caire, 1992, *passim* (*Documents de fouilles*, XXVI).

26. D. N. EDWARDS, *Archaeology and Settlement in Upper Nubia in the 1st Millenium A.D.*, Oxford, 1989, *passim* (*BAR International Series*, 537).

27. A. EFFENBERGER, H.-G. SEVERIN, *Das Museum für Spätantike und Byzantinische Kunst*, Berlin, 1992, *passim* .

28. *Egitto e storia antica dall'Ellenismo all'età araba. Bilancio di un confronto. Atti del colloquio internazionale , Bologne, 31 agosto . 2 settembre 1987*, édités par L. CRISCUOLO et G. GERACI, Bologne, 1989, pp. 88-103, 291-299, 469-473.

29. *Egypt and Africa. Nubia from Prehistory to Islam*, édité par W. V. DAVIES, Londres, 1991, *passim*.

30. *L'Égypte au début de l'ère chrétienne = Le monde de la Bible. Archéologie et histoire*, 63, mars-avril 1990, sp. p. 1-39.

31. *Égypte* [au Musée Royal de Mariemont], *Choix d'Oeuvres*, choix et texte de Cl. DERRIKS, Morlanwelz, 1990, n° 42-50.

32. *Egyptian-Netherlands Cooperation in Coptic Art Preservation 1991-1995*, Leiden, *passim*.

33. S. P. ELLIS, *Graeco-Roman Egypt*, Buckinghamshire, 1992, *passim* (*Shire Egyptology Series*, 17).

34. J. FRÖSÉN, *Brev från antiken. Mumiekartonnager och papyri*, Stockholm, 1990, *passim* (*Medelhavsmuseet*, Skrifter ,15).

35. P. M. GARTKIEWICZ, *Dongola 2 : The Cathedral in Old Dongola and Its Antecedents*, Varsovie, 1990, *passim* (*Nubia*, I).

36. *Le grand guide de l'Égypte*, traduit de l'anglais, Paris, 1992, pp. 41-54, 144-145, 217, 227-228, 233, 244-245; 255, 265 (*Bibliothèque du voyageur*).

37. P. GROSSMANN, *Abu Mina I. Die Gruftkirche und die Gruft*, Mayence, 1989, *passim* (*Archäologische Veröffentlichungen*, 44).

38. R. HOLTHOER, *Kopterna och deras konst-nationellt eller provinsialbysantinsk*

= *Bysans och Norden. Figura Acta Universitatis Uppsaliensis*, N.S. 23, Uppsala, 1989, pp. 167. 190.

39. U. HORAK, *Illuminierte Papyri Pergamente und Papiere* I, Vienne, 1992, (*Pegasus Oriens*, 1).

40. V. HUHTALA, *Koptilainen tekstiilikokoelma Suomen Kansallismuseossa*, Helsinki, 1988.

41. V. HUHTALA, *Koptien Egypti (Egypt of the Copts)* dans *Egyptiajatuksia ihmisestä ja historiasta*, Helsinki, 1989 (l'article traite de la vie des coptes en général, mais l'art y est évoqué).

42. *L'icône Copte. I. A travers les âges*, Limoges, 1990, *passim (MC*, 18).

43. *L'icône Copte. II. L'iconographie copte contemporaine*, Limoges, 1991, *passim (MC*, 19).

44. K. C. INNEMÉE, *Ecclesiastical Dress in the Medieval Near East*, Leyde-New York-Cologne, 1992, *passim (Studies in Textile and Costume History*, I).

45. *Intellectual Heritage of Egypt. Studies presented to Laszlo Kakosy by Friends and Colleagues on the Occasion of His 60th Birthday*, Budapest, 1992 (*Studia Aegyptiaca*, XIV) (plusieurs articles intéressent notre domaine, ainsi F. De Salvia, *Horo sui coccodrilli nella Roma costantiniana*, pp. 509-518, P. Grossmann, *Kirchenruine von Sallal*, pp. 235- 244 et S. Donadoni, *Un relievo con santo cavaliere*, pp. 117-118).

46. *An International Directory of Institutions holding Collections of Coptic Antiquities outside of Egypt*, édité par St. EMMEL, Rome, 1990.

47. *Itinéraires d'Égypte. Mélanges offerts au père Maurice Martin s.j.*, réunis par Ch. DÉCOBERT, Le Caire, 1992, *passim (BdE*, 107).

48. *JCoptS*, founded by the International Association for Coptic Studies, I. *To A. I. Elanskaja*, Louvain, 1990.

49. A. KAKOVKINE, *La collection copte de l'Ermitage* dans *L'histoire de l'Ermitage et de ses collections*, Leningrad, 1989, sp. pp. 93-94.

50. J. KAMIL, *Coptic Egypt. History and Guide*, Revised Edition, Le Caire, 1990, *passim* et sp. "Coptic Art", pp. 61-73.

51. Z. KISS, *Les ampoules de saint Ménas découvertes à Kôm el-Dikka (1961-1981)*, Varsovie, 1989 (*Alexandrie*, V).

52. Z. KISS, *Sculptures des fouilles polonaises à Kôm el-Dikka (1960-1982)*, Varsovie, 1988, *passim (Alexandrie*, IV).

53. *Life in a Multi-cultural Society : Egypt from Cambyses to Constantine and Beyond*, Chicago, 1991 (*SAOC*, 51), *passim* = *Acts of the Fourth International Congress of Demotists, The Oriental Institute, The University of Chicago, September 4-8, 1990*

54. D. LE FUR, M.-H. RUTSCHOWSCAYA, A. DESPRAIRIES, P. TREMBLAY, *Les pigments dans la peinture copte* dans *Conservation . restauration des biens culturels*, décembre 1990, pp. 45-50.

55. N. LEVALLOIS, *Les déserts d'Égypte*, Paris, 1992, *passim*.

56. A. LORQUIN, *Les tissus coptes au Musée national du Moyen Age, Thermes de Cluny*, Paris, 1992.

57. *Marina El Alamein*, I *Archaeological Background and Conservation Problems*; *the Polish-Egyptian Preservation Mission at Marina 1988; the Polish Excavation Mission at Marina 1987-1989*, Varsovie, 1991, *passim* (dorénavant cité : *Marina El Alamein*).

58. *Mélanges Antoine Guillaumont. Contributions à l'étude des christianismes orientaux* (avec une bibliographie du dédicataire), Genève, 1988, *passim* (*Les Cahiers de l'Orientalisme*, XX).

59. *Musée Égyptien de Berlin*, Berlin, 1989, *passim*.

60. *Musée Égyptien de Turin. Civilisation des Égyptiens*, sous la direction de A.M. DONADONI-ROVERI, I *La vie quotidienne*, Turin, 1988, pp. 102-103, 204-208, 211-217.

61. *Musée Égyptien de Turin. Civilisation des Égyptiens*, sous la direction de A.M. DONADONI-ROVERI, II *Les croyances religieuses*, Turin, 1988, pp. 226-237 et 238-245.

62. *Musée Égyptien de Turin. Civilisation des Égyptiens*, sous la direction de A.M. DONADONI-ROVERI, III. *Les arts de la célébration*, Turin, 1989, pp. 180-185.

63. *The National Museum in Warsaw. Painting*, Varsovie, 1990, n° 1-10.

64. Cl. NAUERTH, *Herakles. Ikonographische Vorarbeiten zu mythologischen Themen der koptischen Kunst*, Heidelberg, 1989 (*DBAT*, Beiheft 8).

65. Cl. NAUERTH, mit beiträgen von D. AHRENS, B. BORKOPP, S. SCHALICKE, *Die koptischen Textilien der Sammlung Wilhelm Rautenstrauch im Staatlichen Museum Simeonstift Trier*, Trèves, 1992.

66. *Nubica I/II (1987-1988)*, édité par P. SCHOLZ et C.D.G. MÜLLER, Cologne, 1990, *passim*.

67. *Orbis Aethiopicus. Studia in honorem Stanislaus Chojnacki natali septuagesimo quinto dicata, septuagesimo septimo oblata*, ed. P. SCHOLZ cum collaboratione R. Pankhurst et W. Witakowski, Albstadt, 1992, *passim* (= *Bibliotheca nubica* 3, 1990) (avec des informations sur Naqloun par J. Dobrowolski, sur Faras par W. Godlewski et M. Martens et une étude icononographique sur "l'Entrée à Jérusalem" par P. Scholz).

68. *Polish Archaeology in the Mediterranean 1988-1989*, édité par W. A. DASZEWSKI et M. GAWLIKOWSKI, Varsovie, 1990, *passim* (dorénavant cité : *PAM*, I).

69. *Polish Archaeology in the Mediterranean, II. Reports 1989-1990*, édité par W. A. DASZEWSKI et M. GAWLIKOWSKI, Varsovie, 1991, *passim* (dorénavant cité : *PAM*, II).

70. *Polish Archaeology in the Mediterranean, III Reports 1991*, édité par W. A.

DASZEWSKI et M. GAWLIKOWSKI, Varsovie, 1992, *passim* (dorénavant cité : *PAM*, III).

71. K.-H. PRIESE, *Das Gold von Meroe*, Berlin, 1992, *passim*.
72. L. RÉGNAULT, *La vie quotidienne des Pères du désert en Égypte au IVe siècle*, Paris, 1990, *passim*.
73. *Report from El Ashmunein. Polish-Egyptian Archaeological and Preservation Mission at El Ashmunein 1988*, Varsovie, 1991, *passim*.
74. M.-H. RUTSCHOWSCAYA, *L'art copte* dans *Le Louvre. Trésors du plus grand musée du monde*, Paris, 1991, pp. 134-135.
75. M.-H. RUTSCHOWSCAYA, *L'Égypte copte* dans *Le Louvre, les Antiquités Égyptiennes*, Paris, 1990, pp. 87-95.
76. M.-H. RUTSCHOWSCAYA, *Musée du Louvre, Département des Antiquités Égyptiennes. La peinture copte*, Paris, 1992.
77. M.-H. RUTSCHOWSKAYA, *Tissus coptes*, Paris, 1990.
78. N. SAMAIN, *L'Égypte pharaonique à travers les Coptes*, s. l., 1989, *passim*.
79. *Saint-Antoine et les moines du désert. Les moines du désert des Kellia* = DosHA, 133, décembre1988.
80. R. A. L. SCHEURLEER, *Egypte, geschenk van de Nijl*, Amsterdam, 1992, sp. *De Kopten*, pp. 191-200.
81. G. S. SCRON, *Otecestvennye publikatsil po koptologii i greko- rimskomu Egiptu* (= *National publications in Coptology and Graeco-Roman Egypt*), Leningrad, 1989.
82. A. STAUFFER, *Spätantike und koptische Wirkereien. Untersuchungen zur ikonographischen Tradition in spätantiken und frühmittelalterlichen Textilwerkstätten*, Berne-Berlin..., 1992.
83. A. et H. STIERLIN, *Orient byzantin. De Constantinople à l'Arménie et de Syrie en Éthiopie*, Fribourg, 1991, pp. 112-115 (L'Art antique du Proche-Orient).
84. Samwil al-SYRIANI et BADI' HABIB, *Guide to Ancient Coptic Churches and Monasteries in Upper Egypt*, [Le Caire], 1990.
85. *Tesserae. Festschrift für Josef Engelmann* = JAC Ergängzungsband 18, 1991, *passim*.
86. Th. K. THOMAS, *Niche Decorations from the Tombs of Byzantine Egypt (Heracleopolis Magna and Oxyrhynchus, A.D. 300. 500)* : *Visions of the Afterlife*, Dissertation New York University 1990, 2 voll. publiés par UMI, Ann Arbor, 1993.
87. *Torino alla scoperta della civiltà del Nilo* = AAP, 79, settembre 1991, *passim*.
88. L. TÖRÖK, *Coptic Antiquities*, I et II, Rome, sous presse (*Monumenta antiquitatis extra fines Hungariae reperta*, 2 et 3).
89. K. URBANIAK-WALCZAK, *Die "conceptio per aurem". Berücksichtigung der Malereien in El-Bagawat*, Altenberge, 1992, *passim* (ASKÄ, 2).
90. K. WEITZMANN et G. GALAVARIS, *The Monastery of Saint Catherine at Mount Sinai, the Illuminated Manuscripts*, I. *From the Ninth to the Twelfth Cen-*

tury, Princeton, 1991, *passim*.
91. C. WIETHEGER, *Das Jeremias-Kloster zu Saqqara unter besonderer Berücksichtigung der Inschriften*, Altenberge, 1992, *passim* (*ASKÄ*, 1).
92. L. WILCKENS, *Die textilen Künste von der Spätantike bis um 1500*, Munich, 1991, *passim* .
93. H. ZALOSCER, *Zur Genese der koptische Kunst*, 1991.

2. EXPOSITIONS

Elles ont été relativement nombreuses et trois d'entre elles se tinrent aux États-Unis. L'exposition *"Cleopatra's Egypt"* venait à peine de quitter les États Unis pour l'Europe, que s'ouvrait, à Providence, au "Museum of Art, Rhode Island School of Design", celle consacrée à l'Égypte postpharaonique; *Beyond the Pharaohs* se tint ensuite (du 21 mai au 16 juillet) à Baltimore, à la "Walters Gallery"; annoncée par l'un des organisateurs, G. Vikan, dans *BulWAG* de mai 1989 (pp. 1-4), elle connut un tel succès que le volume qu'édita F. Friedman fut épuisé avant même la fin de l'exposition; une réédition serait souhaitable !

Le catalogue proprement dit (près de 200 pièces) est d'un grand intérêt car il fait connaître des objets peu connus et dont on avait parfois perdu trace; en outre, l'ouvrage contient sous la plume de Fl. Friedman ("Ancient Egyptian Religion" et "Pharaonic Themes"), L. Lesko ("Christianity" et "Monasticism in Egypt"), Th. K. Thomas ("An Introduction to the Sculpture of Late Roman and Early Byzantine Egypt"), A. Cognoscová ("Textiles"), S. Auth ("Pottery and Glass"), G. Vikan ("The Minor Arts of Late Antique Egypt : from Relics to Icons"), P. Grossmann ("Early Christian Architecture in the Nile Valley"), B. A. Pearson et L. S. B. Maccoull ("Greek and Coptic Manuscripts") des considérations générales replaçant les objets dans un contexte plus général. Peu après, *Art and Holy Powers* se tint successivement à Urbana (au "Krannert Art Museum of the University of Illinois at Urbana-Champaign", du 25 août au 1er octobre 1989) et à Ann Arbor (au "Kelsey Museum of Archaeology of the University of Michigan in Ann Arbor", du 27 octobre 1989 au 29 avril 1990); son but, parfaitement atteint, était de retracer la vie quotidienne des chrétiens des IIIe-VIIe siècles.

J'aimerais enfin combler un oubli (*Actes*, pp. 25-26) : en 1986, une exposition a eu lieu au Musée de Newark (New Jersey), avec un catalogue rédigé par Susan H. Auth; on peut y admirer des pièces de qualité parmi lesquelles un beau saint Georges peint sur bois (icône ou coffret) : *Coptic Art of Ancient Egypt. Treasures from the Nadler Collection and the Newark Museum, May 30-November 30, 1986.*

On distinguera au sein des expositions européennes, celles relatives à l'Égypte en général, qui faisaient une place plus ou moins grande aux objets tardifs et coptes, et celles dont but était de mettre en lumière l'un ou l'autre aspect de l'Égypte chrétienne.

Parmi les premières, on notera les manifestations organisées par de nombreuses villes françaises à l'occasion du bicentenaire de Champollion; dans l'évocation de la carrière du grand homme, on ne manqua pas de souligner le rôle de la culture copte dans ses découvertes. Ainsi, dans le catalogue de la grande exposition itinérante "Mémoires d'Égypte" qui se déplaça même à Berlin, M.-H. Rutschowscaya insista-t-elle sur cet aspect. En outre, la plupart des musées français eurent à coeur d'organiser la présentation de leurs collections sans négliger la période copte.

Comme toujours, ce sont les tissus coptes qui sont à l'origine de la plupart des autres expositions; l'explication est simple et multiple : chaque musée en possède, les collections privées, souvent inédites, sont nombreuses, le matériel lui-même, une fois restauré et convenablement présenté, est particulièrement parlant.

L'exposition qui se tint à Genève durant l'hiver 1989-1990 fait exception à cette règle : des peintures et des céramiques provenant des Kellia y ont été présentées, replacées dans leurs cadres historique et archéologique; matériel, maquettes, photos, reconstitution grandeur nature d'un oratoire monacal permettaient de se faire une idée de la vie dans un ermitage des VIe-VIIe s.

D'autres encore, dont le souvenir n'a pas toujours été perpétué par un catalogue, furent organisées autour de la personnalité de grands égyptologues; rappelons qu'en octobre 1990, Strasbourg célébrait le Chanoine Etienne Drioton par deux journées de communications et une petite exposition, où son rôle de coptologue était évoqué.

Quelques mois plus tard, Périgueux rendait hommage à un autre grand
savant, ami de l'Égypte, Jean Clédat, par toute une série de manifestations : une rue porte maintenant son nom, une exposition avec catalogue aux nombreux inédits et un colloque furent organisés avec l'aide
du Louvre et de l'Association Francophone de Coptologie.

Liste chronologique

Cleopatra's Egypt. Age of the Ptolemies, [New York], The Brooklyn Museum, 1988,
    passim ("Brooklyn Museum, October 7, 1988-January 2, 1989; "The Detroit In-
    stitute of Art", February 14-April 30, 1989"; "Kunsthalle der Hypo-
    Kulturstiftung" de Munich enfin, du 8 juin au 10 septembre 1989).
P. BICHLER (ed.), *Schallaburg 1989 9. Juni bis 15. Oktober*, *Antike Koptische Tex-
    tilien aus Österreichischem Privatbesitz*, Vienne, 1989 (= *Katalog des NO Lan-
    desmuseums*, Neue Folge, 233).
Fl. D. FRIEDMAN (ed.), *Beyond the Pharaohs. Egypt and the Copts in the 2nd to
    7th Centuries A.D.*, Providence, Museum of Art. Rhode Island School of De-
    sign,1989, *passim*.
E. D. MAGUIRE, H. P. MAGUIRE, M.J. DUNCAN-FLOWERS (ed.), *Art and Holy
    Powers in the Early Christian House*, Urbana, 1989, *passim*.
*Les Kellia. Ermitages coptes en Basse-Égypte. Genève, Musée d'Art et d'Histoire,
    12 octobre 1989 - 7 janvier 1990*, Genève, 1989.
*Égypte-Égypte. Chefs-d'oeuvre de tous les temps. Paris, 16 juillet 1989-14 janvier
    1990*, avec un chapitre consacré à l'Égypte gréco-romaine par M. REDDÉ et à
    l'Égypte copte par D. BÉNAZETH et G. GABRA.
Mémoires d'Égypte, Strasbourg, Paris, Berlin, 1990, sp. : "Champollion et les études
    coptes" par M.-H. Rutschowscaya, pp. 30-35, *passim*.
"De l'Égypte pharaonique à l'Égypte chrétienne", Musée de Guéret, 3 mars - 30
    avril 1990", *passim* (j'ignore si le catalogue annoncé a bien été publié).
"L'Égypte à Colmar" au Museum d'Histoire Naturelle de Colmar du 15 juin au 1er
    octobre 1990 (un catalogue de la collection égyptienne est en cours, rédigé par
    Cl. TRAUNECKER pour l'Égypte tardive, par A. SCHWEITZER et M. RAS-
    SART-DEBERGH pour les objets d'Égypte romaine et chrétienne).
Ch. BONNET (éd.), *Kerma, royaume de Nubie. L'antiquité africaine au temps des
    pharaons. Exposition organisée au Musée d'art et d'histoire, Genève, 14 juin-25
    novembre 1990*, Genève, 1990, *passim*.
Exposition papyrologique (avec quelques objets coptes) durant l'été 1990 au "Muse-
    um of Mediterranean Archaeology" de Stockholm; à cette occasion, un volume
    intitulé "Letters from the Antique World" fut édité : *supra* J. FRÖSÉN, *Brev från
    antiken*, *passim*.

"Voyage en Égypte", Menton, Musée de la Préhistoire régionale, 16 septembre-29 octobre 1990; le catalogue, réalisé par R.F. Galliano et la "Société des Amis de l'Orient" s'intitule : *Voyage en Égypte, Exposition égyptologique, Musée de la Préhistoire régionale, Menton, 4 août-29 octobre 1990*, Menton, 1990, *passim*.

Exposition au "centre Drioton" et à la Bibliothèque Nationale et Universitaire, en octobre 1990, à l'occasion des Journées d'études en hommage à Étienne Drioton (1889-1961) : "L'Égyptologie et ses publics".

Götter, Gräber & Grotesken. Tonfiguren aus dem Alltagsleben im römischen Ägypten. Museum für Kunst und Gewerbe Hamburg, 15. März bis 12. Mai 1991, Glinde, 1991, *passim*.

Van Nijl tot Schelde. Du Nil à l'Escaut, BBL, 5 april-9 juni 1991, 5 avril-9 juin 1991, [Bruxelles, 1991], les n° 337-367 concernent l'Égypte tardive et chrétienne.

Dans les pas de Jean Clédat: "l'Égypte en Périgord", Musée du Périgord, Paris-Louvain, 1991, *passim (Cahiers de la Bibliothèque Copte, 7)*.

A. STAUFFER, *Die mittelalterlichen Textilien von St. Servatius in Maastricht*, Riggisberg, 1991; les n° 28, 32, 33 proviennent d'Égypte (*Schriften der Abegg-Stiftung Riggisberg*, VIII).

M. MARTINIANI-REBER, avec coll. de Cl. RITSCHARD, G. CORNU, B. RASTER, *Tissus coptes. Musée d'Art et d'Histoire de Genève*, 2 voll., Genève, 1991.

M. CUOGHI COSTANTINI et J. SILVESTRI (ed.), *Capolavori restaurati dell'arte tessile*, Ferrare, 1991, avec un important chapitre sur les tissus antiques provenant souvent d'Égypte : M. FLURY LEMBERG, *La conservazione dei tessuti antichi*, pp. 21-86, *passim*.

A. STAUFFER, *Textiles d'Égypte de la collection Bouvier. Antiquité tardive, période copte, premiers temps de l'Islam. Textilien aus Ägypten aus der Sammlung Bouvier...*, Berne, 1991, avec une contribution de A. SCHMIDT- COLINET, *Deux carrés entrelacés inscrits dans un cercle. De la signification d'un ornement géométrique*, pp. 21-34, *passim*.

États du lin. Musée d'Art et d'Industrie de Roubais, Roubais, 1992 avec un chapitre sur l'Égypte chrétienne par M. H. RUTSCHOWSCAYA, *Le textile dans l'Égypte copte*, pp. 36-61.

"Textiles précieux, beauté fragile. Conservation et reconstitution 1990-1992"; Musée de la Fondation Abbeg, 3 mai-1er novembre 1992, passim (je n'en avais pas encore consulté le catalogue au moment de rentrer ce texte).

Souvenirs de voyages. Autographes et dessins français du XIXe siècle. 99e exposition du cabinet des dessins, Musée du Louvre, 27 février-18 mai 1992, Paris, 1992 : travaux de J. Clédat, n° 76-78, sp. 77 relatif à Baouit.

Byzance. L'art byzantin dans les collections publiques françaises. Musée du Louvre, 3 novembre 1992-1er février 1993, Paris, 1992, *passim*.

3. CONGRÈS

Chaque année a connu un ou plusieurs congrès, où l'Égypte a tenu une place plus ou moins importante; les textes de ces réunions scientifiques étant souvent publiés avec retard, j'ai cru utile de mentionner le titre des communications relatives à notre domaine.

Liste Chronologique

Actes du "Colloquio internazionale, Bologne, 31 agosto 2 settembre 1987" : *Egitto e storia antica dall'Ellenismo all'età araba. Bilancio di un confronto*, édités par L. CRISCUOLO et G. GERACI, Bologne, 1989.

N. BONACASA, *Cento anni di archeologia italiana per la conoscenza dell'Egitto greco-romano*, pp. 291-299.

A. GIARDINA, *Egitto bizantino o tardoantico? Problemi della terminologia e della periodizzazione*, pp. 88-103.

J. IRMSCHER, *Le origini della civiltà copta*, pp. 469-473.

"Fifth International Congress of Egyptology - Cinquième Congrès International d'Egyptologie, October 29-November 3, Cairo 1988"; la plupart des résumés figurent dans les *Abstracts of Papers*, Le Caire, 1988.

N. ALLAM-HAMI, *Survival of Ancient Egyptian Motifs in Coptic Art*, p. 8.

P. BALLET, *Prospection d'ateliers de potiers dans l'Égypte romaine tardive et byzantine*, sans résumé.

El-FAKHARANI, *The View concerning the Localisation of the Tomb of Alexander the Great*, p. 68.

W. GODLEWSKI, *Polish Excavations in Deir Naqlun, Fayoum* sans résumé.

M. HAGGAG, *Classical Elements in the Egyptian Temples of Graeco-Roman Period*, p. 120.

Z. KISS, *Quelques portraits impériaux romains d'Égypte*, p. 157.

W. KOLATAJ, *Baths of Late Antiquity on the Kom-el-Dikka in Alexandria*, p. 161.

G. MAJCHEREK, *Remarks on Roman Pottery from Newly Discovered Site at Marina (El-Alamein)*, sans résumé.

K. MYSLIEWIEC, *Polish Archaeological Works at Tell Atrib and Saqqara*, p. 201.

M. RASSART-DEBERGH, *Peinture des Kellia. Technique et iconographie*, p. 227.

M. RODZIEWICZ, *Ancient Mareotic Harbours*, p. 232.

E. SOUVALTZI, *Siwa the Oasis of Alexander the Great and his Tomb there*, p. 255.

G. WEILL-GOUDCHAUX, *Une nouvelle lecture de la mosaïque de Palestrina*, p. 287.

"The Nubian Wall Paintings". International Symposium, Nieborów, August 29-31 1989". Centré sur les découvertes en Nubie (Faras, Abdallah Nirqi, Tamit, Sonqi Tino, Meinarti, Kulubnarti, Nag'el-Sheima, Abd el-Gadir, Dongola), ce symposium évoqua et discuta les rapports de la peinture chrétienne de Nubie avec celle de régions voisines : Égypte, Syro-Palestine et Byzance.

W. Y. ADAMS, *The Wall Paintings of Meinarti and Kulubnarti.*

R. CORMACK, *The Mosaics of St Demetrios in Thessaloniki and Nubian Wall-paintings.*

S. DONADONI, *The Wall Paintings of Tamit and Sonqi Tino.*

W. GODLEWSKI, *The Wall Paintings of Old Dongola.*

K. INNEMEE, *Iconic and Narrative Images in Nubian Wall-paintings.*

S. JAKOBIELSKI, *The Wall Paintings of Faras (10th-13th centuries).*

B. et G. KÜHNEL, *Syro-Palestinian and Byzantine Sources of Nubian Paintings.*

M. MARTENS-CZARNECKA, *The Wall Paintings of Faras (8th-10th Centuries).*

M. MARTENS-CZARNECKA, *The Wall Paintings of Abd el Gadir.*

B. MIERZEJEWSKA, *Nubian "Protection" Scenes, their Iconography and Provenance.*

J. PARTYKA, *L'expression de la liturgie byzantine dans le programme iconographique de la cathédrale de Faras.*

M. RASSART-DEBERGH, *Quelques réflexions sur les rapports entre peintures copte et nubienne au VIIIe s.*

B. ROSTKOWSKA, *Christian Painting in the Northern Nubia.*

P. SCHOLZ, *Old Egyptian Ikon. Basis of the Iconographical Message in the Nubian Wall Paintings.*

M. SCHWARZ, *Nag'el-Sheima, the Wall Paintings of the Fortress Church.*

P. VAN MOORSEL, *The Wall Paintings of the Central Church in Abdallah Nirqi.*

"L'armée romaine et les Barbares du IVe au VIIe s." Colloque international organisé par le Musée des Antiquités Nationales et l'URA 880 du CNRS, du 24 au 28 février 1990 à Saint-Germain-en-Laye; Preprints, Saint-Germain, 1990. Les actes du congrès sont sous presse.

D. BÉNAZETH et P. DAL PRA, *Quelques remarques à propos d'un ensemble de vêtements de cavaliers découverts dans des tombes égyptiennes*, p. n. n.; *Idem*, dans *RL*, 41, 1991, n° 3, pp. 16-29.

K. HOLLAND-HEWITT, *Problèmes d'iconographie militaire* sans résumé.

M. RASSART-DEBERGH, *Divinités et saints militaires dans l'Égypte romaine et byzantine*, p. n.n.

"Journée copte" le 2 juillet 1990 à Munster à l'occasion de la visite de moines coptes chez le professeur M. Krause (compte rendu dans *MC*, 18, 1990, p. 130).

"Journées d'études en hommage à Étienne Drioton (1889-1961). L'égyptologie aujourd'hui et ses publics. Strasbourg, 15 et 16 octobre 1990". Organisées par l'Université des Sciences Humaines et la Bibliothèque Nationale et Universitaire de Strasbourg. L'intérêt du savant pour l'Égypte tardive et chrétienne ne fut pas oublié dans les discussions de ces deux journées de travail

"Seventh International Conference for Nubian Studies, Geneva, 3-6 September 1990"; seuls les "Rapports Généraux" ont été édités dans la *Pre-Publication* :
Ch. BONNET (éd.), *Seventh International Conference for Nubian Studies, Pre-Publication of Main Papers* (pagination non continue), Genève, 1990; sp. pour les rapports avec l'art chrétien d'Égypte :
W. GODLEWSKI, *The Early Period of Nubian Art. Middle of 6th - Beginning of 9th Centuries*, env. 70 p. avec la bibliographie et l'illustration.
M. MARTENS-CZARNECKA, *Late Christian Painting in Nubia*, 13 p.
La communication de F. W. Hinkel a fait l'objet d'un fascicule séparé (75 pages) : F. W. HINKEL, *Preservation and Restauration of Monuments. Cause of deterioration and measures for Protection.*

"Ateliers de potiers et productions céramiques en Égypte". Table-Ronde tenue à l'IFAO du 26 au 30 novembre 1990 : les actes constitueront le troisième volume des *CCE*. Concerne le néolithique et les premières dynasties, l'Égypte pharaonique, gréco-romaine, chrétienne et contemporaine :
P. BALLET et M. VICHY, *Artisanat de la céramique dans l'Égypte grecque et romaine. Ateliers du Delta, d'Assouan et de Kharga.*
J.Y. EMPEREUR et M. PICON, *La reconnaissance des productions des ateliers céramiques : l'exemple de la Maréotide.*
J. ENGELMANN, *A propos des amphores d'Abou Mina.*
P. FRENCH, *A Preliminary Study of Pottery in Lower Egypt in the Late Dynastics and Ptolemaic Periods.*
H. GHALY, *Pottery Workshop of Saint-Jeremiah (Saqqara).*
G. LECUYOT et G. PIERRAT, *A propos des lieux de production de quelques groupes céramiques trouvés à Tôd et dans la Vallée des Reines.*
G. MAJCHEREK et Abd el Aziz SHENNAWI, *Research on Amphora Production on the Northwestern Coast of Egypt.*
A. POLUDNIKIEWICZ, *Local Imitations of Greek Pottery Found in Tell Atrib.*
M. RODZIEWIECZ, *Field Notes from Elephantine on the Early Aswan Pink Clay Pottery.*
M. SEIF el-DIN, *Technical Aspects and Workshop Centers of the Pilgrim Flasks in the Graeco-Roman Egypt.*
R. TOMBER, *Early Roman Pottery from Mons Claudianus.*

"Présence des chrétiens orientaux", Paris, Grand Palais, 15 novembre-6 décembre 1990.

A. BOUD'HORS, *Dans quelles circonstances se sont constituées les collections de Manuscrits Coptes.*

M. DEWACHTER, *Champollion et les Coptes.*

M.-H. RUTSCHOWSCAYA, *L'iconographie chrétienne dans l'art des tissus coptes.*

À Périgueux, colloque de l'Association Francophone de Coptologie consacrée à Jean Clédat : les 16-18 mai 1991, "Ve Journée d'Etudes Coptes 'Jean Clédat'",

D. BÉNAZETH, *Les avatars d'un monument copte : l'église sud du monastère de Baouît.*

E. GAILLARD, *Jean Clédat.*

E. LUCCHESI-PALLI, *Un détail oriental dans les costumes des peintures de Baouît.*

M. RASSART-DEBERGH, *Les peintures des églises de Baouît à travers les photos de Clédat.*

M.-H. RUTSCHOWSCAYA, *Sur un fragment de peinture du Louvre.*

"IVth International Congress on Graeco-Oriental and African Studies", Delphi, 18-21 July 1991 ; les actes constitueront les volumes V et VI des *Graeco-Arabica*, Athènes, 1992/3.

L. BASCH, *La marine copte : continuation et rupture. Position des problèmes en 1991.*

W. GODLEWSKI, *Naqloun.*

M. RASSART-DEBERGH, *Monachisme copte et bateaux.*

L. SOUVALTZI, *Siwa the Oasis of Alexander the Great and the Excavations there.*

G. al TAHIR, *The Nubian Archers in the Pre-Islamic and Islamic Periods.*

L. TÖRÖK, *Amasis and Ergamenes, Philhellenes from Egypt and Meroe.*

Congrès d'Égyptologie à Moscou, en juillet 1991 (information fournie par Alexandre Kakovkine; je n'en ai pas l'intitulé exact). A ma connaissance, l'ouvrage prévu à cette occasion n'a pas encore été publié mais j'en mentionne le titre tel qu'il me fut annoncé : O. ETINGHOF, A. KAKOVKINE, *Les monuments de l'Égypte Antique dans les musées d'URSS*, Rome, 1992.

"XVIIIe Congrès International des Études Byzantines à Moscou, 8-15 août 1991" (titre en russe, en anglais et en français), *Résumés des communications*, Moscou, 1991, 2 volumes :

D. BÉNAZETH, *Deux catalogues d'objets coptes en métal (Louvre et Musée copte du Caire)*, p. 125.

H. BUSCHHAUSEN, *Die Ausgrabungen in Dayr Abu Fano in Mittelägypten. Ein*

Koptisches Kloster aus der Justinianischen Renaissance, p. 186.

K. CORRIGAN, *An Icon of the Crucifixion at Mount Sinai*, p. 245.

A. GONOSOVA, *The Production of Textiles in Egypt : Household or Market Consumption*, pp. 375-376.

A. KAKOVKINE, *Égypte copte et Byzance. Rapports culturels et artistiques réciproques (en russe)*, pp. 503-504.

A. KAKOVKINE, *Représentations coptes de Daphné* (en russe), p. 505.

M.-H. RUTSCHOWSCAYA, *Les salles coptes dans le futur Grand Louvre*, p. 973.

Z. SKALOVA, *A Little Known Group of Copto-Arabic Icons in Egypt*, pp. 1080-1081.

M. E. VAN LOHUIZEN-MULDER, *Capitals and Stuccoes in Ravenna of Coptic Manufacture*, pp. 1207-1208.

P. VAN MOORSEL, *How Greek is Coptic Art?*, pp. 1209-1210.

À l'occasion de ce congrès, une série de conférences et d'expositions se sont tenues dans plusieurs villes et plusieurs ouvrages ont été publiés; j'en retiendrai :

A. KAKOVKINE, *Égypte copte* (en russe) dans *Byzance et traditions byzantines*, Leningrad, 1991, pp. 29-34.

A. KAKOVKINE, B. G Bok. *V. Boch et les collections coptes de l'Ermitage* (en russe) dans *Byzantinologie à l'Ermitage. Pour le Congrès International des Byzantinologues à Moscou, 8-15 août 1991*, Leningrad, 1991, pp. 40-48.

"Sesto Congresso Internazionale di Egittologia. Sixth International Congress of Egyptology, Torino, September 1st-8th 1991"; la plupart des textes ont été publiés dans les *Abstracts of Papers*, Turin, 1991 :

S. AUTH, *The Newark Museum*, pp. 90-91.

M. BARRA BAGNASCO, *Bes-Sileno, un'iconografia tra mondo egizio e greco : nuovi documenti*.

N. BONACASA, *Aspetti e problemi della scultura alessandrina*.

M. CICERONI, *Le testimonianze figurate del Navigium Isidis*, pp. 128-129.

L. DEL FRANCIA, *Osiris, Dionysos, l'arbre*, pp. non numérotées.

F. DE SALVIA, *La collezione egiziana di Napoli : aspetti e problemi d'arte egiziana ed egittizzante*

M. A. GARCÍA MARTÍNEZ, *Egyptianizing Preroman Documents from Iberian Peninsula Slope*, pp. 178-179.

M. O. JENTEL, *Un pastiche d'époque romaine : un buste égyptien à la mode grecque archaïsante*, pp. 234-235.

A. KAKOVKINE, *The Image of Daphnae in Coptic Art*, pp. 248-249.

J. KOSCIUK, *Typological Observations on Early Medieval Houses in Abu Mina*, pp. 256-257.

G. LECUYOT, *Un sanctuaire romain transformé en monastère : le Deir-er-Roumi*, p. 262.

M. I. PASQUALI, *Simboli Isiaci sulla monetazione repubblicana*, p. 57.

S. PENNESTRI, *Piombi monetiformi dell'Egitto greco-romano nelle collezioni numismatiche torinese*, p. 320.

M. RASSART-DEBERGH, *A l'origine de la découverte du monachisme copte*, pp. non numérotées.

P. O. SCHOLZ, *Die Kontinuität des Altägyptischen in der Ikonozität und Theologie des orientalistischen Christentums*, pp. 358-359.

M. SADEK, *The Baths at Ancient Harbour of Marea*, pp. 354-355.

K. SADR, *Graeco-Roman Remains in the Eastern Desert, Bir Abraq Area*, p. 64.

V. TRAN TAM TINH, *Interpretatio Romana de l'iconographie isiaque*, pp. 392-393.

"12. International Kongress für Christliche Archäologie, Bonn 22. bis 28. September 1991"; le thème du congrès était "Voyages et but des pèlerinages"; je mentionnerai toutes les communications ayant trait à l'Égypte, même si elles ne traitent pas exclusivement d'histoire de l'art :

M. DESCOEUDRES, *Mönche als Pilger und als Pilgerziel. Ein Martyrium in der Eremitensiedlung Kellia in Unterägypten.*

W. GODLEWSKI, *The Commemorative Building BX at Old Dongola.*

P. GROSSMANN, *Grabungen im Wallfahrtszentrum von Abu Mina, Neue Funde.*

E. JASTRZEBOWSKA, *Neutestamentliche Dekoration der Pilgerdevotionalien.*

Z. KADAR, *Die Menasampulle von Szombathely (Steinamanger, Ungarn) in Beziehung zu anderen frühchristlichen Pilgerandenken.*

A. KAKOVKINE, *Sur certains monuments coptes de l'Ermitage.*

B. KLAUSEN, *Eulogien, Transport und Weitergabe von Degenskraft.*

J. KOSCIUK, *The Last Face of Abu Mina Settlement.*

P. LINSCHEID, *Untersuchungen zur Verbreitung von Menasampullen nördlich der Alpen.*

L. B. MacCOULL, *Pilgrimage to Deir El-Muharraq (Egypt) in Late Antiquity.*

E. MAKOWIECKA, *Pilgrimage Center at Kellia.*

A. MINCHEV, *Early Christian Clay Ampullae of the Western Black Sea-Coast : Pilgrim Souvenirs and Local Imitations.*

A. OVADIAH, *Deir el-Adra (Egyp) : The Resting Place of the Holy Family on the Flight to Egypt.*

C. WIETHEGER, *Das Jeremias-Kloster zu Saqqara als Wallfahrsstätte. Ein Untersuchung der Bodenplatten mit Fussabdrücken in Raum 1772.*

4. TRAVAUX, DÉCOUVERTES ET RESTAURATIONS

Les découvertes archéologiques de ces quatre dernières années, présentées par Wodek Godlewski et par Peter Grossmann, seront publiées ici même. Je ne souhaite nullement empiéter sur leur domaine, ni donner texte et bibliographie qui feraient double emploi. Il convient néanmoins de tenir compte ici de découvertes fortuites ou de recherches programmées, lorsque les objets mis au jour sont d'importance pour l'histoire de l'art. Trois aspects seront donc rapidement envisagés : "publications" de matériel existant et connu, "protection et restauration" englobant des études techniques précises; "fouilles" enfin mentionnées de façon particulièrement brève.

A. *Publications*

En 1988, G. Gabra annonçait la naissance d'un vaste projet, mené en étroite collaboration par l'Égypte et les instituts étrangers, le *Catalogue du Musée Copte;*[1] H. Buchhausen[2] et Pascale Ballet[3] mentionnaient l'état d'avancement des volumes dont la rédaction leur avait été confiée. G. Gabra a évoqué ici même les progrès réalisés durant les quatre années qui se sont écoulées,[4] Fatma Mahmoud[5] a présenté le travail réalisé avec P. Ballet; j'ai rappelé que le catalogue des peintures des Kellia était en bonne voie.[6]

---

1.   G. GABRA, *Das Projekt "Catalogue Général du Musée Copte". Stand der Arbeiten bis Dezember 1988* dans *Actes*, pp. 27-32.
2.   H. BUCHHAUSEN, *Neuauflage der Catalogue General des Koptischen Museums in Alt -Kairo*, III. Teil. *Holzarbeiten, Elfenbein, Knochenarbeiten* dans *Actes*, pp. 33-37.
3.   P. BALLET, *Lampes du Musée Copte (Vieux-Caire). Brève présentation* dans *Actes*, pp. 124-126.
4.   G. GABRA, *Progress of the Work untill 1991.*
5.   F. MAHMOUD, *Catalogue des céramiques du Musée Copte.*
6.   Le catalogue détaillé de la centaine de peintures restaurées en vue de leur exposition au Musée copte (partie dans les salles, partie dans les réserves) sera précédé d'une introduction générale, de l'historique des fouilles, d'une présentation des ermitages dont elles proviennent; il sera suivi d'une bibliographie exhaustive.

De son côté, Hans den Heijer a indiqué les lignes maîtresses du projet de coopération[7] auquel participent, depuis quelques années déjà, L. et H. Hondelinck[8] et Z. Skalova:[9] publication du catalogue des icônes du Musée Copte et consolidation des objets eux-mêmes; Z. Skalova s'est donnée tout entière à ce projet et prépare un petit volume de conseils, qui sera distribué partout où sont conservées des icônes.

Durant ces quatre années, D. Bénazeth a activement préparé des ouvrages consacrés aux objets en métal, tant ceux conservés au Louvre que ceux du Musée Copte.[10]

Les rapports définitifs des missions suisse et française aux Kellia sont en cours de publication. Le second volume de la série EK81-84 est sous presse;[11] on prépare activement le troisième.[12] De même, la mission de l'Institut Français effectue les dernières vérifications avant de donner à l'impression les deux volumes[13] qui seront consacrés à l'ermitage 195 des Qouçour er-Roub'iyat.

---

7.   H. DEN NEIJER, *Conservation Problems in Egypt*; en outre, à l'initiative du père Van Moorsel, une petite collection a été créée dans le cadre du projet de "preventive education", spécialement des moines : ENCCAP 1991-1995, dont le second volume est consacré aux icônes (*Coptic Icons*, a Reader composed by Mat Immerzeel with a Preface by Paul Van Moorsel); il fait le point sur la collection du Musée Copte (les idées ne diffèrent guère de celles émises par Linda Langen dans *MC*, 18, pp. 7- 18) et établit la fiche type ; rappelons qu'un projet de cataloguer aussi les icônes des églises et monastères fut présenté par le père Samuel (*MC*, 18, p. 129)
8.   L. LANGEN, *Icon-Painting in Egypt* dans *Coptic Art*, pp. 55-72; aussi *BIA*, 1, p. 68.
9.   Z. SKALOVA, *Conservation Problems in Egypt : Introductory Report on the Condition and Restoration of Post-Medieval Coptic Icons* dans *Coptic Art*, pp. 73-87 et *Conservation Problems in Egypt : Some Remarks on the Technology of Post-Medieval Coptic Icons* dans *BSAC*, XXIX, 1990, pp. 55-56; *BIA*, 3, p. 28.
10.   Les objets provenant de Tôd sont publiés déjà, le catalogue du Louvre aussi (supra, 10 et 11); pour le catalogue du Musée Copte, voyez *BIA*, 1, p. 61.
11.   MSAC, EK8184, II *Explorations aux Qouçour er-Roub'iyat. Rapport des campagnes 1982 et 1983, suivi d'une étude des 24 ermitages mis au jour en 1976 par l'EAO*, Louvain, 1993.
12.   MSAC, EK8184, III *Explorations aux Qouçour el-Izeila, les monastères à "église"*, Louvain, sous presse.

B. *Protection et restauration*

En vue d'une meilleure protection et d'une connaissance accrue des objets coptes et musulmans de la part des populations locales, de petits musées ont été aménagés sur plusieurs sites comme Marsa Matrouh, Sohag, Miniah, Assouan.[14]

On a déjà souligné l'importance du travail de Z. Skalova, qui s'occupe non seulement des icônes du Musée Copte, mais aussi de celles conservées dans les monastères; en outre, elle donne des cours de formation pour la préservation et la restauration.[15]

Je mentionnerai aussi rapidement les travaux de consolidation et de restauration des monuments tardifs et chrétiens[16] par les missions polonaises et ceux des collègues égyptiens, sous l'égide du SAE tant au Caire (ensemble du Vieux-Caire Copte et Musulman)[17] que dans sa région (à Matarya, au couvent d'al-Mansouriya); de plus amples informations sont données dans les fascicules du *BIA*.

Dans le même *BIA* et dans la chronique "travaux" du *BIFAO*, on trouvera détaillée la mission que dirige l'IFAO pour la consolidation, la restauration et la présentation des objets provenant des Kellia[18] et

---

13.   L'histoire du site, l'historique de la fouille du bâtiment QR195 (avec liste des participants), l'état de conservation du monument et la méthode de fouille, les étapes de construction, les matériaux et l'architecture en général seront présentés par N. HEINEN et M. WUTTMANN, les céramiques par P. BALLET, les peintures par M. RASSART-DEBERGH; pour ces dernières, voyez *BIA*, 2, pp. 50-51.

14.   *BIA*, 2, pp. 18-21; 3, pp. 12-13.

15.   *Supra* n. 9 et Z. SKALOVA, *Conservation Problems in Egypt : Icons. Preliminary Classification and some Case-Studies* dans *ICOM, Committee for Conservation. 9th Triennial Meeting, Dresden, 26 -31 August 1990, Preprints*, Los Angeles, 1990, II, pp. 777-782.

16.   À Alexandrie (W. DASZEWSKI, H. el SHEIKH, St. MEDEKSZA, *An Unknown Christian Complex in Alexandria* dans *Coptic Studies*, pp. 87-195; dans *PAM*, II, pp. 15-18 et dans *PAM*, III, pp. 15-18), à Marina (*PAM*, II, pp. 38-47 et *PAM*, III, pp. 39-48) et surtout à Ashmunein (*Report from El Ashmunein* (*supra*) et dans *PAM*, III, pp. 19-23).

17.   *BIA*, 1, pp. 12-14 et 38-39; *BIA*, 3, pp. 11 et 21-23.

du Ouadi Natroun,[19] au couvent des Syriens,[20] au Deir el-Baramous[21] et au Deir Amba Bishoi.[22]

L'intérêt de plus en plus marqué pour les matériaux et leur composition va de pair avec les recherches spécifiques en vue d'une meilleure conservation; plusieurs articles ont été consacrés aux peintures[23] et aux textiles.[24]

C. *Fouilles*

On se reportera bien évidemment pour une vision complète au "Rapport" de W. Godlewski publié ici même.

Rappelons d'abord que si les fouilles des missions française et suisse se sont arrêtées aux Kellia, celles de nos collègues égyptiens se poursuivent et seront publiées en collaboration avec plusieurs chercheurs de l'IFAO.

Dans le Ouadi Natrun, un violent incendie au Deir al-Syriani provoqua la chute partielle de l'"Ascension" peinte (1225) dans

---

18. *BIA*, 1, p. 55; *BIA*, 2, pp. 50-51 et n. 1, p. 52.
19. Le directeur de l'IFAO, Nicolas Grimal, a présenté l'ensemble de ces travaux d'abord au Centre culturel français d'Alexandrie en juin 1991, puis en septembre, au congrès d'égyptologie de Turin. Il en a donné un compte rendu détaillé dans la chronique du *BIFAO*, "Travaux..." ; N. GRIMAL, Mission d'étude et de restauration des peintures coptes au Ouadi Natroun dans *BIFAO*, 90-91, 1991, pp. 310-315. En outre, M. Wuttmann prépare une description technique de l'ensemble des travaux de restauration : M. WUTTMANN, *Mission d'étude et de restauration des peintures coptes du Wadi Natroun*; cf. *BIA*, 2, pp. 51-52.
20. N. GRIMAL, *BIFAO*, 90-91, 1991, pp. 312-315; *BIA*, 1, p. 55; *BIA*, 3, pp. 34-35.
21. Spécialement *BIA*, 1, p. 55; *BIA*, 2, pp. 51-52.
22. N. GRIMAL, *BIFAO*, 90-91, 1991, pp. 311-312; BIA, 1, p. 37; M. IMMERZEEL, *Discovery of Wall-paintings in Deir anba Bishoi (Wadi 'n Natrun)* dans *NewsIACS*, 30, February 1992, pp. 8-11
23. D. LE FUR *et alii*, *Les pigments dans la peinture copte* dans *Conservation - restauration des biens culturels*, décembre 1990, pp. 45-50.
24. Par exemple : T. BILSON, *The Conservation of a Roman Egyptian Painted Shroud Fragment* dans *The Conservator*, 16, 1992, pp. 3-11 et S. LANDI, *The Textile Conservator's Manual*, 2d Ed., Oxford, 1992, sp., pp. 104-195 et 317-318.

l'église de la Vierge; durant les travaux de restauration effectués par l'IFAO, on découvrit ainsi une peinture antérieure; cette "Annonciation", remarquable tant par l'iconographie que par le style, n'a pas fini d'intéresser le monde savant.[25]

A Abou Ménas, les fouilles de l'Institut Allemand fournissent régulièrement du matériel de grand intérêt; ainsi, parmi les bâtiments découverts en 1989, une chapelle funéraire richement décorée a retenu l'attention par les ressemblances qu'elle présente avec la décoration kelliote : quelques-unes des nouvelles peintures ont été décrites au congrès d'égyptologie de Turin.[26]

Il me faut encore mentionner, vu leur intérêt dans le domaine de l'histoire de l'art en général:

– les trouvailles de sculptures, de peintures et de momies à Marina (W. A. DASZEWSKI, *Excavations at Marina el-Alamein 1987- 1988* dans *MDAIK*, 46, 1990, pp. 16-51; aussi dans *PAM*, II, pp. 31-37 et III, pp. 29-38; pour les fouilles du Service : *BIA*, 1, pp. 22-23).

– l'ensemble des céramiques, cuirs, tissus, et fragments peints de Naqloun (mise au point ici même : W. GODLEWSKI, *Recent Excavations at Naqlun (1988-1992)*, pp. 00-00; aussi dans *PAM*, I, pp. 29-34; II, pp. 48-53 et III, pp. 49-54; *Nubica I/II*, pp. 171-207).

– les importantes peintures[27] et les momies[28] découvertes à Abou Fana.

– Les édifices tardifs et chrétiens (parfois peints) de Thèbes (*BIA* 2, pp. 48-49. Aussi G. LECUYOT, *Un sanctuaire romain transformé en monastère : le Deir-er-Roumi* dans *Abstracts* [du] *Sesto Congresso In-*

---

25. L'annonce de cette découverte fortuite fut faite par le directeur de l'IFAO, N. Grimal (*supra*, n. 19) et par P. VAN MOORSEL (en date du 29 mai 1991) dans *NewsIACS*, 30, February 1992, p. 12; le père Van Moorsel lui a en outre consacré une première étude : *Deir es Sourian revisited* dans les *NubL*, 17, (August 1991), Leyde, 1992.

26. J. KOSCIUK, *Typological Observations on Early Medieval Houses in Abu Mina* dans *Abstracts. Sesto Congresso Internazionale di Egittologia*, p. 256-257; sur l'ensemble des monuments, voyez P. GROSSMANN, *Abu Mina I* (*supra*, 36).

28. *Les momies d'Abou Fana (VIe s.) ont été autopsiées à la clinique radiologique de l'Université de Tübingen par Wolfgang Pahl : Antike Welt, 22, 1991, p. 69.*

ternazionale di Egittologia, p. 262 et ici, au Ve Congrès Copte, G. LECUYOT, *Valley of the Queens in the Christian Period* (avec bibliographie antérieure), et ceux du Nord Sinai (prospections et fouilles allemandes, égyptiennes et françaises dans *BIA*, 1, pp. 25 et 32-33; *BIA*, 3, p. 35. Ici même : M. Abd el-SAMIE, *The Eastern Basilica of Pelusium*, ainsi que W. GODLEWSKI et P. GROSSMANN respectivement aux pp. 00- 00 et 00-00).

– Enfin les cuirs et les textiles du Mons Claudianus (aperçu des travaux et trouvailles dans *BIA*, 1, pp. 35 et 52-53).

Tous ces objets viennent enrichir considérablement notre documentation.

En guise de "conclusions" :

A travers des exemples choisis, on a tenté de montrer combien fructueuses avaient été ces quatre années. La quantité des articles comme l'imminence de la publication de plusieurs ouvrages (dont des actes de congrès) m'ont amenée à donner ici une bibliographie raisonnée, réservant à une prochaine livraison du *JcoptS* ou du *BSAC* une liste plus exhaustive, semblable à celle publiée dans le "Rapport" de Louvain-la-Neuve.

Signalons encore que quelques-uns des résumés présentés à Washington ont été (à la demande de leurs auteurs) publiés dans *Le Monde Copte* 21-22. Qu'il nous soit permis de remercier une fois encore l'ensemble du Bureau de l'IACS et les organisateurs du Congrès de Washington qui, par leur compréhension, ont permis une plus large diffusion des découvertes et études depuis 1988.

---

27. Elles ont été présentées à notre précédent congrès : H. BUCHHAUSEN, *Die Ausgrabungen von Dayr Abu Fana in Mittelägypten im Jahre 1987* dans *Actes*, pp 216-226 et ont ensuite fait l'objet de brefs rapports dans le *Jahrbuch der Österreichischen Byzantinistik* (*Die Ausgrabungen von Dayr Abu Fana in Mittelägypten im Jahre 1987* dans *JÖB*, 38, 1988, pp. 353-362, sp. fig. 2 et *Die Ausgrabungen in Abu Fana in Ägypten im Jahre 1988* dans *JÖB*, 39, 1989, pp 241-259, sp. fig. 7-9 et 16-18); aussi : *Die Ausgrabungen von Dair Abu Fana in Oberägypten im Jahr 1989 dans Ägypten und Levante. ZAAN, II, Vienne, 1991, pp. 121-146.*

ARMAND VEILLEUX

REPORT ON RESEARCH IN COPTIC MONASTICISM
1988-1992

A presentation of the publications on «Coptic Monasticism» cannot be limited to texts in the Coptic language, since writings of some Coptic monks—or about them—have been preserved in various languages other than Coptic; and also since some monks, like Evagrius, who had an enormous influence on Coptic monasticism did not write in Coptic.

It seems that Coptic monasticism has been the object of scholarly studies less during the last four years than during the preceding four-year period—or the former decades, for that matter. I certainly have much less to report this year, in terms of publications on Coptic monasticism, than I had to report at Louvain, four years ago. That, however, will allow me to dwell a little longer on a few really important publications.

The book by Samuel Rubenson on «The Letters of St. Antony» has been mentioned more than once since the beginning of this Congress. I will speak more about this in a moment; at this point I would like simply to mention that perhaps the most important aspect of Rubenson's work is to have made us a little more aware of the fact that we know pretty little about the first monastic generation in Lower Egypt, that is, the monasticism of Lower Egypt prior to the Origenist controversy. It obliges us to divide the story of Egyptian monasticism into two main sections, the year of Evagrius' death serving as watershed.

I said «Lower Egypt», because few studies have been made on Pachomian cenobitism during the past four years, as well as any concerning Egyptian monasticism in general. So let us begin with the first period, that is made famous especially by two great names: Antony and Evagrius.

BEFORE EVAGRIUS. ANTONY OF EGYPT

The most famous of all the early Coptic monks was obviously Antony. Both his life, attributed to Athanasius, and his Letters continued to be the object of interesting studies during the last four years.

First, let us say a few words about the Life. You will remember that René Draguet, when he published his critical edition of the Syriac version of the *Vita Antonii*, in 1980 claimed that it was not dependent on the Greek Life attributed to Athanasius but was the translation of its source. At our last Congress, I mentioned the article of T. Barnes, followed by Andrew Louth, trying to give new life to that position. Since then the arguments put forward by Draguet and Barnes have been convincingly refuted by Rudolf Lorenz and most of all by Louise Abramowski in her article «Vertritt die syrische Fassung die ursprüngliche Gestalt der Vita Antonii? Eine Auseinadersetzung mit der These Draguets» which appeared in the «Mélanges Guillaumont» (p. 47-56). That question can be put to rest. But we are still waiting for the publication of the Greek text announced by G.J.M. Bartelink at Oxford in 1983 (article published in 1989).

Of saint Antony himself we have seven letters that have been preserved fragmentarily in Coptic and with various degrees of completeness in Arabic, Syriac, Georgian and Latin. They have been known for a number of years, especially since the excellent edition of the Georgian version along with the Coptic fragments by Garitte in 1955. Everyone who read them realized that if they were really from Antony, they revealed an Antony that was rather different from the one presented by Athanasius in his Life of Antony. That was probably the reason why nobody in the past dared to deal seriously with the question of their authenticity. This is precisely what Rubenson has done.

People may question some of Rubenson's lines of argumentation, but as a whole, his conclusion on that point seems inescapable: There is no serious reason to doubt that these letters are from Antony himself. They are attributed to him both in the Coptic original and in the Greek translation; they are mentioned by Jerome and quoted by fifth century authors. Their authenticity is as firmly attested as that of any other ancient writing.

The full title of Rubenson's book is: «The Letters of St. Antony. Origenist Theology, Monastic Tradition and the Making of a Saint». It is, therefore much more than a simple analysis of the Letters. In the second part of his book Rubenson studies the Image of St. Antony, as we can gather not only from these Letters but also from the Life of Antony, the Apophtegmata and other contemporary monastic sources, and compares the whole to what we know about the daily life in Egypt from the papyri and the gnostic texts.

His analysis shows that «the notion of Antony and his companions as ignorant and illiterate is a view that mirrors modern prejudice rather than historical reality». Antony appears as a cultured man who was in touch with the Alexandrine theology of his time, shows a clear dependence on Origen and some striking similarities with the theology of texts such as the *Teachings of Silvanus* and, to some degree, Athanasius' *Contra gentes*.

One of the conclusions of Rubenson is that «monasticism (was) not the product (...) of people on the margin of society, but of intellectuals dissatisfied with what tradition had to offer.»

Although there is a basic accord between the Letters and the *Vita*, the difference between the two is explained before all by the fact that the latter is marked by the Arian conflict that was so decisive for Athanasius' entire life and literary production.

The difference between the Letters and the type of asceticm described by the *Apophtegmata* and the monastic literature of the 5th century is due to the fact that the Origenist crisis of 400 (the year after Evagrius' death) deeply changed not only the life of the monks, but also their interpretation of the tradition. The collections of *Apophtegmata* that were preserved all date after the Origenist controversy, and have all been purged of their origenist elements. It now seems more and more probable that the origenist tradition did not come to the desert with Evagrius and a few intellectuals, but that Antony himself may have played an important role in the making of that tradition.

Another work on Antony's letters could be mentioned: Wincenty Myszor has published a study on the relationship between the Letters of Antony and the Nag-Hammadi texts in *Jahrbuch für Antike und*

Christentum (32 (1989) 73-88). He finds in both works the same thought system, which, following Jan Zandee, he attributes to the influence of Plato's «Gedankenwelt». Nevertheless, he underlines the profound difference between the spirituality of the Letters and gnosticism, specially in the fact that according to the Letters of Antony, the unity resides in the subordination of the whole man under the Spirit, in which the body also takes part (the positive appreciation of the body should be noted). He claims that early monasticism could very well have had contacts with the authors of the Nag Hammadi texts, and that there could be contacts with the contents of works like «Authentikos Logos», «Teaching of Sylvanus», «Exegesis of the Soul», etc... No specific contact, however, can be documented.

EVAGRIUS AND POST-EVAGRIAN PERIOD

Evagrius.

Another great figure of Coptic monasticism is Evagrius. Although he was born in Pontus and wrote in Greek, he did live in the Egyptian desert for the last 16 years of his life, and had a deep and lasting influence on Coptic monasticism. Everything published about him belongs to a presentation of scholarly publications concerning Coptic monasticism.

For several years Antoine and Claire Guillaumont have provided us with excellent editions of Evagrius' works and as excellent introductions and commentaries. After their edition of the *Praktikos*, several years ago, they published the *Gnosticos* in 1989: («Le Gnostique ou celui qui est devenu digne de la science.») It is a critical edition of the Greek fragments, and a full translation made with the help of the Syriac and Armenian versions.

Another specialist of Evagrius has emerged these past few years: G. Bunge, who gave us in 1989 an excellent German translation of the *Praktikos*. The table of Biblical quotations contains a number of additional items to that of Guillaumont. His commentary, although excellent, remains a commentary «of Evagrius by Evagrius». The commentary of Guillaumont went further in explaining the sources of Evagrius as well as his influence.

In another publication («Geistliche Vaterschaft...»), Bunge demonstrated that Evagrius belongs to a tradition of «Spiritual fatherhood» which goes back to the Apostle Paul, finds its full expression in Clement of Alexandria and its embodiment in the Desert Fathers, and that this type of gnosis is at the antipode of gnosticism. In another article («Mysterium Unitatis...»), he shows the deeply orthodox character of Evagrius' teaching on Creation.

Finally, another important publication on Evagrius is Jeremy Driscoll's dissertation on the «Ad monachos» published a few months ago in Rome. (*The «Ad Monachos» of Evagrius Ponticus: Its Structure and a Select Commentary...*). He had published an article on Evagrius in *Cist. Stud.* in 1989: «Listlessness in the Mirror for Monks of Evagrius Ponticus».

Apophtegmata.

The *Apophtegmata* continue to be the object of a few translations and of a large number of studies on their spirituality, among which those of P. Regnault are certainly the best. To be published in September 1992 is a very good book by Douglas Burton-Christie (*The Word in the Desert*). The author studies the interpretation of Scripture by the monks of the Desert, and instead of limiting himself to analyzing the relatively few texts of the Scripture that are actually quoted in the *Apophtegmata*, he describes how their monastic life was a concrete interpretation of the Scripture.

Palladius.

Palladius, in his *Historia Lausiaca* describes monasticism around the year 420. Unfortunately we do not have, yet, an absolutely reliable critical edition of that work. On the one hand, Butler's edition was a pioneer's work; on the other hand, few if any will go along with Draguet in his theories about the Coptic sources of the *Historia Lausi-*

aca. But recent publications of Bunge and De Vogüé seem to give credence to at least some of Draguet's insights. These two authors used what could be called the «lateral tradition», in particular the several documents found in the Coptic synaxaries, that seem to have clear Palladian characteristics. Examining the fragments on Evagrius, Bunge suggests that Palladius, prior to his *Historia Lausiaca*, wrote a first History of the Egyptian monks, for a more select audience. It would be that first work that inspired the Coptic synaxaries and also the historian Socrates in his notice on Evagrius. Palladius would have chosen stories from that first work in order to compose a shorter form for the chamberlain Lausus. In two subsequent articles A. De Vogüé published the Coptic version of the Life of Pambo and of the Life of Evagrius (with A. Bunge). A subsequent article will give the Life of Macarios.

Historia monachorum in Aegypto.

Eva Schulz-Fügel, who gave some good communications on the *Apophtegmata Patrum* at the 1983 and the 1987 Oxford Patristic Conferences, (both published in 1989) has also published an excellent critical edition of the *Historia Monachorum* in the Latin version of Rufinus, dedicating a large part of her introduction to trying to solve the problem of what in that Latin version is really from Rufinus.

Pachomius.

Pachomius and Pachomian monasticism were not the object of any large basic study during the period we are concerned with. Among the various articles that did study some aspects of that monasticism, one should mentioned that of James E. Goehring: «The World Engaged: The Social and Economic World of Early Egyptian Monasticism».

A few other publications.

Moses of Abydos was a Coptic monk of the 6th century.

René-Georges Coquin, who had presented him in an early study, published of him a short fragment that was still unpublished, in the Mélanges Guillaumont: «La 'Règle' de Moïse d'Abybos».

Of course, several of the articles of the *Coptic Encyclopaedia* concern monastic authors and monastic topics. There is no need here to give a list that would be rather long.

Bibliography

ANTOINE (St.), Sw. Atanazy Aleksandryjski. Zywot swietego Antoniego. Sw. Antoni Pustelnik. Pisma. Przeklad Zofia Brzostowska i inni, wstepami i komentarzem opatrzyla Ewa Wipszycka. Instytut wydawniczy Pas, Warszawa, 1987, 268.

ABRAMOWSKI, L., «Vertritt die syrische Fassung die ursprüngliche Gestalt der Vita Antonii? Eine Auseinandersetzung mit der These Draguets», in: Mélanges Guillaumont, p. 47-56.

AL SYRIANY, Samuel and Badii Habib, Guide to Ancient Coptic Churches and Monasteries in Upper Egypt [Le Caire], 1990, 164 p., cartes, ill.

(APOPHTEGMES), Enseignements des Pères du désert: Hyperéchios, Étienne de Thèbes, Zosime. Préf. de Dom M. van Parys. Introd., trad. et notes par Dom P. Tirot, Dom M. van Parys et Dom L. Regnault (= Spir. orien., 51) Abbaye de Bellefontaine, 1991, 141 p.

AVRIL, Joseph, «Observance monastique et spiritualité dans les préambules des Actes (Xe-XIIIe s.)», Rev. d'Hist. Eccl. 85 (1990), 5-29.

BARTELINK, G.J.M., «L'édition du texte grec de la Vita Antonii d'Athanase» in: Studia Patristica XVIII/2. Critica, Classica, Ascetica, Liturgica. (Oxford 1983). - Louvain, Peeters, 1989, p. 1-6.

BARTELINK, G.J.M., (review of Rubenson): Vigiliae Christianae 45 (1991) p. 185-186.

BAUMEISTER, Th., «Der aktuelle Forschungsstand zu den Pachomiusregeln», Münchener Theologische Zeitschrift, 40 (1989), p. 313-321.

BELLET, P., «Nou Testimoni de les lletres de sant Antoni (Cambridge, University Lib. Add. 1876.2)», Studia monastica 31 (1989) 251-258.

BERTRANB, D., «St. Antoine, le discernement des esprits et la santé de l'homme». in: Résonances de Saint Antoine, Bulletin 11 (1989), p. 2-27.

BOURGUET, Pierre du, «Pierres d'attente dans l'Égypte antique pour le monachisme chrétien», dans: Mélanges Antoine Guillaumont, p. 41-46.

BUNGE, G., «Palladiana. I. Introduction aux fragments coptes de l'Histoire Lausiaque», Studia Monastica 32 (1990) 79-129.

BUNGE, G., Evagrios Pontikos, Praktikos oder Der Mönch. Hundert Kapitel über das geistliche Leben. Cologne, Luther-Verlag, 1989, 287 p. (Koinonia-Oriens 32).

BUNGE, G., Geistliche Vaterschaft. Christliche Gnosis bei Evagrios Pontikos. Einl. von Wilhelm NYSSEN, Ratisbonne, Kommissionsverlag Fr. Pustet. 1988, 96p. (Beiheft zu den Studia Patristica et Liturgica 23).

BUNGE, G., «Mysterium Unitatis. Der Gedanke der Einheit von Schöpfer und Geschöpf in der evagrianischen Mystik», Freiburger Zeitschrift für Philosophie und Theologie 36 (1989) 449-469.

BUNGE, G., «Hénade ou Monade? Au sujet de deux notions centrales de la terminologie évagrienne», Le Muséon 102 (1989) 69-91.

BURTON-CHRISTIE, Douglas, «Practice Makes Perfect: Interpretation of Scripture in the Apophtegmata Patrum», in: Studia Patristica vol. XX... p. 213-218.

BURTON-CHRISTIE, Douglas, The Word in the Desert: Scripture and the Quest for Holiness in Early Christian Monasticism, Oxford University Press (to be published in Sept. 1992).

COLIN, G., «La version éthiopienne de la prière de Pachôme», in: Mélanges Guillaumont, p. 63-67.

DRISCOLL, J., «A key for reading the Ad monachos of Evagrius Ponticus» Augustinianum, 1990, XXX, 361-392.

DRISCOLL, J., «Listlessness in The Mirror for Monks of Evagrius Ponticus», Cist. Studies 24 (1989) 206-214.

DRISCOLL, J., The «Ad Monachos» of Evagrius Ponticus: Its Structure and a Select Commentary. Rome: Studia Anselmiana, 1991.

ELM, S., «The Sententiae ad virginem by Evagrius Ponticus and the problem of the early monastic rules», Augustinianum. 1990, XXX, 393-404.

FRANK, K.S., «Arsenios der Grosse. Vom Apophtegmata zum hagiographischen Text», in: Mémorial Dom Jean Gribomont (1920-1986). Rome, Inst. Patrist. Augustinianum 1988, p. 271-287.

GOEHRING, J.E., «The World Engaged: The Social and Economic World of Early Egyptian Monasticism», in: Gnosticism and the Early Christian World: In Honor of James M. Robinson, edited by J.E. Goehring et al. Sonoma. CA: Polebridge, 1990.

GOULD, Graham E., «Moving and Staying Put in the Apophtegmata Patrum», in: Studia Patristica, Vol. XX... (1987) 1989, p. 231-237.

GOULD, Graham E., The Desert Fathers on Personal Relationships. Ph. D. disser., Oxford University, 1988.

GOULD, Graham E., «Early Egyptian Monasticism and the Church», in: Monastic Studies: The Continuity of Tradition, edited by J. Loades, Bangor: 1989.

GOULD, Graham E., «The Life of Antony and the Origins of Christian Monasticism in Fourth-Century Egypt», Medieval History 1 (1991).

GRIGGS, C.W., Early Egyptian Christianity. From its origins to 451 C.E. (= Coptic Studies, 2) 2nd ed., Leiden, Brill, 1991, VII-276.

GUILLAUMONT, A., «L'enseignement spirituel des moines d'Égypte: la formation d'une tradition», in: M. Meslin, Maître et disciples dans les traditions religieuses (=

Patrimoines: histoire des religions). Paris, Cerf, s.d., p. 143-154.

GUILLAUMONT, Antoine et Claire, Évagre le Pontique, «Le Gnostique» ou «A celui qui est devenu digne de la science». Édition critique des fragments grecs. Traduction intégrale établie au moyen des versions syriaques et arménienne. Commentaire et tables. (S.C. Vol. 356), Paris, Le Cerf, 1989, 208p.

HANAKAN, Hans, Antonios der Grosse, Stern der Wüste. Ausgewählt, übersetzt und vorgestellt von Hans Hanakan, Feiburg im Breisgau, Herder, 1989, 158 p. (Texte zum Nachdenken 1625).

HESSE, Otmar, «Das Verhältnis von Stadt und Land in den Apophthegmen», in: Studia Patristica XX, pp. 250-255.

HOLZE, H., «Könobitische Gebetspraxis und individuelle Gebetserfahrung in dem pachomianischen Klöstern», in Wort und Dienst 21 (1991), 132-148.

JOEST, Christoph, «.. alle Tage den Menschen dienen: Pachomius (+346) und seine ursprüngliche Inspiration zum koinobitischen Leben», Erbe und Auftrag 67 (1991) 35-50.

JUNOD, Éric, Les sages du désert. Genève, Labor et Fides, 1991, 106 p.

KARDONG, T.G., «The Monastic Practices of Pachomius and the Pachomians», Studia monastica 32 (1990) 59-78.

KOK, F., «L'office pachômien: psallere, orare, legere», in Ecclesia orans 9 (1992), 69-95.

LELOIR, L., «Les Pères du désert à l'école de leurs andres juifs». in: Cristianesimo e Giudaismo: Eredità e confronti, Augustinianum, t. 28, 1988), p. 405-428.

LORENZ, R., «Die griechische Vita Antonii des Athanasius und ihre syrische Fassung. Bemerkungen zu einer These von R. Draguet» Zeitschrift für Kirchengeschichte 100 (1989) 77-84.

LUCCHESI, Enzo, «Chénouté a-t-il écrit en grec?» in: Mélanges Guillaumont, p. 201-210.

METZLER, K., «Kontamination in der Athanasius-Überlieferung», RÉB 1990, XLVIII, 213-232.

MYSZOR, W., «Antonius-Briefe und Nag-Hammadi-Texte», JAC 1989, XXXII, 72-88.

MÉLANGES..., Mélanges Antoine Guillaumont. Contributions à l'étude des Christianismes orientaux. Avec une bibliographie du dédicataire.—Genève, P. Cramer, 1988 (1989), XII-312 p. (Cahiers d'Orientalisme-20).

PEZIN, M., «Un texte copte de la prière attribuée à Chenouti», in: Mélanges Guillaumont, p. 63-67.

QUECKE, H., «Auszüge aus Evagrius' Mönchsspiegel in koptischer Übersetzung», Orientalia, 58 (1989), p. 453-463, 1 pl.

REGNAULT, Lucien, «Aux origines des collections d'apophtegmes», in: Studia patristica, XVIII, vol. 2: Critica, Classica, Ascetica, Liturgica. Papers of the Ninth International Conference on Patristic Studies, Oxford 1983, Ed. by E.A. Livingstone. Leuven, Peeters,

REGNAULT, Lucien, La vie quotidienne des Pères du désert en Égypte au IVe siècle. Hachette, Paris, 1990, 321 p. 1 carte.

REGNAULT, Lucien, Abba, dis-moi une parole. Paroles mémorables des Pères du désert choisies et traduites. Solesmes, 1984, 191 p.

REGNAULT, Lucien, A l'écoute des Pères du désert aujourd'hui. Apophtegmes des Pères traduits et commentés. Solesmes, 1989, 160p.

REGNAULT, Lucien, L'Évangile vécu au désert. Paroles des Pères du désert traduites et commentées (= Collection Paroles de lumière). Paris, Le Sarment, Fayard 1990, 197 p.

RUBENSON, S., The Letters of St. Antony. Origenist Theology, Monastic Tradition and the Making of a Saint. (= Bibliotheca historico-ecclesiastica Lundensis, 24), Lund, 1990.

RUFINUS (Tyrannius Rufinus), Historia monachorum sive de vita Sanctorum Patrum hrg. von E. Schulz-Flügel (= Patristische Texte und Studien, 34). Berlin New York, de Gruyter, 1990, XXV-423p.

SANCHEZ, M., Diego, «El Comentario al Eclesiastés de Dídimo Alejandrino», Teresianum (Rome) 1990, XLI, 231-242.

SCHULZ-FLÜGEL, Eva, «The Function of Apophtegmata in Vitae and Itineraria», in: Studia Patristica XVIII/2. Critica. Classica, Ascetica, Liturgica. (Oxford 1983)—Louvain, Peeters, 1989, p. 281-291.

SCHULZ-FLÜGEL, Eva, «Zur Entstehung der Corpora Vitae Patrum», in: Studia Patristica, Vol. XX. Critica. Classica. Orientalia. Ascetica. Liturgica. (Oxford 1987). Leuven, Peeters, 1989, 289-300.

STAROWIEYSKI, M., «Remarques sur les sources de quelques apophtegmes des Pères du désert», in: Studia Patristica vol. XVIII,2: papers of the 1983 Oxford Pat. Conf... Ed. E. A. Livingstone, Kalamazoo, Cist. Publ. - Leuven, Peeters, 1989, p. 293-298.

VAN DER VLIET, Jacques, «S. Pachôme et S. Athanase: un entretien apocryphe», Analecta Bollandiana, 110 (1992), p. 21-27.

VAN PARYS, Michel, «Abba Silvain et ses disciples. Une famille monastique entre Scété et la Palestine à la fin du IVe et dans la première moitié du Ve siècles», Irénikon 61 (1988) 451-480.

VOGUÉ, Adalbert de, «Les fragments coptes de l'Histoire Lausiaque. L'édition d'Amélineau et le manuscrit», Orientalia 1989 LVIII, 326-332.

VOGÜÉ, Adalbert de, «Palladiana. II. La version copte de l'Histoire Lausiaque. I. Le Prologue et la Vie de Pambo», Studia Monastica 32 (1990) 323-339.

VOGÜÉ, Adalbert de, and G. Bunge, «Palladiana. III. La version copte de l'Histoire Lausiaque. II. La vie d'Évagre», Studia Monastica 33 (1991) 7-21.

ZANETTI, Ugo, «Du nouveau sur S. Antoine et ses Lettres». Review of Rubenson, Analecta Bollandiana, 108 (1990), p. 278.

ZANETTI, Ugo, «Les Lettres de saint Antoine et la naissance du monachisme. A propos d'un ouvrage récent». (About Rubenson's book), N.R.T. 113 (1991) 87-93.

CENTRO ITALIANO MICROFICHES
Piazzale di Ponte Milvio 28 - 00191 Roma (Italy)

PUBLICATIONS OF THE "CORPUS DEI MANOSCRITTI COPTI LETTERARI"

KB.NL + KB.[93] - *Coptic Bibliography*: Complete bibliography for Coptic studies. Subjects complete from the beginning of the studies: BIBBIA; GNOSTICISMO; APOCRYPHA; LETTERATURA; AGIOGRAFIA; STORIA; GENERALIA (partially); MANOSCRITTI (partially). The other subjects (LINGUISTICA; ARCHEOLOGIA, and parts of GENERALIA, MANOSCRITTI and STORIA) start from 1980, and the previous titles will be completed in the future.

KB.NL - Numerical List. ca. 200 p. Contains all the entries, with full bibliographical information. To be acquired once for all, and adjourned yearly with supplements and with replacements (where mistakes are corrected, etc.), which are sent together with the yearly issues (next item).

KB.[93] - Yearly Indexes. 3 vols., ca. 280, 60, 20 p. Contains the entries, distributed according to the subject, and (within the subjects) in alphabetical order of author name; the index in alphabetical order of the names of the authors; the supplement, with the new entries of the current year. The Yearly Indexes are distributed each year, and each issue completely replaces the previous one. Last year published: 1993.

ST.08 - Birger PEARSON and Tim VIVIAN, with the assistance of D. B. Spanel, *Two Coptic Homilies Attributed to Saint Peter of Alexandria*, 1993, 180 p., ISBN 88-85354-01-7 [Introduction, Coptic text, and English translation of the homily *On Riches*; introduction and English translation of the homily *On the Epiphany*.]

ST.06 - Alberto CAMPLANI, *Le lettere festali di Atanasio di Alessandria*, 1989, V 340 p. [Chapter I offers a general view of the transmission of the letters; chapter II relates to the question of the chronology of the letters and the introduction of the Tessarakoste in Egypt; chapter III, after showing the catechetical and propagandistic character of these texts, deals with some peculiarities of the polemics against Arianism and Meletian church, Athanasius' relations with the Nile valley, the way of selecting bishops all over Egypt. (In Italian).]

ST.01 - Tito ORLANDI, *Elementi di Grammatica Copto-Saidica,* 1983, III 56 p. [Elementary Grammar for Sahidic-Coptic for use in University courses (no exercises or chrestomathy; in Italian).]

ST.02 - T. ORLANDI, F. WISSE (eds.), *Acts of the IInd International Congress of Coptic Studies,* 1985, 371 p. [Covers all topics in the field of Coptic studies.]

ST.03 - Tito ORLANDI, *Shenute Contra Origenistas. Testo, introduzione, traduzione e concordanze,* 1985, 143 p. [Homily by Shenute against Origenism, apocryphal books, gnostic tendencies, etc. Italian translation.]

ST.05 - Tito ORLANDI, *Paolo di Tamma, Opere. Introduzione, testo, traduzione e concordanze,* 1988, 197 p. + 1 microfiche. [Aphorisms on monastic subjects by a IVth Century anchorite in the Middle Egypt. Italian translation. Microfiche reproduction of the manuscripts.]

PUBLICATIONS OF THE
INTERNATIONAL ASSOCIATION FOR COPTIC STUDIES

ST.09 - Tito ORLANDI (ed.), *Acts or the Fifth International Congress of Coptic Studies, Washington, 12-15 August 1992. Vol. 1: Reports on Recent Research,* 1993, 150 p., ISBN 88-85354-02-5.

ST.10 - David W. JOHNSON (ed.), *Acts or the Fifth International Congress of Coptic Studies, Washington, 12-15 August 1992. Vol. 2: Papers from the Sections (Part 1 and 2),* 1993, 270 and 270 p., ISBN 88-85354-03-3.

ST.07 - Stephen EMMEL (ed.), *An International Directory of Institutions Holding Collections of Coptic Antiquities outside of Egypt,* 1990, VI-122 p., ISBN 88-85354-00-9 [This directory provides a comprehensive list of names and addresses of institutions that possess collections of Coptic antiquities outside of Egypt. The scope of each collection is indicated briefly, based mostly on written responses to questionnaires. The directory includes more than 400 entries, from twenty-seven countries. Written in English.]

Riproduzione anastatica: 10 dicembre 1993
Tipografia Poliglotta della Pontificia Università Gregoriana
Piazza della Pilotta, 4 – 00187 Roma